The Game Maker's Apprentice

Game Development for Beginners

Jacob Habgood
Mark Overmars

Apress®

The Game Maker's Apprentice: Game Development for Beginners

Copyright © 2006 by Jacob Habgood and Mark Overmars

ISBN-13 (pbk): 978-1-59059-615-9

ISBN-10 (pbk): 1-59059-615-3

Printed and bound in China 9 8 7 6 5 4 3

Lead Editor: Chris Mills
Development Editor: Adam Thomas
Technical Reviewer/Additional Material: Sean Davies
Editorial Board: Steve Anglin, Ewan Buckingham, Gary Cornell, Jason Gilmore, Jonathan Gennick, Jonathan Hassell, James Huddleston, Chris Mills, Matthew Moodie, Dominic Shakeshaft, Jim Sumser, Keir Thomas, Matt Wade
Project Manager: Richard Dal Porto
Copy Edit Manager: Nicole LeClerc
Copy Editor: Liz Welch
Assistant Production Director: Kari Brooks-Copony
Production Editor: Ellie Fountain
Compositor: Dina Quan
Proofreader: Lori Bring
Indexer: Present Day Indexing
Artist: Kinetic Publishing Services, LLC
Illustrations and Cover Art: Kevin Crossley
Game Artists: Kevin Crossley, Matty Splatt and Ari Feldman
Cover Designer: Kurt Krames
Manufacturing Director: Tom Debolski

Distributed to the book trade worldwide by Springer-Verlag New York, Inc., 233 Spring Street, 6th Floor, New York, NY 10013. Phone 1-800-SPRINGER, fax 201-348-4505, e-mail orders-ny@springer-sbm.com, or visit http://www.springeronline.com.

For information on translations, please contact Apress directly at 2560 Ninth Street, Suite 219, Berkeley, CA 94710. Phone 510-549-5930, fax 510-549-5939, e-mail info@apress.com, or visit http://www.apress.com.

*To halcyon days
with a frog,
a parrot,
and a talented bunch of gremlins.*

Contents at a Glance

PART 4 ■ ■ ■ Multiplayer Games

PART 5 ■ ■ ■ Enemies and Intelligence

Contents

PART 1 ■■■ Getting Started

PART 2 ▪▪▪ Action Games

▪**CHAPTER 3**   **More Actions: A Galaxy of Possibilities** 41

▪**CHAPTER 4**   **Target the Player: It's Fun Being Squished** 65

PART 3 ■ ■ ■ Level Design

PART 4 ■ ■ ■ Multiplayer Games

PART 5 ▮▮▮ Enemies and Intelligence

Foreword

Way back when Mario was still a mere twinkling in Miyamoto's eye, I was the proud owner of a state-of-the-art Commodore 64 microcomputer. It came with a game development system called "The Quill," which allowed anyone to create their own text-based adventure games. It may have been incredibly crude, but it suddenly put at my fingertips the thrill of entertaining my nearest and dearest by devising "interactive challenges" of my own. Unfortunately, I knew little about game design, and rather than easing my players into a new and alien world, I treated them as opponents that had to be defeated before they could reach the end. Their spirits crushed, they left, never to return . . .

It took me years of playing a variety of good (and bad) games to eventually learn how to treat the player to the game-playing experience that their investment of time and money deserved. It took just hours of reading this book to wish I'd had its invaluable guidelines and the accompanying Game Maker tool to help me take my own first steps into game development all those years ago.

Two decades later, I now work for Real Time Worlds as the producer of Crackdown, an imminent Xbox 360 title developed exclusively for Microsoft. Crackdown is the result of over three years of development from a team that's now nearly 70 strong in Dundee (Scotland), with many more contributors across North America and Eastern Europe. This game has cost millions of pounds to create, and already consists of over two and half million lines of programming code! Blood, sweat, and tears have been poured into this title to provide cutting-edge graphics technology, stunning art assets, and dramatic surround sound. We've spent days (and nights) wrestling with new technologies to provide the player with a "playground" and "toy set" that was previously only the stuff of dreams.

Nonetheless, once you strip away the gloss, Crackdown boils down to a handful of gameplay linchpins, or what we term the "pillars of play." Take it from me that when charged with building such a grand gaming monument, it is vitally important to have absolute faith in the basic foundations! I was therefore very pleased to see that this book encourages you to identify these pillars (or game mechanics) and discover how a system of simple rules can combine in unique and compelling ways to create a spellbinding experience.

As you progress through the book you'll build a series of excellent games that you might never have even dreamed you could be capable of creating right now. The instructions are clear and concise, but also encourage you to experiment with your own designs. For example, your version of the captivating and original Koalabr8 game (Chapter 7) will almost certainly be a unique piece of software. The crazy devices you invent, and the way you lay out your levels, will certainly differ from mine. Watch out for Lazarus too (Chapter 4)—it may interest you to know that this eponymous hero first appeared in Jacob's student portfolio, and was partly responsible for securing his first programming job in the industry!

Mark and Jacob have brought together decades of game development expertise in this book. As well as being a professor of computing, and the creator of Game Maker, Mark first cut his game-programming teeth creating versions of games like Super Breakout for the Atari ST. Jacob has a string of titles to his name, and his in-depth knowledge of "the craft" consistently yields outstanding results. Never more so was this the case than when I had the pleasure of working with him on the team that created the PlayStation hit Hogs of War (also mentioned in this book). Where Jacob differs from his peers is in his mastery of all four of the fundamental game development disciplines: programming, sound, art, and, of course, design. Now, thanks to Mark's Game Maker software, you can find out what it feels like in their world!

One of the key messages I hope you'll take away from this book is that there's a world of difference between having a great idea for a game and being a great game designer. The initial idea is simply the seed from which the game grows, or the stone from which the pillars are hewn. The role of a designer is to fully realize the vision: conceiving and continually refining the various supporting mechanisms to make them mesh like the components of a Swiss time-piece. As is repeatedly stated in these pages, there is no correct solution to game design—only a great idea, well executed and injected with personal flair and enthusiasm. Even if you're struggling to pin down that idea right now, I'm sure you will have wrestled it onto the screen and into the hands of friends and family before finishing the final chapter of *The Game Maker's Apprentice*.

Good luck!

Phil Wilson
Producer, Real Time Worlds

Crackdown

About the Authors

JACOB HABGOOD is 30 years old and has been writing computer games since he was 10. He wanted to be a psychologist when he grew up, but somehow he ended up with a computer science degree and went into the games industry instead. He worked as a professional game developer for seven years, programming console games for Gremlin Interactive and Infogrames/Atari in the north of England. During this time he contributed to a range of successful titles and led the programming teams on Micro Machines (PlayStation 2, Xbox, and Nintendo GameCube) and Hogs of War (PlayStation).

Jacob is now a doctoral student at the University of Nottingham, researching the educational potential of computer games. As part of this research, Jacob runs clubs and workshops teaching children and teenagers how to make their own computer games and provides free teaching resources through his website: gamelearning.net. All being well, this work will soon earn him a Ph.D. from Nottingham's Department of Psychology so that he can finally consider himself grown up.

MARK OVERMARS is a full professor in computer science at Utrecht University in the Netherlands. There he heads the research center for Advanced Gaming and Simulation (www.gameresearch.nl) in which researchers from different disciplines collaborate on all aspects of gaming and simulation. One of Mark's prime research domains is computer games. He is also one of the founders of the Utrecht Platform for Game Education and Research (www.upgear.nl), a collaboration of different game-related educational programs in the Netherlands. For many years he has taught courses on computer game design at Utrecht University, and has given lectures on game design to many types of people (high school kids, teachers, researchers, and politicians). Mark is the author of a number of popular software packages, in particular, the Game Maker software package used as the development tool in this book.

About the Technical Reviewer

SEAN DAVIES is 28 years old and has been fascinated by computer games from an early age. He grew up fairly certain that he would become a novelist—or possibly a rock star, but eventually came to a number of important realizations:

1. He's probably never going to be a rock star.

2. Game programming is quite cool, though.

3. Badgers are just really big weasels (the exchange rate is approximately 20 weasels to the badger if you're interested).

4. Any attempts to construct a serious calculus of the family Mustelidae are probably best kept to yourself—people think you're strange (see above).

Having made these startling realizations at such an early stage, the rest of his career path was pretty much decided. After graduating with a degree in computer science, he joined Infogrames in Sheffield, UK, and has worked in the games industry ever since. When Infogrames Sheffield closed its doors in 2002, he joined Sumo Digital, where he still is today. Sean is currently Xbox platform lead on Outrun 2006: Coast to Coast, which Sumo is developing for SEGA, and is looking forward to working on some next-generation console programming in the near future. He currently has no intention at all of ever becoming properly grown up.

Outrun 2006: Coast to Coast

About the Illustrator

The first things **Kev Crossley** remembers drawing as a child were some Daleks and the Incredible Hulk, and he knew from that point on that he would grow up to be one or the other. When Kev was five, his dad brought home the videogame Pong, and Kev has been trying to come to grips with it ever since. Nonetheless, he has managed to get through a couple of Zelda games and has spent many a happy hour blasting the head off one of this book's authors with a Rail Gun.

Kev spent some time in a university, but eventually realized that an art degree was not going to give him access to Time Lords or gamma rays, so he decided to work in a bakery instead. Eventually he got sick of eating coconut macaroons and biscuits and applied for a job making videogames for a little green monster. For the next third of his life, he had a great time producing graphics and animation for over 20 titles—some of which were quite good.

These days Kev is a concept artist at Core Design in Derby, UK, where he has occasionally been known to hang out with women obsessed with tombs. He has also done copious amounts of freelance illustration and writing for publishers all over the world, including a series of instructional drawing books and sequential work for Rebellion's sci-fi comic *2000AD*. His one regret is that he can't ride a skateboard, because a cross between the Daleks and Tony Hawk would be unstoppable.

Acknowledgments

By rights, this book really shouldn't exist, because it's required far too much effort from far too many people to make it a profitable endeavor. Nonetheless, it does exist, and as a result there are a lot of people who need to receive our heartfelt thanks in helping us to realize this labor of love.

First and foremost, we need to thank all those people closest to the individuals directly involved in bringing this book into existence. Their influence may not be obvious to the reader, but projects like this could never happen without the support and understanding of the wives, girlfriends, and families of all the people involved in this book. In particular, Jacob would like to thank Jenny, Fiona, Michelle, and Amelia, all of whose names should adorn the credits of many a videogame for the sacrifices that they regularly make to indulge the creative passions of their loved ones.

The next biggest thanks should go to Matty Splatt, who has shied away from a full billing in the "About the" sections but did a fantastic job of bringing Koalabr8 and Pyramid Panic to life with his comical and beautifully polished graphics. We would also like to give a special thanks to Ari Feldman for allowing us to use and modify his game sprites for the Wingman Sam game.

More thanks go to Jenny and Marguerite Habgood for their grammatical critiques, and the following people for all their comments and input into the project: Sarah Peacock, Judy Robertson, John Sear, and Phil Wilson. Additional thanks goes to all the staff and students at Sheffield West City Learning Centre, who suffered the book's instruction in its earliest form.

Quick thanks also to everyone who enthusiastically play-tested the games in the book, including Gail Clipson, Fiona Crossley, Katie Fraser, Giulia Gelmini, Jasmin Habgood, Martijn Overmars, Ronald Overmars, and Stuart Reeves.

Finally, we would like to thank everyone at Apress for their support, and for sticking with us even after it became plainly obvious that both authors were far too busy to write a book!

Introduction

Who wouldn't want to make computer games? It's creative, rewarding, and these days even pretty darn cool too. You can make them to share with your school friends, your work colleagues, your grandchildren, or even the entire gaming world. This book is not specifically for the young or old, but anyone who loves computer games and wants to have a go at making them for themselves. We've all painted a picture, written a story, and made a wobbly piece of pottery at some point in our lives, so it's now time to embrace the art form of the future and try making computer games too.

This book provides a collection of engaging tutorials that introduce you to the Game Maker tool and teach you how to use it. The first four parts of the book take you step by step through seven different projects using Game Maker's simple drag-and-drop programming system. By the time you've finished making Evil Clutches, Galactic Mail, Lazarus, Super Rainbow Reef, Koalabr8, Wingman Sam, and Tank War, you'll have a well-rounded experience of making games with Game Maker. Parts 2, 3, and 4 also end with game design chapters that encourage you to stand back from your creations and consider how principles of game design can be used to make them more fun. Moreover, we don't just talk about it, but we provide new versions of the games with improved features so that you can experience for yourself how solid game design can lead to good gameplay.

Game Maker provides a simple environment that allows complete beginners to quickly start building games, using an icon-based system of events and actions (see Figure 1). This drag-and-drop programming technique provides an easy way to learn about game development and allows you to create complete games without going near a traditional programming language.

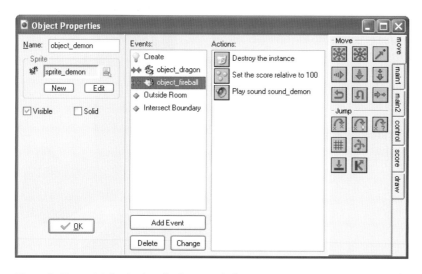

Figure 1. *Game Maker's simple drag-and-drop system uses iconic events and actions to program computer games.*

However, once you become more experienced, traditional languages can provide a more powerful way to program games. Consequently, Game Maker also provides the Game Maker Language (GML), which underpins Game Maker and makes it such a powerful tool (see Figure 2). The last part of the book uses several simple examples to introduce you to GML, before we demonstrate how you can use it to create artificial intelligence for undead creatures in the Pyramid Panic game.

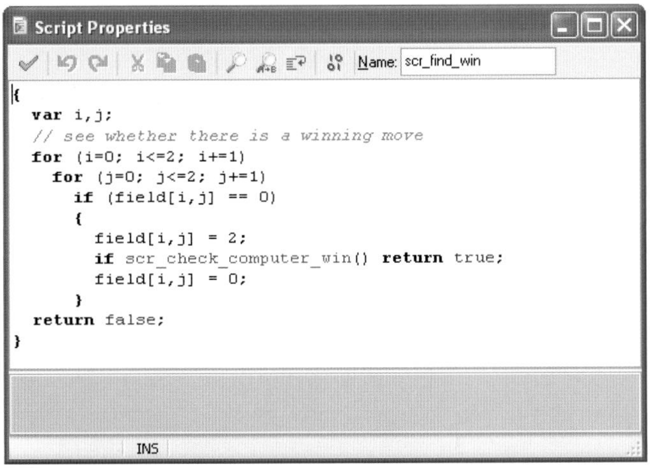

Script Properties
Name: scr_find_win
{
var i,j;
// see whether there is a winning move
for (i=0; i<=2; i+=1)
for (j=0; j<=2; j+=1)
if (field[i,j] == 0)
{
field[i,j] = 2;
if scr_check_computer_win() return true;
field[i,j] = 0;
}
return false;
}
INS

Figure 2. *Game Maker Language (GML) provides extra power for advanced users.*

The example games in this book have been brought to life with graphics and illustrations by real games industry artists. Furthermore, you can use all the professional resources provided on the CD in your own Game Maker projects with the blessing of the publisher and authors. We only ask that you share your creations with the online Game Maker community so that we can see what you have created with them. We want you to enjoy the creative journey ahead and hope that it will help you to share in our passion and enthusiasm for creating computer games!

PART 1

■ ■ ■

Getting Started

Welcome to the world of game development. Playing games can be a lot of fun, but you're about to discover why making them is so much better!

Welcome to Game Maker

If you're looking for an enjoyable way to learn how to make computer games, then this is the book for you. You don't need a degree in computer science and you won't have to read a book the size of a telephone directory—everything you need is right here. As long as you can use Windows without breaking into a cold sweat, you have all the qualifications you need to start making your own games. In the chapters ahead, we'll show you how to make nine complete games and pass on some of our hard-earned professional experience in game design along the way. Already, you are just two chapters away from completing your first game and have taken your first step along the path of the game maker's apprentice!

Every trade has its tools, and every tradesman knows how to choose the right tool for the job. In this book we will be creating all the games using a software tool for Windows called *Game Maker*. Game Maker is ideal for learning game development as it allows you to start making games without having to study a completely new language. This makes the whole learning experience a lot easier and allows you to concentrate on creating great game designs rather than getting bogged down with the technicalities of programming. Nonetheless, programming languages can offer many advantages to experienced users and so Game Maker also includes its own language, which is there for you to discover when you feel ready to use it.

You'll be pleased to hear that there is a free version of Game Maker included on the CD accompanying this book. All the games can be made using this free version; however, there are some special effects in the later chapters that will only work with a registered version of Game Maker. If you want to register your version for this, or any of the other extra features that it unlocks, then it can be obtained from the Game Maker website for a very small fee (currently US $20): www.gamemaker.nl.

Installing the Software

You can't begin making the games in this book until you have the Game Maker software installed on your PC. You'll find the install program in the Program folder on the CD, so insert the disc, navigate to the Program folder, and start the program called gmaker_inst.exe. The form shown in Figure 1-1 should then appear on the screen.

Figure 1-1. *Install Game Maker by following the instructions on the screen.*

Click **Next** and follow the instructions as they appear. We strongly recommend installing the program in the default directory.

Note Game Maker requires a fairly modern PC running Windows 98SE, Me, 2000, or XP—although Windows XP is preferable. You'll need a DirectX-compatible graphics card with at least 32MB of memory and DirectX 8 or later installed on your machine. A DirectX-compatible sound card is also required for sound and music. If your machine does not meet these requirements, you might have problems running Game Maker or the games created with it. Don't worry if all this techno-babble makes no sense—just try it out because you're not likely to have any problems unless your PC is very old. See the readme file in the Program folder on the CD for further details.

Game Maker should start automatically once the installation has completed. You can also launch it directly from the Windows Start menu or by double-clicking the Game Maker icon on your desktop. The first time you run Game Maker on a new computer, you will be asked if you want to run the program in Advanced mode (see Figure 1-2). Click **No** as it will be easier to stick with the Simple mode for the time being—we'll show you how to switch to Advanced mode later on.

Figure 1-2. *Click* **No** *at the prompt, as we want to start by using Simple mode.*

Registration

The free version of Game Maker provided with this book is fine for learning how to make all the games in this book, but some of Game Maker's more exciting features are disabled unless you register the program. Registering will also allow you to create more professional-looking games by removing the Game Maker pop-up message that appears at the start of any game. Until you register, a reminder message will appear from time to time like the one shown in Figure 1-3. Clicking **Close this Form** will make it disappear, but if you use Game Maker a lot we strongly encourage you to register it. Registration will support the further development of Game Maker and ensure that everyone who uses it can continue to enjoy making games for years to come. Information about registration can be obtained by clicking **Go to Registration Webpage** or by simply visiting the Game Maker website at www.gamemaker.nl.

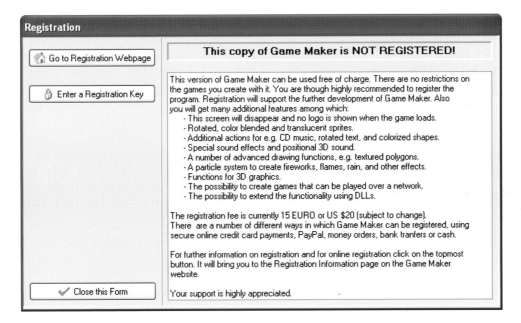

Figure 1-3. *Select* **Close this Form** *to start working with Game Maker or* **Go to Registration Webpage** *to learn more about registration.*

The Global User Interface

If everything has gone according to plan, then you should now be looking at the window shown in Figure 1-4. If not, consult the readme file in the Program folder on the CD for possible causes and further instructions.

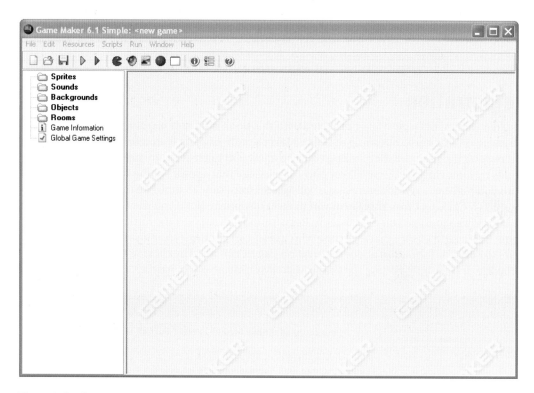

Figure 1-4. *This is Game Maker's main window.*

We'll describe the user interface in more detail in the next chapter, but for the moment just notice that there's a standard-looking menu and toolbar at the top of the screen, and a *folder tree* on the left-hand side. This tree is where we will add all the different *game resources* that are used to make Game Maker games. More about resources later, but first let's make sure Game Maker is working properly by running a simple game.

Running a Game

Loading and running a game that has been created using Game Maker couldn't be simpler. Just complete the following instructions.

Running the sample game:

1. Click the **File** menu and select **Open** from the drop-down menu. This will bring up the standard Windows file requester.

2. Make sure the CD is in your CD drive. Navigate to the Games/Chapter01 folder on the CD and look for bouncing.gm6 (all Game Maker files end with this .gm6 extension). Select this file and click **Open**.

It may not seem as if anything has changed, but if you look carefully, there are now plus signs in front of the different folders on the left-hand side. Clicking these plus signs will open up the folders to show the resources that they contain.

Let's run the game. Don't expect too much, though; this is just a simple demo to check whether Game Maker works correctly on your machine. Click the green play button on the toolbar. The Game Maker window should disappear and the image in Figure 1-5 will appear. This is the pop-up that is only shown in the free version of the program and can be removed by registering your copy of Game Maker.

Figure 1-5. *This pop-up message appears in the free version of Game Maker.*

After a short pause, a game window should appear like the one in Figure 1-6. You should hear music and see a number of balls bouncing around the screen. If you like, you can try to destroy the balls by clicking on them with the left mouse button, or you can press F4 to make the game window fill the screen. When you have seen enough, press the Esc key to end the game.

Figure 1-6. *In the bouncing ball demo, you can try to destroy the balls by clicking on them with the left mouse button.*

If something went wrong (for example, you got an error message or you didn't hear the music), then consult the readme document in the Program folder on the CD for possible causes and further instructions. You can now close Game Maker by choosing **Exit** from the **File** menu.

How to Get More Information

This book will show you how to make some cool games with Game Maker, but it is not a complete manual for everything that Game Maker can do. Fortunately, the Game Maker help file contains all the facts, and you can access it at any time through the program's **Help** menu or the Windows Start menu. A copy of this document is also available in the Documents folder on the CD.

You are also strongly advised to check out the official Game Maker website at www.gamemaker.nl. Here you'll find the latest version of the program and lots of games that have been created with it—as well as additional resources and documents. The website also gives you access to the Game Maker user forum. This is a very active forum and a great place to get help from other users or just to exchange ideas and games.

What's Next?

Now that the boring stuff is out of the way, so I think it's about time we made our first game. You're probably thinking your first game will be pretty dull—something with more bouncing balls, perhaps? Not likely!

CHAPTER 2

■ ■ ■

Your First Game: Devilishly Easy

Learning something new is always a little daunting at first, but things will start to become familiar in no time. In fact, by the end of this chapter, you'll have completed your very first gaming masterpiece!

Designing the Game: Evil Clutches

Before you start making a game, it's a good idea to have an idea of what you're aiming for. Commercial game developers usually prepare long design documents before they start creating a game. Nonetheless, writing documents isn't a fun way to learn how to make games, so we'll keep our designs as short as possible. We're calling the game in this chapter *Evil Clutches*, and this is its design:

> *You play a mother dragon who must rescue her hatchlings from an unpleasant band of demons that have kidnapped them. The band's boss sends a stream of demons to destroy the dragon as the hatchlings make their escape. The mother can fend off the boss's minions by shooting fireballs, but must be careful not to accidentally shoot the hatchlings!*
>
> *The arrow keys will move the dragon up and down and the spacebar will shoot fireballs. The player will gain points for shooting demons and rescuing young dragons, but will lose points for any hatchlings that accidentally get shot. The game is over if the dragon is hit by a demon, and a high-score table will be displayed. Figure 2-1 shows an impression of what the final game will look like.*

Using this description, we can list all the different elements needed to create our game: a dragon, a boss, demons, hatchlings, and fireballs. Making the game will require pictures of each of these as well as a background image, some sound effects, and music. We call all these different parts that make up the game *resources*, and the resources for this game have already been created for you in the Resources/Chapter02 folder on the CD. For the remainder of the chapter, we will learn how to put these resources together into a game and bring them to life.

Figure 2-1. *Here's the Evil Clutches game in action.*

Sprites

In Game Maker, pictures of dragons, demons, and other game objects are all called *sprites*. Sprites are one kind of resource used in games, and they can be made from images that have been created in art packages or downloaded from the Internet. Game Maker includes a simple sprite editor for drawing your own sprites, but you can use any drawing package you like for this purpose. However, creating sprites is time consuming, so we've already provided professionally drawn sprites for each game.

If you've not done so already, start up Game Maker. Figure 2-2 shows the (rather empty) main window that appears.

■**Note** If your window doesn't look exactly the same as shown in Figure 2-2, then you're probably running Game Maker in Advanced mode. To switch to Simple mode, choose **Advanced Mode** from the **File** menu and the checkmark beside it will disappear.

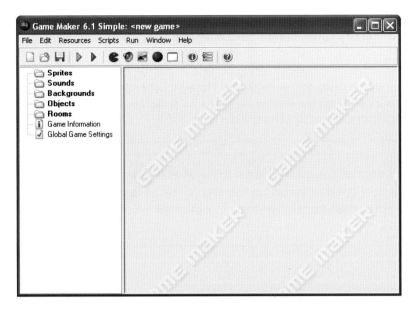

Figure 2-2. *In the main window of Game Maker (in Simple mode), the menu and toolbar runs along the top of the window and a list of resources down the left side.*

The left side of the window shows the different types of resources that make up the game: sprites, backgrounds, sounds, and so forth. These are currently empty, but the names of new resources will appear here as they are added to the game. The menu bar along the top of the window contains all the commands that allow us to work with resources—although most common tasks can also be accessed using the buttons on the toolbar. We'll begin by using the **Create Sprite** command to create a new sprite.

Creating a new sprite resource for the game:

1. From the **Resources** menu, choose **Create Sprite**. The Sprite Properties form appears, like the one shown in Figure 2-3.

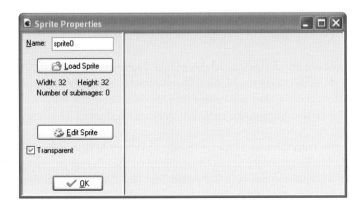

Figure 2-3. *Open the Sprite Properties form for a new sprite.*

2. Click the **Name** field, where it currently says sprite0. This is the default name created by Game Maker for the new sprite, but you should rename it to sprite_dragon.

3. Click the **Load Sprite** button. This opens the standard Windows file requester.

4. Select the required image using the file requester. The image for the dragon is called Dragon.gif, and you'll find it in the Resources/Chapter02 folder on the CD. Your Sprite Properties form should now look like Figure 2-4.

Note Always avoid using spaces and punctuation in names for resources as they will confuse Game Maker when you try to use some of its more advanced functions later on. You can use the underscore (_) symbol instead of spaces, which is usually found on the same key as the minus symbol (press Shift and the minus key).

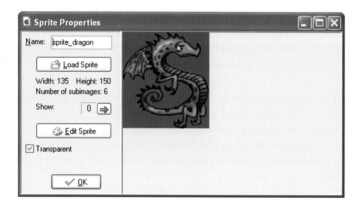

Figure 2-4. *The Sprite Properties form looks like this after we load the dragon sprite.*

5. Click **OK** to close the form. You have now created a sprite.

The dragon sprite should now have been added to the list of sprites in the resource list. If you ever need to change a resource, you can reopen its properties form by double-clicking on its name in the resource list. Do this now and take another look at the dragon sprite's properties (Figure 2-4).

The form shows that there are six subimages to this sprite. Sprites often consist of several images shown one after the other to create the illusion of movement. If you move through the subimages using the blue arrow button, you will notice that there are actually only two different images for this sprite. The extra copies make sure that the dragon doesn't flap its wings too quickly when it's animating.

The checkmark next to the **Transparent** property means that the background of the dragon sprite is see-through. Most sprites are set to transparent so that the surrounding rectangle won't be drawn when the sprite appears in the game. Figure 2-5 shows the difference that the **Transparent** option makes—the advantages are obvious to see!

Figure 2-5. *Here's the dragon sprite with the Transparent option set (left) compared to the same dragon without the Transparent option (right).*

■**Note** Game Maker works out which color to make transparent based on the color in the bottom leftmost corner of each image. This is worth remembering when you want to create your own sprites.

Okay, let's create the other sprites for the game in the same way.

Creating the remaining Evil Clutches sprites:

1. From the **Resources** menu, choose **Create Sprite**.

2. In the **Name** field in the Sprite Properties form, type the name sprite_boss.

3. Click the **Load Sprite** button and choose the file Boss.gif.

4. Click **OK** to close the Sprite Properties form.

5. Now create a demon sprite, baby sprite, and fireball sprite using the Demon.gif, Baby.gif, and Fireball.gif files in the same way. Give each sprite an appropriate name (using only letters and the underscore symbol).

This completes all the sprites needed to create the Evil Clutches game.

Objects

Sprites don't do anything on their own; they just store pictures of the different elements in the game. *Objects* are the parts of the game that control how these elements move around and react to each other. We'll begin by creating our first object to tell Game Maker how we want the demon boss to behave.

The Boss Object

The following steps create a new object and assign it a sprite so that Game Maker knows how it should look on the screen.

Creating a new object and assigning it a sprite:

1. From the **Resources** menu, choose **Create Object**. An Object Properties form like the one in Figure 2-6 appears.

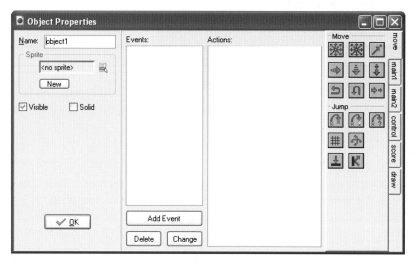

Figure 2-6. *Open the Object Properties form for your new object.*

2. In the **Name** field, give the object a name. You should call this one object_boss.

3. Click the icon at the end of the sprite field and a list of all the available sprites will appear. Select the sprite_boss sprite.

Caution Always make sure that you give your object resources names that are different from your sprite resources. Ending up with an object and a sprite both called "dragon," or two objects called "demon," can confuse Game Maker when you try to use its more advanced functions later on. Adding prefixes like "sprite_" or "object_" to names is a good way to achieve this without having to think of new names.

Events and Actions

Game Maker uses *events* and *actions* to specify how objects should behave. *Events* are important things that happen in the game, such as when objects collide or when the player presses a key on the keyboard. *Actions* are things that happen in response to an event, such as changing an object's direction, setting the score, or playing a sound. Game Maker games are basically just a collection of objects with actions to tell them how they should react to different events. Therefore, to set the behavior of an object in Game Maker you must define which events the object should react to and what actions they should perform in response.

The boss object's lists of events and actions are currently empty. We're going to begin by adding an event and action that will start the boss moving up the screen at the beginning of the game. This will be complemented by an action that reverses the vertical direction of the boss in the event that it collides with the edge of the screen. As a result, the boss will continually move up and down between the top and bottom of the screen.

Adding a create event for the boss object:

1. Click the **Add Event** button. The Event Selector appears, as shown in Figure 2-7.

Figure 2-7. *Click **Add Event** to open the Event Selector pop-up form.*

2. Click the **Create** event to add it to the list of events. A new event is automatically selected (with a blue highlight) in the event list, as shown in Figure 2-8. This means we're already looking at this event's **Actions** list alongside it (which is currently empty).

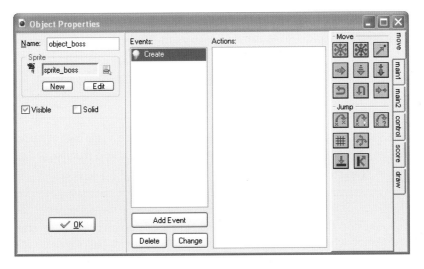

Figure 2-8. *This is how the Object Properties form should look once the name, sprite, and **Create** event have been added.*

3. Next you need to include the **Move Fixed** action in the list of actions. To do this, press and hold the left mouse button on the action image with eight red arrows, drag it to the empty **Actions** list box, and release the mouse button. An action form will then pop up asking for particular information about this action (see Figure 2-9).

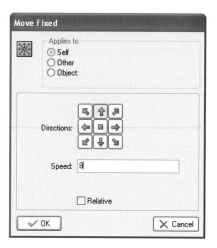

Figure 2-9. *Here's the action form for the **Move Fixed** action.*

■**Note** Whenever we use an action in the instructions, that action's image is shown in the left margin to help you find the correct one.

4. Select the up arrow and enter a value of 8 for the **Speed**. This will make the object move vertically 8 pixels (the tiny squares that make up a monitor display) for every step that it takes.

5. Press **OK** to close the action form and it will be included in the list of actions.

■**Note** All of Game Maker's actions are organized into tabbed pages of icons on the right of the **Actions** list. Browse through the different action tabs to see all the various actions and hold your mouse over one to reveal its name.

This event should start the boss moving upward. Now we'll add an event to reverse an object's vertical direction when it collides with the edge of the screen. This event is called the Intersect Boundary event because it gets called when the object's sprite intersects the screen's boundary by being partly in and partly out of the screen.

Adding an intersect boundary event for the boss object:

1. Click the **Add Event** button.

2. Choose **Other** from the Event Selector pop-up form and select **Intersect boundary** from the drop-down menu that appears. This action will then be added and selected in the list of events.

3. Include the **Reverse Vertical** action in the list of actions for this event. You'll now see the form shown in Figure 2-10.

Figure 2-10. *The action form for the* ***Reverse Direction*** *action looks like this.*

4. Nothing needs changing on this form, so just click **OK**. The Object Properties form for the boss object now looks like the one shown in Figure 2-11.

Figure 2-11. *In the Object Properties form for the boss object, we've added two events, along with their corresponding actions.*

These are all the events and actions we need for the boss right now. You can switch between the different events by clicking on them in the **Events** list. The selected event is highlighted in blue and the actions for that event are then shown in the **Actions** list. You can edit the properties of each action by double-clicking on them, but we're done with the boss object for now.

5. Click **OK** at the bottom left of the form to close it.

The Dragon Object

Now let's turn our attention to the heroine of the game. We'll begin by creating an object for the dragon in the same way as for the boss.

Creating a dragon object:

1. From the **Resources** menu, choose **Create Object**.

2. Give the object a name by entering object_dragon in the **Name** field.

3. Select the sprite_dragon sprite from the drop-down sprite menu.

The dragon also needs actions to make it move up and down the screen, but this time only when the appropriate keys are pressed on the keyboard. We do this by using keyboard events.

Adding keyboard events for the dragon object:

1. Click the **Add Event** button.

2. Choose a **Keyboard** event and select **<Up>** from the pop-up menu (to indicate the up arrow key).

3. Include the **Move Fixed** action in the **Actions** list.

4. In the action form, select the upward direction and set **Speed** to 16.

5. Repeat the previous process to add a **Keyboard** event for the **<Down>** key that includes a **Move Fixed** action with a downward direction and a speed of 16. The Object Properties form should now look like the one shown in Figure 2-12.

We just need one more event and action to make the dragon's movement work correctly. Our **Keyboard** events will start the dragon moving when the player presses the arrow keys, but there are currently no events to stop it from moving again when the keys are no longer being pressed. We use the **Keyboard, <no key>** event to test for when the player is no longer pressing any keys.

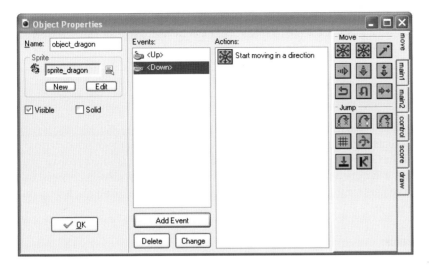

Figure 2-12. *The Object Properties form for the dragon looks like this once we add the <**Up**> and <**Down**> events.*

Adding a no key event for the dragon object:

1. Click the **Add Event** button.

2. Choose a **Keyboard** event and select **<no key>** from the pop-up menu.

 3. Include the **Move Fixed** action in the **Actions** list for this event.

4. Select the center square in the action form, to indicate no movement, and set **Speed** to 0. The form should now look like Figure 2-13.

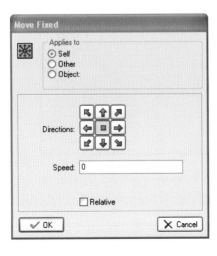

Figure 2-13. *These settings stop the movement of the dragon.*

5. That's all the actions we need to make our dragon move up and down, so click **OK** to close the Object Properties form for the dragon object.

■**Caution** When setting a **Move Fixed** action with a speed of 0, you must also select the center square of the direction grid. If no direction square is selected at all, then the action is ignored!

Rooms

Our dragon and boss objects are all ready to go now, but in order to see them we need to put them into a level. Levels in Game Maker are made using *rooms*, and putting objects into a room defines where they will appear at the start of the game. However, not all objects need to be there at the start of the game, and they can be created on the fly as well (fireballs, for example). Let's create a new room.

Creating a new room resource:

1. Select **Create Room** from the **Resources** menu. A Room Properties form will appear (see Figure 2-14).

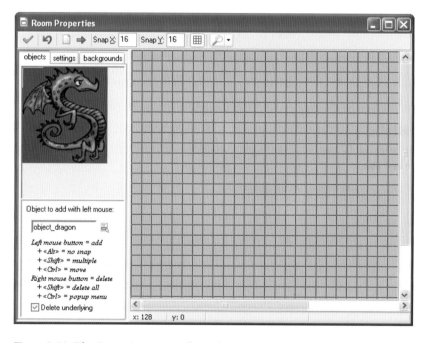

Figure 2-14. *The Room Properties form for a new room opens.*

■**Note** If there are sliders along the edges of the room grid, then the window is not currently large enough to see the entire room. Maximize the Game Maker window and the Room Properties form to see more of the room, or use the sliders to scroll around the entire room.

2. Click the **settings** tab in the top left of the form.

3. Enter a name for the room in the **Name** field. Call this one room_first.

4. Enter a caption for the title bar of the window when the game is running. "Evil Clutches" seems appropriate for this game. The room settings should now look like Figure 2-15.

Figure 2-15. *Here's the **settings** tab of the Room Properties form, with the name and caption filled in.*

Now we can place our objects in the new room.

Adding a dragon and boss to the room:

1. Click the **objects** tab in the top left of the form. You should see that the dragon object is already selected as the object "to add with left mouse."

2. Click on the room grid with the left mouse button. An instance of the dragon object will be placed with its top-left corner at the point at which you click. The position you place the dragon becomes its starting position in the game, so put just one dragon close to the left boundary of the room area. If you add it in the wrong place, use the right mouse button to remove it again.

3. Click on the dragon's image on the **objects** tab (or on the image of the pop-up menu next to where it says object_dragon) and select the boss object from the menu that appears.

4. Place an instance of the boss close to the right edge of the room, but make sure that the whole of his sprite is completely inside the room—otherwise his events will not work correctly! The room should now look something like Figure 2-16.

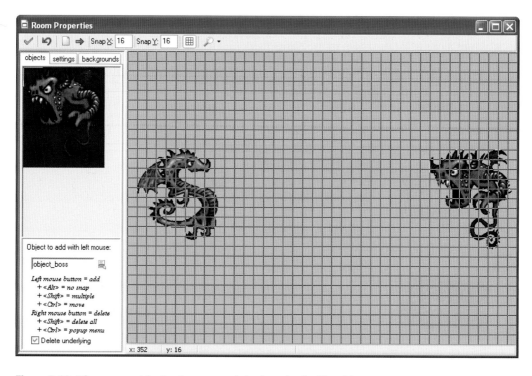

Figure 2-16. The room with the dragon and the boss looks like this.

Our very first version of the game is now ready. Click the green checkmark in the top-left corner of the form to close it and you can see the results of your labor . . .

■**Tip**　You can also click and hold the mouse button to move instances within a room.

Save and Run

It's always a good idea to save your work as often as possible—just in case your computer crashes. In case you haven't already worked it out for yourself, then the steps for this process are given here. However, in the future you'll have to remember to save your work regularly yourself! This works in the same way as most programs.

Saving your work and running the game:

1. Choose **Save** from the **File** menu (or click the disk icon).

2. The first time you save the game, you will be prompted for a location and filename in the normal way. Note that Game Maker files always end with the extension .gm6. Save this game in a place where you can easily find it again (on the desktop, for example).

3. To run the game, select **Run Normally** from the **Run** menu. After a brief pause, a game window should appear, like the one shown in Figure 2-17.

Figure 2-17. *Here's the first version of the Evil Clutches game in action.*

You should now be able to move the dragon up and down using the arrow keys, and the boss should float up and down by itself. If your game doesn't work in this way, then you might want to check through all your steps in the previous sections. You may also need to ensure that your game window is selected (by clicking on it with the mouse) before your keyboard input has any effect. All games we make in the book are stored on the CD in stages, and the current version of the game can be found on the CD in the file Games/Chapter02/evil1.gm6.

Although we now have a running game, it's not much fun to play yet as there are no goals or challenges. We'll spend the remainder of the chapter turning it into a playable game. Press Esc to stop the game.

Tip Pressing F4 while the game is running will maximize the game to fill the entire screen. Press F4 again to return to the windowed version.

Instances and Objects

So far we have two object resources in our game and two characters appearing on the screen. However, there is an important distinction to be made between object resources and *instances* of objects that appear on screen. It may seem odd, but now that we have made dragon and boss objects, we can put as many *instances* of dragons and bosses on the screen as we like. Try it—go back and place more dragons and bosses in the room. If you run the game, you will find that they all behave in exactly the same way as the original instances! (Don't forget to remove them again afterward using the right mouse button.) A good way to think of the relationship between objects and instances is to think of objects as jelly molds and instances as the jellies that you make with them. You only need one mold to make any number of jellies, yet the mold defines the appearance of all of them (see Figure 2-18). From now on we will talk about instances and objects in this way, so it is important that you appreciate the difference.

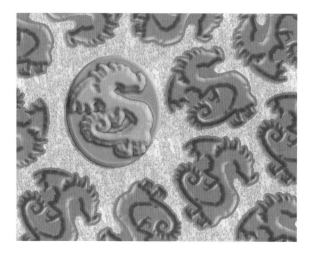

Figure 2-18. *Object resources are like jelly molds, and they can be used to create any number of object instances on the screen at once.*

Demons, Baby Dragons, and Fireballs

To create some challenges and goals, we're going to need to bring our remaining objects into the game. Let's start by giving the dragon the ability to breathe fireballs—as dragons often do!

The Fireball Object

To create the fireball object you'll need the fireball sprite. If you didn't get around to doing this earlier, then quickly flick back a few pages and add it in the way that was described in the "Sprites" section. You should remember the basic steps required to making a new object by now, but here they are one more time, just in case.

Creating the fireball object:

1. Select **Create Object** from the **Resources** menu.

2. Call the object `object_fireball`.

3. Select the fireball sprite.

We now need to think about how we want fireballs to behave. When the dragon creates a fireball, we want it to move across the screen toward the boss and get destroyed when it reaches the other side of the screen.

Adding the fireball object's events:

1. Click the **Add Event** button and choose the **Create** event.

 2. Include the **Move Fixed** action in the **Actions** list. Select the right arrow to indicate the direction and set **Speed** to 32 (fireballs fly fast!).

3. Click the **Add Event** button again, select **Other** events, and pick **Outside room**.

 4. Select the **main1** action tab and include the **Destroy Instance** action in the **Actions** list. In the action form that pops up, simply click **OK**. The fireball Object Properties form should now look like Figure 2-19.

5. Click **OK** to close the fireball Object Properties form.

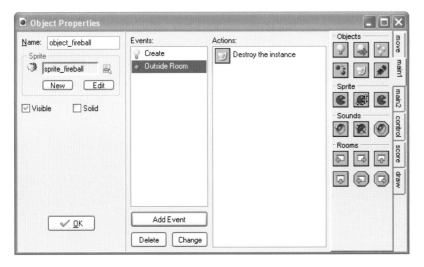

Figure 2-19. *The properties form for the fireball object should now look like this.*

■**Caution** It is always a good idea to make sure that instances are deleted when they're not needed any more (when they go off the edge of the screen, for example). Even though you can't see them, Game Maker still has to spend time updating them, and too many instances will eventually slow down the program.

Now we need to tell the dragon object to create instances of the fireball object when the player presses the spacebar. We do this in a similar way to the events that make the dragon move, but this time using a **Key Press** event rather than a **Keyboard** event. **Keyboard** events happen as long as the player continues to hold down the key, but **Key Press** events happen only once when the key is first pressed. Using a **Keyboard** event for the fireballs would create a continuous stream of fireballs and make the game too easy, so that's why we're using **Key Press** instead.

Creating a Key Press event for the dragon object:

1. Double-click the dragon object in the resource list (not the dragon sprite). This will bring back the Object Properties form for the dragon object.

2. Click the **Add Event** button. Select the **Key Press** event and then choose **<Space>** from the pop-up menu.

3. Select the **main1** action tab and include the **Create Instance** action in the **Actions** list.

4. In the action form that appears, we need to specify which type of instance to create and where on the screen it should be created. Select the fireball object from the menu, enter a value of 100 into **X** and 10 into **Y**, and select the **Relative** checkbox. Figure 2-20 shows what the completed action form should look like.

5. Click **OK** to close the action form and click **OK** again to close the Object Properties form.

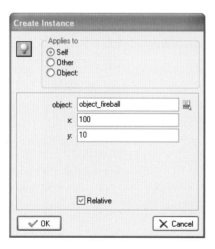

Figure 2-20. *Note that we checked the **Relative** property to make the fireball appear relative to the position of the dragon.*

The x and y values you just entered are screen coordinates, which are used to indicate positions on the game screen. Screen coordinates are measured in pixels (the tiny squares that make up a monitor display), with x values indicating the number of pixels horizontally, and y values indicating the number of pixels vertically.

We need to select the **Relative** option because the fireball needs to be created on the screen in front of the dragon, in other words, *relative* to the dragon's position. However, the dragon's position is measured from the top-left corner of its sprite—just above its wings—and this would be a crazy place for the fireball to appear! Giving an x-coordinate of 100 moves the fireball across 100 pixels to the right (to just above its head) and a y-coordinate of 10 brings it 10 pixels down. This creates the fireball right in front of the dragon's mouth and exactly where we need it (see Figure 2-21). Test the game now to check that you can use the spacebar to shoot fireballs, and that they appear in the correct position.

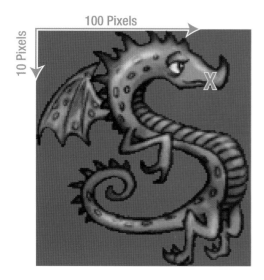

Figure 2-21. *The fireball needs to appear from the dragon's mouth, which is 100 pixels across and 10 pixels down from the origin of the dragon's sprite.*

The Demon Object

The demon object will work in the same way as the fireball, except that demons fly from right to left and are created by the boss. Also, to make demons a bit more interesting, we'll start some moving diagonally as well as horizontally. Those that head diagonally for the top or bottom of the screen will need to reverse their vertical direction when they intersect the boundary—like the boss object does. We'll also need to destroy demons when they go outside the room, like the fireball. Next we provide the steps you need to do all of this; notice that we've started to shorten the steps that you should be familiar with by now.

Creating the demon object:

1. Create a new object called `object_demon` and give it the demon sprite.

2. Add a **Create** event and include the **Move Fixed** action.

3. Select all three left-pointing direction arrows and set **Speed** to 12. Selecting more than one direction causes Game Maker to randomly choose between them when an instance is created. The action form should now look like Figure 2-22.

4. Add an **Intersect boundary** event (in the **Other** events) and include the **Reverse Vertical** action in it.

5. Add an **Outside room** event (also in the **Other** events) and include a **Destroy Instance** action in it.

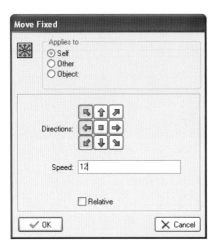

Figure 2-22. *In the move action for the demon, note that all three arrows to the left are pressed, so a random direction out of the three is selected for each demon created.*

The demons will now bounce back and forth between the top and the bottom of the screen, but we also need them to react to collisions with other instances. For this we use a *collision event*, which happens when two sprites of different objects overlap on the screen. The first collision event we need is for when a demon collides with a fireball. This event should destroy the demon, and reward the player by increasing their score. There are a number of different actions dealing with scores, health, and lives in the **score** actions tab. As soon as the score changes, it will automatically be displayed in the game window caption.

Adding an event to the demon object for colliding with the fireball:

1. Click the **Add Event** button, choose the **Collision** event, and select the fireball object from the pop-up menu.

2. Include the **Destroy Instance** action from the **main1** action tab.

3. Also include a **Set Score** action from the **score** tab. This should automatically appear below the **Destroy Instance** action in the **Actions** list. Lists of actions like this are carried out one after another, starting from the top of the list and working down.

4. Enter a value of 100 in the **Set Score** action form, and click the **Relative** property. This property makes the action set the score *relative* to the current score, so 100 will be added to the score rather than setting the score to 100. See Figure 2-23.

If a demon collides with the dragon, then the game is over. When this happens, we want to bring up a high-score table and (when appropriate) let the player enter their name. After showing the high-score table, we want to restart the game. Conveniently, Game Maker provides a **Show Highscore** event that handles most of this automatically.

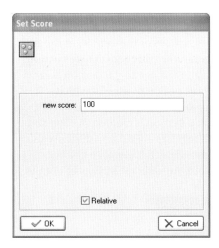

Figure 2-23. *We add 100 to the score by setting the **Relative** property.*

Adding an event to the demon object for colliding with the dragon:

1. Add a **Collision** event for colliding with the dragon object.

2. Include a **Show Highscore** action from the **score** tab.

3. Click **OK** to keep the default settings for this action's properties.

4. Also include a **Restart Game** action from the **main2** tab. This action has no properties.

5. The object properties form for the demon should now look like Figure 2-24. Check that you have included all the demon object's events. We're done with this object for now, so click **OK**.

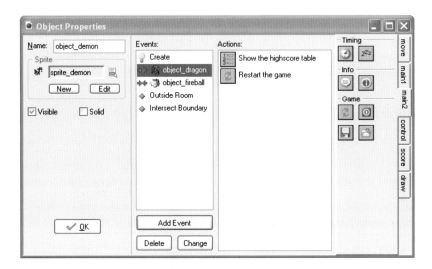

Figure 2-24. *The Object Properties form for the demon object now looks like this.*

Summoning Demons

That's it for the demon, but we still need the boss to create instances of the demon in the first place. However, we don't want the demons to appear at regular intervals because this would make the game too easy. Instead, we want there to be a random chance that a demon is created at each "*step*" of the game. A *step* is essentially just a short period of time in which everything on the screen moves a very small distance. There are normally 30 steps in every second, so we only need there to be a very small chance that a demon is created in each step. We achieve this by using a **Test Chance** action, which acts like throwing a die with many sides (see Figure 2-25). In each step we throw the die, but only one side will trigger the chance action and create a demon. In this way, we create a steady, but unpredictable, flow of demons.

Figure 2-25. *The more sides a die has, the less often Game Maker will throw the one side that triggers the **Test Chance** action.*

Adding a step event to the boss object:

1. Double-click the boss object in the resource list to bring back its Object Properties form.

2. Click the **Add Event** button, select the **Step** event, and choose **Step** again from the pop-up menu.

 3. Include the **Test Chance** action from the **control** tab. Set the sides of the die to 50 in the action's properties.

 4. Also include the **Create Instance** action in the **Actions** list for this event. Set the properties to create a demon object and select the **Relative** option, so that the demon is created relative to the boss's position. The event should now look like Figure 2-26.

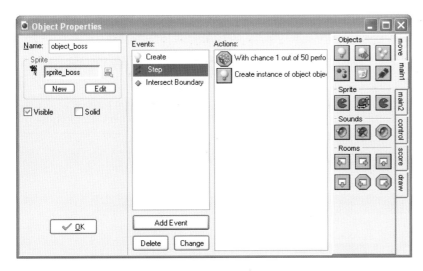

Figure 2-26. *In this step event, demons are randomly created.*

The **Test Chance** action is an example of a *conditional action*. Conditional actions control the action that immediately follows them so that it is only performed if some condition is met. So in this case the **Create Instance** action is only performed if the **Test Chance** action rolls a 1 using a 50-sided die—otherwise it is skipped.

Click **OK**, save your work, and run the game to test it. Demons should now be appearing, and you should be able to shoot them with your fireballs to rack up your score in the window caption. When you eventually get hit by a demon, the high-score table will be displayed and the game restarts. How long can you survive?

The Baby Dragon Object

We now have a game with two goals: shooting demons and staying alive. However, it's still not much fun to play as it's far too easy to provide any real challenge. To increase the challenge, we're going to occasionally throw in a baby dragon along with the demons. If the player shoots a baby dragon, they will lose 300 points, but if they rescue one they will gain 500 points. This will mean that the player will have to be much more careful about when they shoot, thereby increasing the challenge of the game.

Creating a new baby dragon object and its events:

1. Create a new object called object_baby, and give it the baby dragon sprite.

2. Add a **Create** event for the object and include a **Move Fixed** action in it. Set it to move left with a **Speed** of 8 (slower than the demons to make life harder).

3. Add an **Outside room** event (in **Other** events) and include a **Destroy Instance** action from the **main1** tab.

4. Add a **Collision** event with the fireball object and include a **Destroy Instance** action in that as well.

5. Also include a **Set Score** action in the collision event with a value of -300 and the **Relative** property selected. This will subtract 300 from the player's score.

6. Add a **Collision** event with the dragon object and include the **Destroy Instance** action in it.

7. Also include the **Set Score** action with a value of 500 and the **Relative** property selected. This will add 500 to the player's score. The baby dragon object should now look like Figure 2-27.

8. Click **OK** to close the properties form.

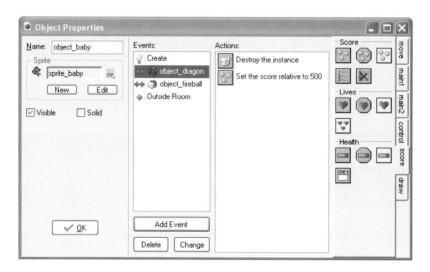

Figure 2-27. The Object Properties form for the baby dragon object looks like this.

Now we need to make the boss randomly release baby dragons as well as demons. This is exactly the same as for the demons except we will use a value of 100 for the die so that they are created less often.

Editing the boss object to randomly create baby dragons:

1. Reopen the Object Properties form for the boss object.

2. Click on the existing **Step** event to select it and view its actions.

3. Include another **Test Chance** action in the **Step** event. Set the sides of the die to be 100 in the action's properties.

4. Include the **Create Instance** action below the new **Test Chance** action in the **Actions** list. Set the properties to create a baby object and select the **Relative** option.

That completes the second phase of our game! All the gameplay elements are now in place. Save the game and carefully test it to make sure it works correctly. You'll also find the current version of the game on the CD in the file Games/Chapter02/evil2.gm6

Backgrounds and Sounds

In this section we'll finish off the look and feel of our game by adding background graphics, sound effects, and music. As you'll see, these finishing touches have quite a dramatic effect on how professional the game seems.

A Background Image

The first improvement we'll make is to add a background to the room. Backgrounds are another type of resource, like sprites, rooms, and objects. We've created an image that is exactly the same size as the game window (640×480 pixels). This needs to be loaded into a new background resource, which can then be assigned to a room.

Creating a new background resource and assigning it to a room:

1. Select **Create Background** from the **Resources** menu.

2. Call the background background_cave, and click the **Load Background** button. Select the Background.bmp image from the Resources/Chapter02 folder on the CD. The Background Properties form should now look like Figure 2-28.

3. Click **OK** to close the Background Properties form.

4. Reopen the properties form for the room by double-clicking on it.

5. Select the **backgrounds** tab in the Room Properties form. Click the menu icon to the right of where it says <no background> and select the new background from the pop-up menu. The Room Properties form now looks like Figure 2-29.

6. Close the Room Properties form by clicking the green checkmark in the top-left corner of the form.

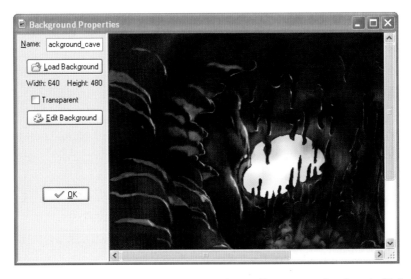

Figure 2-28. *The Background Properties form allows you to load and edit backgrounds.*

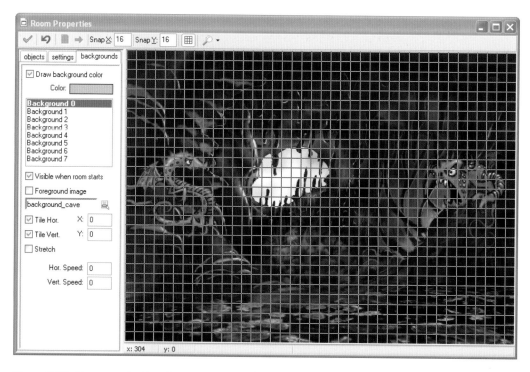

Figure 2-29. *The room looks a lot more atmospheric once you add the background to the room.*

Background Music

The next step is to add some atmospheric music. *Sounds* are another kind of Game Maker resource for including both sound effects and music. We need to create a sound resource for the music and then set up an action to start the music playing. We'll include this action in the **Create** event of the boss object so that it starts playing at the beginning of the game, but it would work just as well in the dragon object too.

Creating a music sound resource and playing it in the boss object:

1. Select **Create Sound** from the **Resources** menu and call it sound_music.

2. In the properties form that appears, click **Load Sound** and select the Music.mp3 file from Resources/Chapter02 on the CD. The Sound Properties form should now look like Figure 2-30.

3. Close the Sound Properties form by clicking **OK**.

4. Reopen the Object Properties form for the boss object.

5. Click the existing **Create** event to select it and view its actions.

 6. Include a **Play Sound** action (**main1** tab) in the **Create** event.

7. In the action properties, select the music sound and set the **Loop** property to true. This makes the music loop back to the start when it finishes. The sound action form should then look like Figure 2-31.

8. Click **OK** to close the action, and click **OK** again to close the boss object.

Figure 2-30. *The Sound Properties form allows you to load, preview, and save sound files.*

Figure 2-31. *This sound action loops the background music.*

Sound Effects

Adding sound effects is another way to enhance the atmosphere of a game, but they also help to inform the player about their actions. For now, we'll just add two sound effects to our game: one for shooting a demon and one for shooting a baby dragon. The baby's sound effect will be much higher-pitched and cuter than the demon's so that the player instantly knows they have done something wrong.

Creating and playing sound effects for shooting babies and demons:

1. Create a new sound resource called sound_demon.

2. Load the Demon.wav file from Resources/Chapter02 on the CD.

3. Close the Sound Properties form.

4. Reopen the Object Properties form for the demon object and select the existing **Collision** event with the fireball object.

5. Include a **Play Sound** action in the collision event and select the new sound. Leave the **Loop** property set to false.

6. Close the action form and demon Object Properties form.

7. Repeat the previous steps to create a sound resource for Baby.wav. Include an action to play it in the baby dragon object's collision event with the fireball.

Congratulations

Congratulations on completing your very first game using Game Maker! If you need it, then you'll also find the final version of the game in the file Games/Chapter02/evil3.gm6, on the CD. When you've finished a game, you can turn it into an executable by choosing **Create Executable** from the **File** menu. Executables don't need Game Maker to run, so it's easy to give them to your friends or put them on a website.

Now that you're a bit more familiar with Game Maker, why not try making some changes to the game to see what effects they have? You could add new objects to the game—there's an image for an "evil baby" in the resources directory that you can use. Perhaps these could be demons in disguise? Also try changing the movement speeds of the different objects. This can have a big impact on the difficulty of the game, as can changing the number of sides on the dice in the **Test Chance** actions. Balancing the settings for all these parameters is one of a game designer's most important jobs, and we'll talk more about this in Chapter 11.

This chapter has introduced you to the basic elements of Game Maker. We've looked at different kinds of game resources and seen how events and actions are used to control the behavior of objects. However, we've only just scratched the surface; there is still much more to discover about Game Maker and lots of even better games to make. Our journey continues in the next chapter with a trip to a moon or two as we learn more about events and actions by playing with spaceships.

PART 2

■ ■ ■

Action Games

There aren't many jobs where you try to put your customers into dangerous situations, but asteroid fields are just occupational hazards in this line of work!

■■■

CHAPTER 3

More Actions: A Galaxy of Possibilities

We hope you enjoyed making Evil Clutches and that it gave you a sense of how easy Game Maker is to use. However, you can achieve so much with a bit more knowledge, so let's move on to our second project and do something a little more adventurous.

Designing the Game: Galactic Mail

As before, it helps to set out a brief description of the game we want to create. We'll call this game *Galactic Mail* because it's about delivering mail in space. Here's the design:

> *You play an intergalactic mail carrier who must deliver mail to a number of inhabited moons. He must safely steer a course from moon to moon while avoiding dangerous asteroids. The mail carrier is paid for each delivery he makes, but pay is deducted for time spent hanging around on moons. This adds pressure to the difficult task of orienting his rickety, old rocket, which he cannot steer very well in space.*
>
> *When the rocket is on a moon, the arrow keys will rotate it to allow the launch direction to be set. The spacebar will launch the rocket, and the moon will be removed from the screen to show that its mail has been delivered. In flight, the rocket will keep moving in the direction it is pointing in, with only a limited amount of control over its steering using the arrow keys. When things move outside the playing area, they reappear on the other side to give the impression of a continuous world. The player will gain points for delivering mail, but points will be deducted while waiting on a moon. This will encourage the player to move as quickly as possible from moon to moon. There will be different levels, with more asteroids to avoid. The game is over if the rocket is hit by an asteroid, and a high-score table will be displayed. Figure 3-1 shows an impression of what the final game will look like.*

This description makes it possible to pick out all the various elements needed to create the game, namely moons, asteroids, and a rocket. For reasons that you will see later, we'll actually use two different moon objects (for a normal moon and an occupied moon) and two different rocket objects (for a "landed rocket" and a "flying rocket"). All the resources for this game can be found in the Resources/Chapter03 folder on the CD.

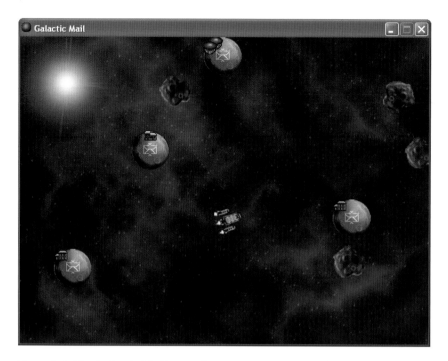

Figure 3-1. *The Galactic Mail game features moons, asteroids, and a rocket ship.*

Sprites and Sounds

Let's begin by adding all the sprites to our game. In the previous chapter, we saw that sprites provide images for each element of the game. In this chapter, we'll use some extra abilities of sprites; however, before we can do this, you must set Game Maker into Advanced mode.

Setting Game Maker into Advanced mode:

1. If you are working on a game, you must save the game before switching modes.

2. Click the **File** menu and look for an item called **Advanced Mode**. If there is a check-mark in front of it, then you are already in Advanced mode. Otherwise, click that menu item to select it, and the main window should change to look like the one in Figure 3-2.

To make things simple, we'll leave Game Maker in Advanced mode for the remainder of the book, even though some of the options will only be used in the final chapters. Now we're going to start a new, empty game.

Note To start a new game, choose **New** from the **File** menu. If you are already editing a game that has had changes made to it, you will be asked whether you want to save these changes.

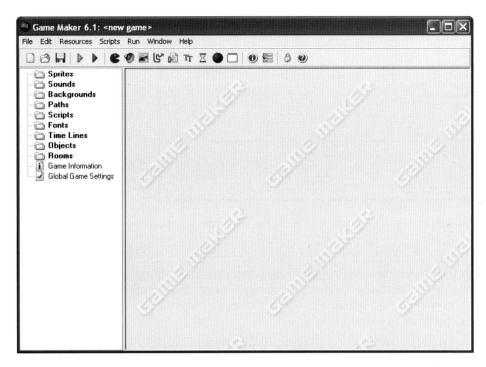

Figure 3-2. *In the main window of Game Maker in Advanced mode, there are a number of additional resources on the left and an additional menu.*

Our first step is to create all the sprites we need for the game. This works in the same way as in the previous chapter, but this time we must complete a couple of additional steps. Each sprite in Game Maker has its own *origin,* which helps to control the exact position in which it appears on the screen. By default, the origin of a sprite is set to be located at the top-left corner of the image. This means that when you move objects around in the game, it is as if you were holding them by their top-left corner. However, because the rockets in Galactic Mail need to sit in the center of the moons, it will be easier if we change the origin of all our sprites to be central.

Creating new sprite resources for the game:

1. From the **Resources** menu, choose **Create Sprite**. The Sprite Properties form with additional Advanced mode options will appear, like the one shown in Figure 3-3.

2. Click in the **Name** field and give the sprite a name. You should call this one `sprite_moon`.

3. Click the **Load Sprite** button. Select `Moon.gif` from the `Resources/Chapter03` folder on the CD.

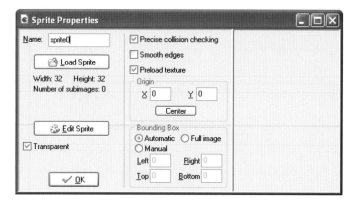

Figure 3-3. *This Sprite Properties form shows the advanced options.*

4. The controls for setting the origin are halfway down the second column of the form. Click the **Center** button to move the origin to the middle of the sprite. You should now see a cross in the middle of the sprite's image indicating the position of the origin. You can also change the origin by clicking on the sprite image with the mouse or typing in the **X** and **Y** values directly.

5. Enable the **Smooth edges** option by clicking on the box next to it. This will make the edges of the sprite look less jagged during the game by making them slightly transparent.

6. Click **OK** to close the form.

7. Now create asteroid and explosion sprites in the same way using Asteroid.gif and Explosion.gif (remember to center their origins too).

8. We'll need two sprites for the rocket: one for when it has landed on a moon and one for when it is flying through space. Create one sprite called sprite_landed using Landed.gif and another called sprite_flying using Flying.gif. Center the origins of these two sprites as before.

Before closing the Sprite Properties form for this last sprite, click the **Edit Sprite** button. A form will appear like the one shown in Figure 3-4. If you scroll down the images contained in this sprite, you'll see that it contains an animation of the rocket turning about a full circle. There are 72 different images at slightly different orientations, making up a complete turn of 360 degrees. We'll use these images to pick the correct appearance for the rocket as it rotates in the game. We can use the Sprite Editor to change the sprite in many ways, but for now simply close it by clicking the button with the green checkmark in the top left of the window.

Your game should now have five different sprites. Next let's add some sound effects and background music so that they are all ready to use later on.

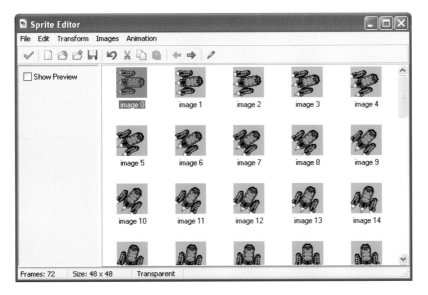

Figure 3-4. *The Sprite Editor shows all the images of the rocket.*

Creating new sound resources for the game:

1. Select **Create Sound** from the **Resources** menu. Note that the Sound Properties form now has additional Advanced mode options, but we don't need to worry about them for now (some of these are only available in the registered version of Game Maker).

2. Call the sound sound_explosion and click **Load Sound**. Select the Explosion.wav file from Resources/Chapter03 on the CD.

3. Close the form by clicking **OK**.

4. Now create the sound_bonus and music_background sounds in the same way using the Bonus.wav and Music.mp3 files.

Adding all these resources at the start will make it easier to drop them into the game as we are going along—so let's get started on some action.

Moons and Asteroids

Both moons and asteroids will fly around the screen in straight lines, jumping to the opposite side of the room when they go off the edge of the screen. In Game Maker this is called *wrapping*, and it is done using the **Wrap Screen** action.

Creating the moon object:

1. From the **Resources** menu, choose **Create Object**. The Advanced mode Object Properties form has additional options and actions too (see Figure 3-5).

2. Call the object object_moon and give it the moon sprite.

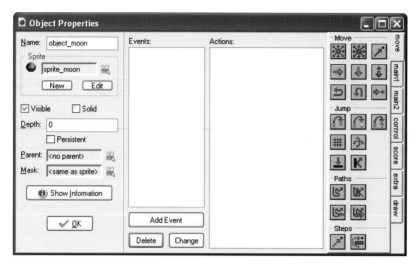

Figure 3-5. *The Object Properties form for the moon object looks like this.*

When a moon is created, we want it to start moving in a completely random direction.

Adding a create event to the moon object:

1. Click the **Add Event** button and choose the **Create** event.

2. Include the **Move Free** action in the **Actions** list for this event.

3. This action form requires a direction and a speed. Enter a **Speed** of 4 and type
   `random(360)` in the **Direction** property. This indicates a random direction between
   0 and 360 degrees. The form should now look like Figure 3-6.

Figure 3-6. *Using the random command in a **Move Free** action will make the moons start moving in a random direction.*

We also need to make sure that when the moon goes off the edge of the room, it reappears at the other side.

Including a wrap action for the moon object:

1. Click the **Add Event** button, choose the **Other** events, and select **Outside Room** from the pop-up menu.

2. Include the **Wrap Screen** action in the **Actions** list.

3. In the form that appears, you should indicate that wrapping should occur in both directions (top to bottom and left to right). Now the form should look like Figure 3-7.

4. The moon object is now ready to go, so you can close the Object Properties form by clicking **OK**.

Figure 3-7. *The **Wrap Screen** action properties form looks like this.*

The asteroid object can be created in exactly the same way as the moon earlier. However, to keep things neat, we want to make sure that asteroids appear behind other objects when they cross paths with them on the screen. Instances of objects are usually drawn in the order in which they are created, so it is hard to be sure whether one type of object will appear in front of another. However, you can change this by setting an object's *depth* value. Instances with a smaller depth are drawn on top of instances with a larger depth, and so appear in front of them. All objects have a default depth of 0, so to make sure the asteroids appear behind other objects we simply give them a depth greater than 0.

Creating the asteroid object:

1. Create a new object called `object_asteroid` and give it the asteroid sprite.

2. On the left-hand side there is a text field labeled **Depth**. Enter `10` in this field to change the depth of the object from 0 to 10.

3. Add the **Create** event and include the **Move Free** action in the **Actions** list. Type `random(360)` in the **Direction** property and enter a **Speed** of 4.

4. Add the **Other, Outside Room** event and include the **Wrap Screen** action in the **Actions** list (indicate wrapping in both directions).

Note From now on we will use commas in event names, such as **Other, Outside Room** to show the two stages involved in selecting the event.

---

5. The Object Properties form should now look like Figure 3-8. Click **OK** to close the form.

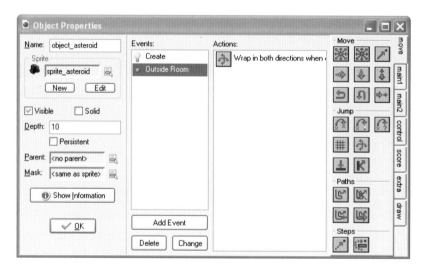

Figure 3-8. *We've set the depth for the asteroid object.*

Now would seem like a good time to check that everything has gone according to plan so far. However, before we can do that we must create a room with some instances of moons and asteroids in it.

Creating a room with moon and asteroid instances:

1. Select **Create Background** from the **Resources** menu.

2. Call the background `background_main`, and click the **Load Background** button. Select the `Background.bmp` image from the `Resources/Chapter03` folder on the CD.

3. Click **OK** to close the Background Properties form.

4. Select **Create Room** from the **Resources** menu. If the whole room isn't visible, then enlarge the window.

5. Select the **settings** tab and call the room room_first. Provide an appropriate caption for the room (for example "Galactic Mail").

6. Select the **backgrounds** tab. Click the menu icon to the right of where it says <no background> and select the background from the pop-up menu.

7. Select the **objects** tab and place a number of asteroids and moons in the room. (Remember that you can choose the object to place by clicking where it says "Object to add with left mouse"). The Room Properties form should now look like Figure 3-9.

8. Close the Room Properties form by clicking the green checkmark in the top-left corner.

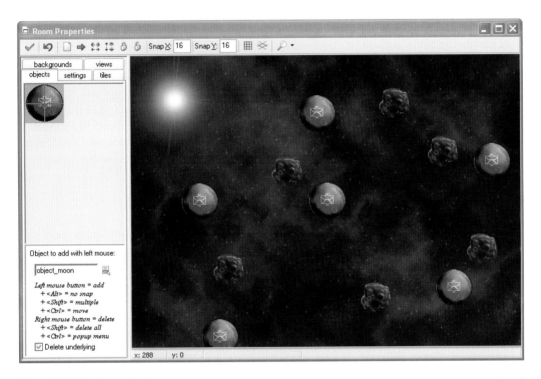

Figure 3-9. *Here's our first room.*

That should give us something to look at, so let's give it a try.

Saving and running the game:

1. Choose **Save** from the **File** menu (or click the disk icon). Save the game somewhere where you can easily find it again (the desktop, for example).

2. Select **Run normally** from the **Run** menu. If all goes well, the game should then appear in a new window.

Before continuing, double-check that everything is working the way it's supposed to. Are the moons and asteroids moving in different random directions? Do they reappear on the other side of the screen when they leave the room? Do the asteroids always pass behind the moons? If any of these are not working, check that you have followed the instructions correctly. Alternatively, you can load the current version from the file Games/Chapter03/galactic1.gm6 on the CD.

Flying Around

This isn't a very interactive experience yet, so let's introduce some gameplay by bringing the rocket into the game. We've already mentioned that we'll make two rocket objects, but let's stop to consider why this is necessary. Our rocket has two different ways of behaving: sitting on top of a moving moon with full control over the ship's direction, and flying through space with only limited control. Having two ways of controlling one object would involve a complicated set of events and actions, but if we separate these behaviors into two different objects, then it becomes quite simple. Provided that both objects look the same, the player will never notice that their ship is actually changing from being a "flying rocket" object to a "landed rocket" object at different stages of the game.

We also need two moon objects, as we want the landed rocket object to follow the path of one particular moon around (the one it has landed on). Making it into a separate object will allow us to single it out from the others in this way. As this second moon object will be almost the same as the normal moon, we can take a shortcut and make a copy of the existing moon object.

Creating the special moon object:

1. Right-click the moon object in the resource list, and select **Duplicate** from the pop-up menu. A copy of the moon object will be added to the resource list and its properties form is displayed.

2. Change the name to object_specialmoon. It is important that you use this exact name (including the underscore) as we will use this to identify this object later on.

3. Set the **Depth** of this object to -5. This will guarantee that instances of this moon are always in front of the other moons as it is lower than 0.

4. We will also make this moon responsible for starting the background music at the beginning of the game. Add an **Other, Game start** event and include a **Play Sound** action in it (**main1** tab). Select the background music sound and set **Loop** to true so that the music plays continuously.

5. Click **OK** to close the properties form.

Now open the first room and add a single instance of this new special moon to the level. Run the game and the music should play. (You won't notice any other difference because the special moon should look and behave exactly like the other moons.)

Now we can make our two rocket objects. We'll begin with the landed rocket, which needs to sit on the special moon object until the player decides to blast off. We'll use a **Jump Position** action to make it follow the special moon's position as it moves around the screen.

Creating the landed rocket object:

1. Create a new object called `object_landed` and give it the landed rocket sprite. Set the **Depth** to `-10` so that it appears in front of the moons and looks like it's sitting on the surface of the special moon.

2. Add a **Step, End Step** event to the new object. An **End Step** allows actions to be performed immediately before instances are drawn at their new position on the screen. Therefore, we can use this event to find out where the special moon has been moved to and place the rocket at the same location—just before both of them are drawn.

■**Note** A **Step** is a short period of time in which everything on the screen moves a very small distance. Game Maker normally takes 30 steps every second, but you can change this by altering the **Speed** in the **settings** tab for each room.

---

3. Include the **Jump Position** action in the **Actions** list for this event. This action allows us to move an object to the coordinates of any position on the screen. Type `object_specialmoon.x` into the **X** value and `object_specialmoon.y` into the **Y** value. These indicate the `x` and `y` positions of the special moon. Make sure that you type the names carefully, including underscores and dots (i.e., periods or full stops) in the correct positions. The action should now look like Figure 3-10.

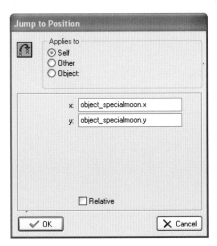

Figure 3-10. *We set the rocket to jump to the x and y positions of the special moon, so that it will follow this moon around.*

4. You might want to test the game now. Place one instance of the rocket at a random position in the room and run the game. The rocket should jump to the position of the special moon and stay on top of it as it moves around.

When you run the game, you will also notice that the rocket continually spins around without any user input. This is because the rocket sprite contains an animation showing the rocket rotating through 360 degrees. By default, Game Maker automatically cycles through a sprite's subimages to create an animation. However, this is not what is needed for this game— we need Game Maker to select the appropriate subimage based on the direction the rocket is moving in.

This requires a small amount of mathematics. There are 72 images representing a turn of 360 degrees, so each image must have been rotated by 5 degrees more than the last (because 360/72 = 5). Game Maker stores the direction of all objects in degrees, so it can work out which rocket subimage to use by dividing the rocket object's current direction by 5. Therefore we can make the rocket face in the right direction by using this rule (direction/5) to set the current subimage in a **Change Sprite** action.

Including a change sprite action in the landed object:

1. With the landed rocket Object Properties form open, include a **Change Sprite** action (**main1** tab) in its **End Step** event. Choose the landed rocket sprite from the menu and type `direction/5` into the **Subimage** property. `direction` is a special term that Game Maker recognizes as meaning the direction that this instance is currently facing in. Finally, set **Speed** to `0` to stop the sprite from animating on its own and changing the subimage. Figure 3-11 shows how this action should now look.

Figure 3-11. *Set the correct subimage in the sprite.*

■**Note** This way of dealing with rotated images might seem rather clumsy, but many old arcade games were made in a similar way so that each rotated image could include realistic lighting effects. Nonetheless, the registered version of Game Maker contains an additional action to rotate a sprite automatically without the need for subimages at all.

We can also make use of this special term for the object's direction to add actions that allow the player to control the direction of the rocket using the arrow keys.

Including keyboard events for the landed rocket object:

1. Add a **Keyboard, <Left>** event to the landed rocket object.

 2. Include the **Move Free** action and type `direction+10` in the **Direction** property. This indicates that the current direction should be increased by 10 degrees. Set **Speed** to `0` because we don't want the rocket to move independently of the special moon. This action should now look like Figure 3-12.

Figure 3-12. *Set the direction to equal itself plus 10.*

 3. Add a similar **Keyboard** event for the **<Right>** key. Include a **Move Free** action and type `direction-10` in the **Direction** property.

The last control we need for the landed rocket will allow the player to launch the rocket using the spacebar. This control will need to turn the landed rocket object into a flying rocket object, but we can't make an action for this as we haven't created the flying rocket object yet! So we'll make the flying rocket now and come back to this later.

Creating the flying rocket object:

1. Create a new object called `object_flying` and select the flying rocket sprite. Set **Depth** to `-10` to make sure that this object appears in front of moons.

 2. Add an **Other, Outside Room** event and include a **Wrap Screen** action to wrap around the screen in both directions.

 3. Add an **End Step** event. Include a **Change Sprite** action, choose the flying rocket sprite, type `direction/5` in the **Subimage** property, and set the **Speed** to `0`.

4. Add a **Keyboard, <Left>** event and include a **Move Free** action. We don't want the player to have too much control over the flying rocket, so type `direction+2` in **Direction** and set **Speed** to 6.

5. Add a **Keyboard, <Right>** event with a **Move Free** action. Type `direction-2` in **Direction** and set **Speed** to 6.

The basic gameplay is nearly there now—just a few more events to tie up. First, the game should end when the rocket hits an asteroid. Next, when the flying rocket reaches a moon, it should turn into a landed rocket, and the moon should turn into the special moon (so that the landed rocket can follow it). We achieve this using the **Change Instance** action, which basically turns an instance from one type of object into another. To return to our jelly comparison, this is a bit like melting down the jelly from one instance and putting it into a new object mold. Although the instance may end up as a completely different kind of object, it keeps many of its original properties, such as its position on the screen and its direction. The fact that these values remain the same is critical—otherwise the launch direction of the landed rocket would get reset as soon as it turned into a flying rocket!

Adding collision events to the flying rocket object:

1. Add a **Collision** event with the asteroid object and include the **Restart Game** action (**main2** tab) in the **Actions** list. Later on we'll include an explosion to make this more interesting.

2. Add a **Collision** event with the moon object and include the **Change Instance** action (**main1** tab). Set the object to change into `object_landed` using the menu button, and leave the other options as they are.

3. Include a second **Change Instance** action for changing the moon into a special moon object. To make this action change the moon object (rather than the rocket), we need to switch the **Applies to** option from **Self** to **Other**. This makes the action apply to the other object involved in the collision, which in this case is the moon. Set the object to change into `object_specialmoon`. Figure 3-13 shows the settings.

Figure 3-13. *Change the other instance involved in the collision into a special moon.*

Finally, we can go back to the landed rocket object. This will need an event that changes it into a flying rocket and deletes the special moon when the spacebar is pressed.

Adding a key press event to the landed rocket object:

1. Reopen the Object Properties form for the landed rocket by double-clicking on it in the resource list.

2. Add a **Key Press, <Space>** event and include a **Move Free** action to set the rocket in motion. Type `direction` in the **Direction** property (this keeps the direction the same) and set **Speed** to `6`.

3. Now include a **Change Instance** action and change the object into an `object_flying`.

4. Finally, we want to delete the special moon because it no longer needs to be visited. Include a **Destroy** action and change the **Applies to** option to **Object**. Click the menu button next to this and select the `object_specialmoon`, as shown in Figure 3-14.

Figure 3-14. *Include a **Destroy** action for the special moon.*

▓Caution Using the **Object** setting for **Applies to** performs an action on all instances of that kind of object in the room. Deleting all of the special moon instances is fine in this case (as there is only one), but you will need to think carefully about the effects this setting will have before using it in your own games.

That completes the second version of our game. Make sure you save it and check that it all works as it should so far. You should now be able to rotate the rocket on a moon, launch it with the spacebar, and steer through the asteroids to land on another moon. Moons should disappear as you visit them, and the game should restart if you hit an asteroid. If something is not working, then check the instructions again, or compare your version with the version on the CD (Games/Chapter03/galactic2.gm6).

There are clearly a number of things still missing from the game, but the game is already quite fun to play. In the next section, we will add a scoring mechanism and a high-score table, as well as advancing the player to a new level once mail has been delivered to all the moons.

Winning and Losing

In this section we'll put a bit more effort into what happens when the player wins or loses the game. Let's begin by making asteroids a bit more explosive!

An Explosion

To get this working, we'll add a new explosion object and create an instance of it when the rocket hits an asteroid. This will play the explosion sound when it is created and end the game with a high-score table after the explosion animation has finished.

Adding an explosion object to the game:

1. Create a new object called `object_explosion`, and select the explosion sprite. Give it a **Depth** of `-10` to make it appear in front of other instances.

2. Add a **Create** event and include a **Play Sound** action (**main1** tab) for the explosion sound.

3. Add an **Other, Animation End** event. This event happens when a sprite reaches the final subimage in its animation.

4. Include the **Show Highscore** action (**score** tab) in the **Actions** list for this event. To make the high-score list look more interesting, set **Background** to the same as the background for the game, set **Other Color** to yellow, and choose a different font (e.g., Arial, bold). The action should now look like Figure 3-15.

Figure 3-15. *You can spice up the high-score table.*

5. Also include a **Restart Game** action to start the game again after the high-score table is closed (**main2** tab).

6. Click **OK** to close the object.

Next we have to change the behavior of the flying rocket when it hits an asteroid.

Editing the flying rocket object:

1. Reopen the properties form for the flying rocket object by double-clicking on it in the resource list.

2. Select the **Collision** event with the asteroid by clicking on it once. Click once on the **Restart Game** action and press the Delete key to remove it from the action list.

3. Include a **Create Instance** action (**main1** tab) in its place, and set it to create the explosion object. Make sure the **Relative** property is enabled so that the explosion is created at the current position of the rocket.

4. Include a **Destroy Instance** action (**main1** tab) and leave it set to **Self** so that the rocket gets deleted. Click **OK** on the properties form to finish.

You might want to run the game now to see how it looks. Try colliding with an asteroid and you should get an explosion followed by the high-score table. Unfortunately, you can't score any points yet, so let's add this next.

Scores

If you've played the game quite a bit already, then you may have noticed a way of "cheating." You can avoid the risk of hitting asteroids by waiting for another moon to fly right next to your own and then quickly hop between moons. The game can become a lot less fun once this technique has been discovered, so our scoring system is designed to discourage the player from playing this way. Although they receive points for delivering mail, they also lose points for waiting on moons. This means that a player that takes risks by launching their rocket as soon as possible not only will have the most enjoyable playing experience but will also score the most points.

Editing game objects to include scoring:

1. Reopen the properties form for the special moon object and select the **Game Start** event. Include a **Set Score** action with a **New Score** of 1000. This gives the player some points to play with at the start. Close the properties form.

2. Reopen the properties form for the landed rocket and select the **End Step** event. Include a **Set Score** action with **New Score** as -1 and the **Relative** option enabled. This will repeatedly take 1 point off the score for as long as the player remains on a moon. As there are 30 steps every second, they will lose 30 points for every second of hanging around. Close the properties form.

3. Reopen the properties form for the flying rocket and select the **Collision** event with the moon object. Include a **Set Score** action with a **New Score** of 500 and the **Relative** option enabled.

 4. Include a **Play Sound** action after setting the score and select the bonus sound.

Levels

At the moment, there is no reward for delivering all the mail. In fact, once all the moons are removed, the rocket just flies through space until it collides with an asteroid! This seems rather unfair, and it would be much better if the player advanced to a more difficult level. Making multiple levels in Game Maker is as simple as making new rooms. We can use actions to move between these rooms, and include more asteroids in the later levels to make them more difficult to play.

Let's begin by creating the new levels. You'll repeat these steps to make two more levels so that there are three in total. You can always add more of your own later on.

▮Note The order of the rooms in the resource list determines the order of your levels in the game, with the top level being first and the bottom level last. If you need to change the order, just drag and drop them into new positions into the list.

Creating more level resources for the game:

1. Right-click on a room in the resource list and choose **Duplicate** from the pop-up menu. This will create a copy of the level.

2. Go to the **settings** tab and give the room an appropriate name (room_first, room_second, etc.).

3. Switch to the **objects** tab, and add or remove instances using the left and right mouse buttons.

4. Make sure that each level contains exactly one special moon and one instance of the landed rocket.

In order to tell Game Maker when to move on to the next room, we have to be able to work out when there are no moons left in the current one. To do this, we will use a *conditional action* that asks the question "Is the total number of remaining moons equal to zero?" If the answer is yes (or in computer terms, **true**), then a block of actions will be performed; otherwise the answer is no (or **false**), and this block of actions is skipped. We'll put this check in the collision event between the flying rocket and the moon, so that players complete the level as soon as they hit the final moon.

▪**Note** All conditional actions ask questions like this, and their icons are octagon-shaped with a blue background so that you can easily recognize them.

Editing the flying rocket object to test for the number of remaining moons:

1. Reopen the properties form for the flying rocket and select the **Collision** event with the moon object.

2. At the end of the current list of actions, include the **Test Instance Count** action (**control** tab). Set the **Object** field to object_moon and the other settings will default to how we need them (**Number**, 0 and **Operation**, Equal to). This is now equivalent to the question "Is the total number of remaining moons equal to zero?" The form should look like Figure 3-16.

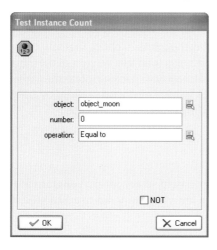

Figure 3-16. *We use the* **Test Instance Count** *action to count the number of moons.*

3. Below this action we need to start a *block*. A block indicates that a number of actions are grouped together as part of a conditional action. This means that all of the actions in the block will be performed if the condition is true and none of them if it is not. Add the **Start Block** action (**control** tab) directly below the condition to test the instances.

4. First, we will pause for a moment to give the player a chance to notice they have reached the final moon. Include the **Sleep** action (**main2** tab) and set **Milliseconds** to 1000. There are 1,000 milliseconds in a second, so this will sleep for 1 second.

5. We'll award the player an extra bonus score of 1,000 points when they finish a level. Include a **Set Score** action (**score** tab) with a **New Score** of 1000 and make sure that the **Relative** option is enabled.

6. Include the **Next Room** action from the **main1** tab to move to the next room. No properties need to be set here.

7. Finally, add the **End Block** action (**control** tab) to end the block of the conditional action. The completed set of actions should now look like Figure 3-17. Note that the actions in the block are indented so that you can easily see that they belong together.

Figure 3-17. *Note that the actions in the block are indented.*

It is time to try out the game again. Save and play the game to check that you can go from one level to the next by visiting all the moons. You can also load this version of the game from the file Games/Chapter03/galactic3.gm6 on the CD. However, if you complete the game you'll get an error message indicating that it has run out of levels. Don't worry—this is something we will fix in a moment, when we add some more finishing touches to the game.

Finishing Touches

To finish our game, we'll add an opening title screen, a help screen, and a congratulatory message upon completing the game. We'll also include a few visual touches to add a little bit of variety in the moons and asteroids.

A Title Screen

To create the title screen, we need a new object to display the name of the game and perform some initial tasks. We'll make it start the music and set the initial score, and then wait for the player to press a key before taking them to the first level.

Creating a new title object resource for the game:

1. Create a new sprite called sprite_title using Title.gif.

2. Create a new object called object_title and give it this sprite. Set the **Depth** property to 1 so that the moons go in front of it and the asteroids behind.

3. Add a **Create** event. This will contain the actions to start the music and set the score, but we've already created these in the special moon object, so we can simply move them over.

4. Open the special moon Object Properties form from the resource list and select the **Game Start** event to view its actions.

5. Drag and drop the two actions from the special moon **Game Start** event into the **Create** event of the title object. The **Game Start** event in the special moon should now be empty, and so it will delete itself automatically when the Object Properties form is closed. Do this now by clicking **OK** on the special moon's properties form.

 6. Add a **Key Press, <Any key>** event to the title object and include the **Next Room** action in the action list for this event (**main1** tab).

Next we need to create a new room for the title screen.

Creating a new title room resource for the game:

1. Create a new room called room_title and give it an appropriate caption. Also set the room's background in the same way as before.

2. Add a few moon and asteroid instances to the room (just for effect).

3. Place an instance of the new title screen object in the center of the room.

4. Close the room properties.

5. To make sure that this is the first room in the game, drag the new room to the top of the list of rooms in the resource list.

Now quickly test the game to check that this all works correctly.

Winning the Game

We also need to stop the game from producing an error at the end and congratulate the player instead. Similar to how we created the title room, we will create a finish room with a finish object to display the message and restart the game.

Creating a new finish object resource for the game:

1. Create a new object called object_finish. It doesn't need a sprite.

 2. Add a **Create** event to the object and include the **Display Message** action in it (**main2** tab). Set the **Message** to something like: "Congratulations! You've delivered all the mail."

 3. Include a **Set Score** action, with a **New Score** of 2000 and the **Relative** option enabled.

 4. Include the **Show Highscore** action, with **Background, Other Color**, and **Font** properties set as before.

 5. Finally, include the **Restart Game** action.

Now that we have the object, we can create a room for it to go in.

Creating a new finish room resource for the game:

1. Create a new room and place one instance of the new finish object inside it. As this object has no sprite, it will appear as a blue ball with a red question mark on it. This will not appear in the game, but it reminds us that this (invisible) object is there when we are editing the room.

Now test the game to check that you can complete it—and that you get the appropriate message when you do (in other words, not an error message!)

Adding Some Visual Variety

At the moment all the moons look exactly the same, and the asteroids even rotate in unison as they move around the screen. However, with a different moon sprite and a little use of the random command, we can soon change this.

Editing the moon and asteroid objects:

1. Open the properties form for the moon object and click the **Edit** button below the name of the object's sprite (this is just another way of opening the moon sprite's properties).

2. In the moon sprite's properties, click **Load Sprite** and select `Bases.gif` instead of the existing sprite. This sprite contains eight subimages showing different kinds of inhabitations on each moon. Click **OK** to close the Sprite Properties form.

 3. Back in the moon Object Properties form, select the **Create** event and include a new **Change Sprite** action. Select the moon sprite and type `random(8)` in the **Subimage** property. This will randomly choose one of the inhabited moon sprites. Also set **Speed** to `0` to stop the sprite from animating on its own and changing the subimage.

4. Close the Action Properties and the moon Object Properties forms.

 5. Include an identical **Change Sprite** action to the **Create** event of the special moon object in the same way. There is no need to edit the moon sprite again, as both objects use the same one.

 6. Open the properties form for the asteroid object and include a new **Change Sprite** action in its **Create** event as well. This time choose the asteroid sprite, and type `random(180)` in the **Subimage** property. There are 180 images in the rotating asteroid animation, so this will start each one at a different angle. Also type `random(4)` in the **Speed** property so that asteroids rotate at different speeds.

Help Information

Once you have finished making a game, it is easy to sit back and bask in your own creative genius, but there is one more important thing you must do before moving onto your next game. It may seem blindingly obvious to you how to play your masterpiece, but remember that it is rarely that obvious to a newcomer. If players get frustrated and stuck in the first few minutes because they can't figure out the controls, then they usually assume it is just a bad game rather than giving it the chance it deserves. Therefore, you should always provide some help in your game to explain the controls and basic idea of the game. Fortunately, Game Maker makes this very easy through its **Game Information**.

Adding game information to the game:

1. Double-click on **Game Information** near the bottom of the resource list.

2. A text editor will open where you can type any text you like in different fonts and colors.

3. Typically you should enter the name of the game, the name of the author(s), a short description of the goals, and a list of the controls.

4. When you're done, click the green checkmark at the top left to close the editor.

That's all there is to it. When the player presses the F1 key during game play, the game is automatically paused until the help window is closed. Test the game one last time to check that this final version works correctly. You can also load the final version of the game from Games/Chapter03/galactic4.gm6 on the CD.

Congratulations

Congratulations! You've now completed your second game with Game Maker. You might want to experiment with the game a bit further before continuing as there is much more you could do with it. To start with, you could make more levels with faster-moving asteroids or smaller moons to make it harder to land on them. We've included both larger planet sprites and smaller planetoids for you to experiment with, so see what you can come up with.

This chapter has introduced you to more features of Game Maker. In particular you've made use of events and actions to change sprites and objects. You've also used the **Depth** property of objects to control the order in which the instances appear on the screen. This chapter has also introduced *variables* for the first time, even though we haven't called them that yet. For example, the word direction is a variable indicating the current direction of an instance. We also used the variables x and y that indicate the position of an instance. There are many variables in Game Maker, and they are extremely useful. We will see plenty more of them in the chapters to follow.

In the next chapter, we'll continue to build on what you've learned so far by creating a crazy action game that requires quick thinking to avoid being squished. It's amazing what can go on in a deserted warehouse . . .

■ ■ ■

CHAPTER 4

Target the Player: It's Fun Being Squished

Our third game will be an action game that challenges players to make quick decisions under pressure—and if they're not fast enough then they'll get squished! We'll introduce some new techniques for putting character animation into the game, and show how a *controller object* can be used to help to manage the game.

Designing the Game: Lazarus

As usual we'll need a description of our game. We've named it *Lazarus*, after the biblical character who was resurrected from the dead, because the game once had to be recovered from an old floppy disk that had become corrupted! Always remember to make backups of your data!

Lazarus has been abducted by the Blob Mob, who are intent on bringing this harmless creature to a sticky end. They've imprisoned him at the Blobfather's (sorry) factory, where they are trying to squish him under a pile of heavy boxes. However, they've not accounted for Lazarus's quick thinking, as the boxes can be used to build a stairway up to the power button that halts the machinery. Do you have the reactions needed to help Lazarus build a way up, or will the evil mob claim one more innocent victim?

Each level traps Lazarus in a pit of boxes stacked up on either side of the screen to contain him within the level. The arrow keys will move Lazarus left and right, and he will automatically jump onto boxes that are in his way. However, he can only jump the height of a single box, and stacks two or more boxes high will block his path. New boxes will periodically appear directly above Lazarus's current position and fall vertically down from the top of the screen until they come to rest. This means that the player will be able to use Lazarus's position to control where boxes fall and build a stairway up to the power button.

There will be four different types of boxes, increasing in weight and strength: cardboard, wood, metal, and stone. Falling boxes will come to rest on boxes that are stronger than them, but will crush boxes that are lighter. The type of each box is chosen at random, but the next box will be shown in the bottom-left corner of the window just before it appears. There will be a number of increasingly difficult levels, with higher stairways to build, and boxes that fall faster. When Lazarus gets squished, the level will restart to give the player another try. See Figure 4-1 for an example of how a level will look.

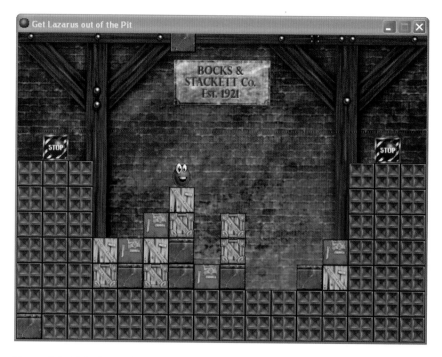

Figure 4-1. *This shows how a typical level might look in the Lazarus game.*

This may sound rather simple, but—as you'll see—it actually makes for a very challenging game! All the resources can be found in the Resources/Chapter04 folder on the CD.

An Animated Character

Our first task will be to create the Lazarus character. We'll give him comical animations for when he's moving, jumping, and being squished to add to the appeal of the game. This will require a number of different sprites and several different Lazarus objects as well. Like the different behaviors of the rocket in Galactic Mail, using several objects helps us to separate the different animations of Lazarus in a simple way.

The animations for Lazarus have been designed around the size of the boxes in the game. All the boxes are exactly 40×40 pixels in size, so the animations that show Lazarus jumping from one box to the next need to be as tall and wide as two boxes (80×80 pixels). This means we'll be working with sprites of different sizes, and have to think carefully about where to place the origin of each sprite so that they match up correctly. Remember that Game Maker acts as if it is holding each sprite by its origin as it moves around the screen; so all the origins need to be at the same position relative to Lazarus—regardless of the size of the sprite. This should begin to make sense as you complete the steps that follow.

▌Tip Setting the **Smooth Edges** property in the Sprite Properties form can often make sprites appear less pixilated (blocky) in the game.

Creating the Lazarus sprite resources for the game:

1. Create a new sprite called `spr_laz_stand` using `Lazarus_stand.gif` from the `Resources/ Chapter04` folder on the CD. This sprite is 40×40 pixels and shows Lazarus in his "normal" position. Remember that the origin for sprites defaults to the top-left corner (**X** and **Y** both set to `0`). We'll leave this where it is and make sure that the origins of all the other sprites match up with this position. Click the **OK** button to close the form.

2. Create another sprite called `spr_laz_right` using `Lazarus_right.gif`. This sprite is 80×80 pixels and shows Lazarus jumping 40 pixels to the right (use the blue arrows to preview the animation). As usual, the origin has defaulted to the top-left corner of the sprite, but the top-left corner is further above Lazarus's head than in the last sprite. To match up with the previous sprite, we need to move the origin down by 40 pixels—so set the **Y** value to `40`. The properties form should now look like Figure 4-2.

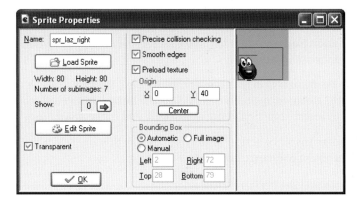

Figure 4-2. *The origin for this sprite has been moved to halfway down the left-hand side.*

3. Create a `spr_laz_jump_right` sprite in exactly the same way using `Lazarus_jump_right.gif` (with an **X** value of `0` and a **Y** value of `40`).

4. Create a `spr_laz_left` sprite using `Lazarus_left.gif`. This sprite is also 80×80 pixels and shows Lazarus jumping 40 pixels to the left, but this time Lazarus starts on the bottom-right side of the sprite. This means we need to move the origin 40 pixels down and 40 pixels right to place it at the same relative position as before. Set both the **X** and **Y** values to `40` and close the form.

5. Create a `spr_laz_jump_left` sprite in exactly the same way using `Lazarus_jump_left.gif` (with an **X** value of `40` and a **Y** value of `40`).

6. Create two more sprites called `spr_laz_afraid` and `spr_laz_squished` using `Lazarus_afraid.gif` and `Lazarus_squished.gif`. These are 40×40 pixels so there's no need to change the origin.

These are all the sprites we need for Lazarus, so our next step is to make some objects for him. The main object will be the "normal" standing Lazarus. This is the most important one, as it will react to the player's keyboard input. The others are only there to play the different animations, after which they turn themselves back into the standing Lazarus. They will also move Lazarus to a new position that corresponds to the final frame of the animation.

We have a bit of a chicken-and-egg situation here, as we did with the two types of rockets in Galactic Mail. The "normal object" will need actions to turn it into "animating objects" (which don't exist yet) and the "animating objects" will need actions to turn them into "normal objects" (which also don't exist yet). So which objects do we create first? Well, the answer is that we create the "normal object" but come back to creating its events and actions after we have created the "animating objects"—crafty, eh?

Creating Lazarus object resources for the game:

1. Create a new object called obj_laz_stand and give it the standing Lazarus sprite.

2. Press **OK** to close the properties form (we will come back to it later).

3. Create a new object called obj_laz_right and give it the sprite that hops one box horizontally to the right (spr_laz_right).

4. Add an **Other, Animation End** event. Remember that this event happens when a sprite reaches the last subimage in its animation.

5. Include the **Jump to Position** action in this event (**move** tab). Set **X** to 40 and **Y** to 0, and make sure that the **Relative** option is enabled. As the boxes are all 40×40 pixels, this will move Lazarus exactly one box to the right at the end of the animation.

6. Also include the **Change Instance** action (**main1** tab) below this and select obj_laz_stand as the object to change back into.

7. Click **OK** to close the object properties form.

8. Create another object called obj_laz_left and give it the sprite that hops one box horizontally to the left (spr_laz_left). Repeat the same process as before (steps 4–7), but set **X** to -40 for the **Jump to Position** action.

9. Create another object called obj_laz_jump_right and give it the sprite that hops up one box diagonally to the right (spr_laz_jump_right). Repeat the process, setting **X** to 40 and **Y** to -40.

10. Add a final object called obj_laz_jump_left and give it the sprite that hops up one box diagonally to the left (spr_laz_jump_left). This time, set **X** to -40 and **Y** to -40.

We may as well get the squished Lazarus object out of the way now too—even though we won't need it for a while. Once its gruesome animation finishes, this object will display a message to tell the player that they've been squished. This isn't because we think they are too stupid to notice, but it provides a useful pause before starting the level again! We're not going to add lives or high scores in this game, so we'll simply restart the level to give the player another try.

Creating the squished Lazarus object resource:

1. Create an object called `obj_laz_squished` and give it the squished Lazarus sprite.

2. Add an **Other, Animation End** event and include the **Display Message** action (**main2** tab) in it.

3. Type something like "`YOU'RE HISTORY!#Better luck next time`" into the message properties. Note that putting the # symbol in the middle of the message will start a new line from that point.

4. Finally, include the **Restart Room** action (**main1** tab) after the message action and press **OK** to close the object properties form.

Okay, so now we have these animation objects in place, we can continue making the main standing Lazarus object we started on the previous page. One of its main jobs is to change into the appropriate animating object when the player presses a key. The appropriate object depends on whether Lazarus is standing next to any boxes. We'll use a conditional collision action to help Game Maker work this out for us.

Adding a right key event for the standing Lazarus object:

1. Reopen the properties form for the `obj_laz_stand` object by double-clicking it in the resource list.

2. We'll start by creating actions to handle moving to the right. Add a **Key Press, <Right>** event and include the **Check Collision** action in it (**control** tab).

3. This action allows us to check that there *would* be a collision if we moved this instance to a particular position on the screen. We need to make sure that Lazarus is on solid ground before allowing him to move, as he shouldn't be able to jump when he is standing on thin air! To check that this is the case, we set **X** to 0 and **Y** to 8 (slightly below his current position), and enable the **Relative** option.

▦Note Conditional collision actions have an **Objects** option, which allows us to choose between checking for collisions with all objects or only ones marked as solid. We're leaving this set to only solid, so we need to remember to set the **Solid** property later when we create the box objects.

---

4. All of the remaining actions in this event depend on the previous condition (they only need to be called if it is **true**). Consequently, we'll need to include them all between **Start Block** and **End Block** actions. Include the **Start Block** action now.

5. Now include the **Check Empty** conditional action. This conditional action is the opposite of the last one: it checks that there *wouldn't* be a collision if we moved to a particular position on the screen. So to check that the space to the right of Lazarus is free, set **X** to 40 (the width of a box), set **Y** to 0, and enable the **Relative** option.

6. Include the **Change Instance** action (**main1** tab) and select the `obj_laz_right` object. Select **yes** to **Perform Events**. This means that the **Create** event of the object we're turning into *will* get called (which is important later when we add sound effects).

Note The **Perform Events** option controls whether the **Destroy** event of the current object and the **Create** event of the new object should be called. This isn't usually necessary so it does not call them by default.

---

7. Next include the **Else** action from the **control** tab (more about this in a moment).

8. Include another **Check Empty** conditional action directly after this. This should verify that there are no boxes diagonally, up, and to the right of Lazarus. Set **X** to 40 and **Y** to -40, and enable the **Relative** option.

9. Next include the **Change Instance** action and select the `obj_laz_jump_right` object. Select **yes** to **Perform Events**.

10. Finally, include an **End Block** action to conclude the actions that should be performed if Lazarus is on solid ground. The list of actions now should look like Figure 4-3.

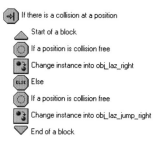

Figure 4-3. *Here are the actions for moving or jumping to the right.*

This is the first time we've used the **Else** action, but it is often used alongside conditional actions in this way. On its own, a conditional action only allows you to specify actions that should be performed if a condition is true. However, in combination with **Else**, you can specify different actions to be performed if that same condition is not true. This has many uses, but in this situation it allows us to ask sequences of questions like this:

Is there solid ground beneath Lazarus's feet? Yes. Well, is there a free space to the right of Lazarus? No—there's a box in the way. Okay, well, is there a free space on top of that box then? Yes—let's jump on top of it.

This is just one possible outcome, but our actions provide outcomes for four different situations: not moving when falling through the air; moving horizontally to the right when no boxes are in the way; jumping diagonally to the right when a single box is in the way; and doing nothing at all when more then one box is in the way. You can think of this action list as reading something like this:

If the position below has something solid in it, then read the next sentence. If the position to the right is collision free, then change into object obj_laz_right*; else, if the position diagonally right is collision free, then change into object* obj_laz_jump_right*.*

Before continuing, go through the actions step by step in your head and try to work out how you end up with each of these different outcomes (move right, move diagonally right, and no movement). When you're happy that this makes sense, we'll move on and do the same thing for the left arrow key.

■Note Like other conditional actions, the **Else** action can be used with or without blocks. If blocks are not used, then the **Else** only affects the action that immediately follows it.

Adding a left key press event to the standing Lazarus object:

1. Add a **Key Press, <Left>** event and include the **Check Collision** action. Set **X** to 0 and **Y** to 8, and enable the **Relative** option (this checks below).

2. Include a **Start Block** action.

3. Include the **Check Empty** conditional action (**control** tab) with **X** set to -40, **Y** set to 0, and the **Relative** option enabled (this checks left).

4. Next, include a **Change Instance** action (**main1** tab) and select obj_laz_left. Choose **yes** to **Perform Events**.

5. Now include **Else** action from the **control** tab.

6. Include a **Check Empty** action with **X** set to -40, **Y** set to -40, and **Relative** enabled (this checks diagonally left).

7. Include a **Change Instance** action and select the obj_laz_jump_left object. Choose **yes** to **Perform Events**.

8. Finally, include an **End Block** action to finish the block of actions.

Although our keyboard events stop Lazarus from jumping in mid-air, there aren't yet any events to make him fall down to the ground when he is. We'll get Game Maker to test for this in a **Step** event so that it is continually checking to see if he should be falling. However, we need to think carefully about how far he should fall in each step. The amount of movement in each step will determine how fast he falls, but it will make our job much simpler if we also choose a number that divides exactly into 40 (the height of the boxes). Can you think why?

Let's imagine that we chose a number that doesn't divide into 40, like 12. Lazarus would have fallen 12 pixels after one step, 24 pixels after two steps, 36 pixels after three steps, and 48 pixels after four. At no stage has Lazarus fallen the exact 40 pixels needed to fall the height of one box; he is either 4 pixels too high (at 36 pixels) or 8 pixels too low (at 48 pixels). This means he would either end up floating above boxes, or jammed someway into them! Using any number that divides into 40 will avoid this problem (1, 2, 4, 5, 8, 10, 20, or 40), so we've chosen a value of 8 because it produces a sensible-looking falling speed.

Adding a step event to the standing Lazarus object to make it fall:

1. Add the **Step, Step** event to the standing Lazarus object. We are using the "standard" **Step** event as we don't really care exactly when Lazarus falls, provided he does.

2. Include a **Check Empty** action in the **Step** event, setting **X** to 0 and **Y** to 8, and enabling the **Relative** option. This action checks for empty space just below Lazarus.

3. Include a **Jump to Position** action directly after it so that it will only be performed if the **Check Empty** condition is true. We need to give it the same relative settings as before, so that it moves into the empty space. Set **X** to 0 and **Y** to 8, and enable the **Relative** option.

A Test Environment

We've gone through quite a lot of steps so far without being able to test our work, so before going any further let's quickly create a test level for Lazarus to move around in. There are no falling boxes yet, so we'll have to create some random stacks of our own to check if the movement is working correctly. We'll create just one box type to do this: the boxes that make up the walls of the pit.

Creating the wall object resource for the game:

1. Create a new sprite called spr_wall using Wall.gif. Disable the **Transparent** option as the walls for this level need to look completely solid.

2. Create a new object called obj_wall and give it the wall sprite. Enable the **Solid** option so that the checks in the standing Lazarus object can detect the wall.

3. Create a new room called room_test and provide a caption in the **settings** tab.

4. Look in the toolbar at the top of the Room Properties form and set both **Snap X** and **Snap Y** to 40. All our boxes are 40×40 pixels, so this will help us to place them neatly on the level. The grid in the room will change accordingly.

5. Switch to the **objects** tab again and select the wall object to place. Create a level with a number of boxes that form flat areas and staircases (remember, you can hold the Shift key to add multiple instances). Also add one instance of the standing Lazarus object. Try to make it look something like Figure 4-4.

■**Note** Sometimes when you close a room form you get a warning message saying that there are instances outside the room. This can happen when you accidentally move the mouse outside the room area while adding objects. You will be asked whether these instances should be removed—simply click the **Yes** button.

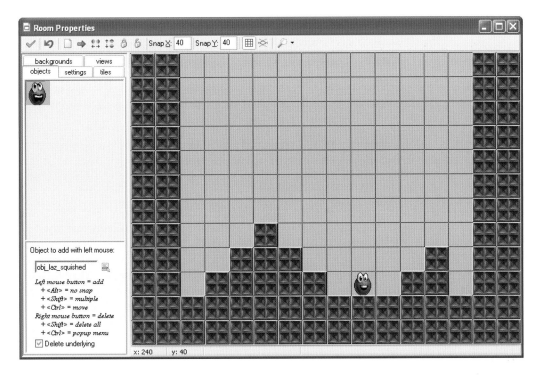

Figure 4-4. *Your test level should look something like this.*

At last, you can finally run the game! Test the character's movement in all the possible situations and make sure that he behaves the way you would expect. If something isn't working right, then check your steps carefully, making sure that you enabled the **Relative** option in all the actions where it was indicated. Alternatively, you can load the current version from the file Games/Chapter04/lazarus1.gm6 on the CD.

Falling Boxes

Our next goal is to create the falling boxes that both threaten the player and provide the means for their escape. As indicated in the game description, there will be four types of boxes in the game: stone boxes, metal boxes, wooden boxes, and cardboard boxes. As you would expect, stone boxes are the heaviest and cardboard boxes are the lightest. Falling boxes are chosen at random and heavier boxes will crush lighter boxes as they fall—making it harder to build a stairway out of the pit. However, to give the player a chance to think ahead, the next box will be shown in the corner of the screen while the last box is still falling.

Each box will need to change its behavior three times in the game: first it appears in the corner, as the "next box"; then it falls down the screen until it lands on another box; and finally it forms a stationary obstacle for Lazarus to negotiate. As you may have guessed, we will achieve this by creating three different objects for each box: one for each behavior. We will start by creating the stationary boxes, as they are the simplest to make. First, though, we need to create some new sprites.

Creating new box sprite and object resources for the game:

1. Create sprites called spr_box_stone and spr_box_card using StoneBox.gif and CardBox.gif. Disable the **Transparent** option on both these sprites.

2. Now create sprites called spr_box_metal and spr_box_wood using MetalBox.gif and WoodBox.gif. This time leave the **Transparent** option enabled, as these two sprites have a small amount of transparency around the edges.

3. Create a new object called obj_box_stone and give it the sprite for the stone box. Set the **Solid** option so that it is detected in collision tests.

4. Repeat the previous step to add objects for obj_box_metal, obj_box_wood and obj_box_card.

Next we'll make the falling boxes. These need to start at the top of the screen, directly above Lazarus's horizontal position, so we'll make use of the x variable of the standing Lazarus object to tell us where that is. Once it starts falling, we'll give it a speed of 5 because that divides exactly into 40 (important for the same reasons as before) and it is slightly slower than the speed that Lazarus falls (otherwise a box might squish Lazarus in the air!). When a box collides with a heavier box, it turns into a stationary box, but when it collides with a lighter box, it destroys that box and continues to fall.

Creating falling box objects for the game:

1. Create a new object called obj_falling_stone, give it the sprite for the stone box, and select the **Solid** option as before.

2. Add a **Create** event and include a **Jump to Position** action in it. Type the variable obj_laz_stand.x (the horizontal position of Lazarus) into **X** and set **Y** to -40. This will make the box start above Lazarus, just out of view at the top of the screen.

3. Next include the **Move Fixed** action, using a downward direction and a **Speed** of 5.

4. Add a **Collision** event with obj_laz_stand and include a **Change Instance** action in it. Change the **Applies to** option to **Other**, so that it changes Lazarus rather than the box. Select the obj_laz_squished and select **yes** to **Perform Events.**

5. Add another **Collision** event, this time with obj_wall. This needs to stop the box moving, so include a **Move Fixed** action and select the middle square with a **Speed** of 0. Also include a **Change Instance** action, and select the stationary box obj_box_stone.

6. Add a third **Collision** event with obj_box_stone and include the same two actions as the **Collision** event with the wall above (you could copy them).

7. Add a fourth **Collision** event with obj_box_metal. The metal box is lighter than the stone box so it must be crushed. Include a **Destroy Instance** action and select the **Other** object.

8. Add fifth and sixth **Collision** events with obj_box_wood and obj_box_card, both including identical **Destroy Instance** actions as we did in step 7 to destroy the **Other** box in the collision.

Okay, that's one of the falling boxes. The other falling boxes are similar but need to behave slightly differently when they collide with different kinds of boxes.

9. Create the remaining three falling objects for the other types (`obj_falling_metal`, `obj_falling_wood`, and `obj_falling_card`). Repeat steps 1–8 for each one, using step 7 when a box crushes another box and step 5 when a box stops moving. Refer to Table 4-1 when deciding which boxes should crush each other.

Table 4-1. *Box Materials That Should Crush Each Other*

Material	Material(s) That It Crushes
Stone	Metal, Wood, and Card
Metal	Wood and Card
Wood	Card
Card	None

Phew! That was quite a lot of work (28 events and 46 actions), made worse by the fact that we had to repeat the same steps over and over again. In Chapter 6 we will see that there is actually a quicker way to do this kind of thing using *parents*. Nonetheless, although this might have seemed like a lot of effort, it may help you to appreciate the work that goes into a commercial game. They usually take at least 18 months to program and require hundreds of thousands of lines of code to make them work!

Now let's set about creating the final set of boxes that appears in the bottom-left corner to show the player which box is coming next. This adds an important element of gameplay, allowing the player to plan ahead and adapt their strategy based on where it would be most useful for the next box to fall. It requires quick thinking and takes a bit of practice, but it helps to create a challenging and rewarding game. The "next box" objects are very simple to make, but we'll need four of them again—one for each type of box.

Creating next box object resources for the game:

1. Create a new object called `obj_next_stone`, give it a stone box sprite, and enable the **Solid** option. That's it, so click **OK** to close the object properties.

2. Create objects for `obj_next_metal`, `obj_next_wood`, and `obj_next_card` in the same way.

I'm sure you'll be relieved to find out that's all the boxes we need to create for this game! However, while the falling boxes have actions to turn them into stationary boxes, there are no actions yet for turning next boxes into falling boxes, or creating next boxes in the first place. That's because we are going to create a *controller object* to do this. A controller object is usually an invisible object (it doesn't have a sprite), which performs important actions on other objects. Our controller object will use a **Step** event to continually check if there is a falling box on the level. If not, then it will turn the current next box into a falling box and create a new next box. In this way, the controller object will maintain a constant cycle of new and falling boxes until the level is completed—or the player gets squished!

Creating a controller object resource for the game:

1. Create a new object called `obj_controller` and leave it without a sprite.

2. Add a **Step, Step** event and include the **Test Instance Count** conditional action (**control** tab). This counts the number of instances of a particular object on the level and tests it against a value. Choose the `obj_falling_stone` object; leave **Number** as **0** and **Operation** as **Equal to**. This creates a condition that is true if the number of falling stone box instances on the level is equal to 0 (i.e., there aren't any!).

3. Include three more **Test Instance Count** conditional actions to check if there are no instances of `obj_falling_metal`, `obj_falling_wood`, and `obj_falling_card` in the same way. When combined, these conditional actions will make sure that there are no falling boxes of any kind on the level before creating a new one.

4. Include a final **Test Instance Count** action for the `obj_laz_stand` object, but set **Number** to 1 and the **Operation** to **Equal to**. This makes sure that there is an instance of the standing Lazarus object on the level, rather than any of the animating objects.

5. Include a **Start Block** action. This will group together all the actions that need to be performed to create the new box.

6. Include a **Change Instance** action and select **Object** for **Applies to,** so that it changes *all* instances of one kind of object on the level into another. Set **Object** to `obj_next_stone`, **Change Into** to `obj_falling_stone`, and select **yes** to perform events (the **Create** event for the falling box needs to be performed to start it in the correct position). This will turn any stone next boxes into stone falling boxes. The action should now look like Figure 4-5.

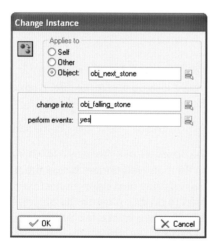

Figure 4-5. *Change the next box into a falling box.*

7. However, because the type of box will be chosen randomly, we don't know what kind of next box object the next box will actually be. To cover all bases, add three more **Change Instance** actions to change `obj_next_metal` objects into `obj_falling_metal` objects, `obj_next_wood` into `obj_falling_wood`, and `obj_next_card` into `obj_falling_card` in the same way.

8. Next we need to randomly create one of the next box objects. Include a **Create Random** action (**main1** tab) and select the four different next box objects. Set **X** to 0 and **Y** to 440, and leave **Relative** disabled. Remember that when **Relative** is disabled, **X** and **Y** are measured from the top-left corner of the screen. These coordinates will therefore put the new next box where it should be in the bottom-left corner of the screen. The action should now look like Figure 4-6.

9. Finally, include an **End Block** action to conclude the block of actions that are dependent on all the conditions above them being true.

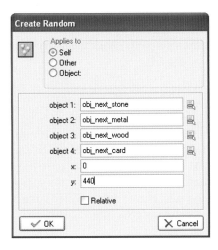

Figure 4-6. *The **Create Random** action allows us to randomly create one of the four next box objects.*

This long list of conditional actions means that the block of actions will only be performed if all these conditions are true. In other words, if there are no instances of `obj_falling_stone` and no instances of `obj_falling_metal` and no instances of `obj_falling_wood` and no instances of `obj_falling_card` and one instance of `obj_laz_stand`, *then* Game Maker will create a new box.

You might have thought it a bit odd that we need to check that there is a standing Lazarus object as part of our conditions for creating new boxes. If you look back at one of the **Jump To Position** actions in the **Create** events of the falling boxes, you will remember that we use the `obj_laz_stand.x` variable to start the object in the correct position. However, Game Maker can't provide that object's x position if it has turned into an animation object, so it will create an error in the program. So to avoid this possibility we check that there's a standing Lazarus instance on the level before creating new falling boxes.

Now it's finally time to test our new objects.

Editing the test room to add new instances:

1. Reopen the test room we created by double-clicking on it in the resource list.

2. Remove all the extra wall instances so that it leaves just a pit with walls on both sides and across the bottom.

3. Add one instance of the controller object into the room (easily forgotten!)

▓**Note** When an object has no sprite, it shows up in the Room Properties form as a blue ball with a red question mark. This will not appear in the game, but reminds us that this (invisible) object is there when we are editing the room.

Now run the game and test it carefully. Make sure that the box that appears in the bottom left is actually the box that falls down the screen next and check that heavier boxes are crushing lighter ones. As usual, if there are any problems, then carefully check the instructions or load the game from Games/Chapter04/lazarus2.gm6 on the CD.

Finishing Touches

We now have all the basic ingredients of the game in place and there are just a few more things to do before we could call it a finished game. There's no way to complete a level yet, so we need to include the stop buttons that will halt the boxes and move the player onto the next level. Some sound effects would also be nice—as would a background and a title screen. We're obviously going to need a few different levels, too. However, before all that we're going to add something cool that will endear the player to Lazarus's plight a little more.

No Way Out!

You may have noticed that there's another animation we haven't used yet that shows Lazarus looking afraid. We're going to show this animation when he's in a hopeless situation and knows he is about to meet his end. However, rather than create a new object for this animation like we did with the others, we're just going to change the sprite of the standing Lazarus object when he becomes afraid. We can do this because "being afraid" does not need any actions of its own: it has exactly the same behavior as standing—it just looks different. We're going to control this animation within the **Step** event, so that the correct animation is chosen at any point in time. We will use **Check Collision** actions to detect if Lazarus is surrounded by stacks of boxes two or more high on both sides. The **Check Collision** action performs actions only when there *is* a collision at a particular point. In this way, we can detect whether Lazarus is trapped on all sides and set his animation to be afraid.

Editing the standing Lazarus object to detect for being trapped:

1. Reopen the standing Lazarus object and select its **Step** event, so that you can see the existing actions for this event.

2. Include the **Check Collision** conditional action (**control** tab) below the last action in the list. Set **X** to 40 and **Y** to 0, and enable the **Relative** option. This checks for a box to the right of Lazarus.

3. Include another **Check Collision** action with **X** set to 40, **Y** set to -40, and the **Relative** option enabled. This checks for a box diagonally to the right of Lazarus.

4. Include two more **Check Collision** actions: one with **X** set to -40 and **Y** set to 0, and the other with **X** set to -40 and **Y** set to -40. Both should have the **Relative** option enabled. These check for boxes to the left and diagonally to the left of Lazarus.

5. Finally, include a **Change Sprite** action, using the "afraid Lazarus" sprite. This will now only happen if the four conditional actions above are true and Lazarus is literally boxed in.

Hopeless as this situation may sound, it is actually possible for Lazarus to be saved from this predicament by a heavy block crushing the stack of boxes on one side of him. If this happens, then we would like Lazarus to stop being afraid. We *could* include conditional actions to check for this happening and change his sprite back to normal. However, we can achieve the same effect simply by including a **Change Sprite** action at the very beginning of the list of actions for this event. Changing into the standing Lazarus sprite by default will make the sprite revert back to normal if he stops being trapped.

Editing the standing Lazarus object to detect for being freed:

1. Select the **Step** event for the standing Lazarus object so that you can see the existing actions for this event.

2. Include a **Change Sprite** event at the very beginning of the list of actions (you can drag actions about if it falls in the wrong place). Set it to change into the standing Lazarus sprite.

You might want to play the game now and make sure that this new feature is working correctly. Features like this don't change the gameplay directly, but add to the playing experience and make the game more entertaining to play.

Adding a Goal

The player's goal is to reach one of the stop buttons, so that it halts the machinery and stops dropping the boxes. However, in practice all the buttons really need to do is move the player onto the next level when the standing Lazarus object collides with them. If there are no more rooms, then it will show a completion message and restart the game.

Creating a new button object resource for the game:

1. Create a new sprite called spr_button using Button.gif.

2. Create a new object called obj_button and give it the button sprite. Set **Depth** to 10 so that it appears behind other objects.

 3. Add a **Collision** event with the standing Lazarus object and include a **Sleep** action in it (**main2** tab). Set **Milliseconds** to 1000 (1 second) and **Redraw** to true. This should give a brief pause for the player to realize they have completed the level.

 4. Include a conditional **Check Next** action (**main1** tab).

 5. Include a **Next Room** action (**main1** tab).

 6. Include an **Else** action followed by a **Start Block** action.

 7. Include a **Display Message** action (**main2** tab) and set **Message** to something like "CONGRATULATIONS#You have completed the game!"

 8. Include a **Different Room** action and set **New Room** to the first room (which is the only room at the moment).

 9. Finally, include an **End Block** action and close the object properties.

10. Edit your test room and add a stop button on either side at the top of the pit.

Starting a Level

At the moment, boxes start falling as soon as the player enters the level, leaving them with no time to gather their thoughts and prepare their strategy. We're going to help them out by creating a starter object that displays the title for a couple of seconds before changing itself into the controller object and starting to drop boxes.

Creating a new starter object resource for the game:

1. Create a new sprite called spr_title using Title.gif.

2. Create a new object called obj_starter and give it the title sprite.

 3. Add a **Create** event and include a **Sleep** action in it. Set **Milliseconds** to 2000, for a wait of two seconds.

 4. Include the **Change Instance** action and select the controller object. Close the object properties.

5. Edit your test room, and remove the controller object using the right mouse button. Add the starter object at an appropriate place instead.

▨**Note** You may have noticed that the title doesn't appear on the first level when you run the game. This is because the starter object's **Create** event is executed before the window appears, so it has already turned into a controller object by the time we see the room. This can be remedied using an **Alarm** action to add a delay, but we won't worry about this for now, and we'll come back to alarms in Chapter 6.

Sounds, Backgrounds, and Help

It's about time we made the game feel a bit more professional by including sound effects and music in the game. This is quite simple and you can probably handle most of this on your own by now, but here are some pointers to help you on your way:

1. All the sound resources can be found in the Resources/Chapter04 folder on the CD.

2. You'll need to add sounds for Music.mp3, Wall.wav, Crush.wav, Squished.wav, Move.wav, and Button.wav and play them at the right times using the **Play Sound** action (**main1** tab).

3. A good place to start playing the music would be in a new **Game Start** event for the controller object. You'll find the **Game start** event in **Other** events. Don't forget to set **Loop** to true in the **Play Sound** action to make the music loop forever.

4. You'll need to add crush or wall sound effects to the existing **Collision** events between falling box objects and stationary box objects.

5. Add a new **Create** event for the squished Lazarus object, and play the squished sound effect there. This will save you the trouble of putting it in each of the four collision events between falling boxes and Lazarus.

6. Adding **Create** events to play the move sound effects would also be a good way of handling the four moving Lazarus objects.

7. Finally, you'll need to play the button sound effect in the **Collision** event between the button and Lazarus.

Test the game and make sure all the sound effects are playing in the correct place. If you don't hear a sound when moving around, check that you set **Perform Events** to **yes** in the **Change Instance** actions that change into the animating objects. If you didn't, then Game Maker won't perform the **Create** events that contain the sound effects.

A backdrop to the levels would also improve the look of the game, and we should put together some kind of help text for the player too.

Creating a background resource and Game Information:

1. Create a background using Background.bmp from Resources/Chapter04 on the CD.

2. Reopen the properties form for the room and select the **backgrounds** tab. Select the new background from the menu halfway down on the left.

3. Double-click on **Game Information** in the resource list and add a help text for the game. Remember to include the name of the game and who it was created by (you), along with a short description of the aims and controls.

Levels

All that is left now is to create a variety of levels for your game. We talk about level design in much more detail in Chapter 8, but it's probably best to start with shallow pits and buttons on each side to keep things fairly easy. However, as the levels progress they can become as deep and narrow as you like! Making the floor of the pit higher will make the level harder, as the player has less time to react to the falling boxes. You could also place stationary boxes in unhelpful places or place the buttons in mid-air to vary the challenge. One sure way to make the game more challenging is to increase the **Speed** setting on the **settings** tab for each level. This controls the number of steps per second on each level. It defaults to 30 steps per second, but higher numbers will make the game faster and harder and lower numbers will make it slower and easier.

Now it's up to you to create some interesting levels for the game. Remember that duplicating rooms will save you a lot of work, so right-click on the room in the resource list and select **Duplicate** from the pop-up menu. Once you've made your levels, let someone else try to play them and see how difficult they find it. Game designers often find their games very easy because they have played them so much, but it is often much harder for everyone else. This is something you should always try to bear in mind when designing your games.

One very last thing: you may find it helpful to add a cheat in your game that allows you to skip between levels. You can do this as follows.

Editing the controller object to add cheats:

1. Open the properties form for the controller object.

2. Add a **Key Press, <N>** event and include the **Next Room** action.

3. Add a **Key Press, <P>** event and include the **Previous Room** action.

Good luck, and don't forget to remove these cheats when the game is finally finished!

Congratulations

You'll find the final version of the game in the file Games/Chapter04/lazarus3.gm6 on the CD. You might want to extend the game a bit further by adding opening and closing screens, or adding a scoring system to the game so that players can compete for the highest score. If you're feeling particularly adventurous, why not try adding some bonuses that sometimes appear when boxes are crushed by each other? One of these could even transform all the stationary boxes into stone boxes—or card boxes if you're feeling mean!

By making this game, you have learned how to animate characters, both by creating different objects and by switching sprites. You have also seen how to use a controller object to manage the game, plus you've learned how to use **Else** actions to provide extra control over the outcome of conditional actions. In fact, you've learned a lot about Game Maker over these past few chapters, and it's about time we gave you a bit of a break. With this in mind, the next chapter is all about game design and you won't have to go near events and actions again until Chapter 6. In the meantime, we'll be thinking more carefully about the designs behind the games we've made so far, and we'll be exploring what makes them fun to play.

CHAPTER 5

■■■

Game Design: Interactive Challenges

Once you've caught the game-making bug, then it's only a matter of time before you'll want to start designing your own games. There's nothing more satisfying than realizing your creative ideas and seeing other people enjoy them, and that's precisely what making games is all about. We don't want you to feel that you have to finish this book before trying out your own ideas—have a go whenever you feel ready, as you can always come back for more knowledge and ideas when you need them. Nonetheless, there is more to designing a good game than having a cool idea for a character or story, so these design chapters are here to provide some helpful advice for designing your own projects.

What Makes a Good Game?

We all know when we're playing one; we become completely absorbed by it and the hours fly by in no time at all, but how do you create a game like that? Well, unsurprisingly there's no formula to guarantee success—otherwise everyone would be doing it! However, there are some general principles that can help you to create better games by thinking more deeply about the way that games work. To become a good game designer, you need to learn to see beyond the surface features of games and consider what makes them fun at a basic level. This is something that takes time and practice, but we'll try to give you a taste of what we mean. Think about a particularly good section of your favorite game for a moment. Visualize where it is set, what your character is doing, and how it is interacting with the other characters and objects in the game. We're going to take fighting giant squids in *Zelda: Wind Waker* as an example:

> *The skies turn black and there is a crack of thunder as a giant squid rises from the surface of the ocean and towers over Link's tiny boat. A whirlpool forms around the monster's enormous body and the boat begins to circle helplessly around it in the current. The music reaches fever pitch and Link's only hope is to destroy all of the squid's bulging eyes with his boomerang before he is inevitably dragged down to a watery grave!*

Now this next part may seem a little strange: imagine that something has gone wrong with your PC or console and all the characters and objects in the game have turned into colored cubes! The music and sound effects have stopped too, but everything else is working just the way it always did. Now try to visualize your scene again:

A giant pink cube appears in front of my brown cube and I begin circling around it, gradually getting closer on each turn. There are eight white cubes attached to the pink cube—all of which must be destroyed before I get too close. To do this I must target white cubes in my line of sight and launch a yellow cube to fly out and destroy them. The yellow cube then returns back to me, and I can target and launch it again.

Now here's the question: would the cube version of the game still be fun to play? Well, it certainly won't be *as much* fun to play, since it has lost most of its original atmosphere and emotional involvement. However, for good games (like Zelda), some of the gameplay that makes it fun to play would still be there. It may look ridiculous—and you definitely wouldn't buy it like that—but part of the game's original magic remains.

Not quite convinced? Okay, take a look in the Games/Chapter05 folder and play the example games, evil_squares.gm6, galactic_squares.gm6, and lazarus_squares.gm6. These are the three games you've already made but with simple shapes and sound effects, instead of the usual backgrounds, characters, and music. Give each game a chance and you'll soon see that there is still fun to be had once all the pretty graphics, characters, and stories have been completely stripped away (see Figure 5-1). Once you're convinced, read on . . .

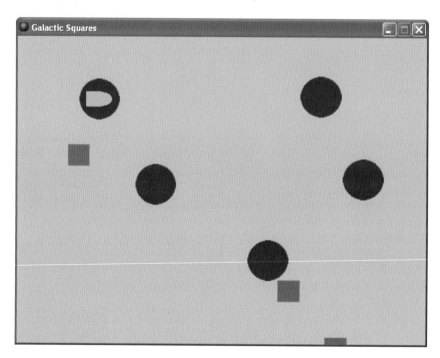

Figure 5-1. *Galactic Squares is not very pretty, but it's still fun to play.*

Game Mechanics

Okay, so good games are still playable even after all the fancy graphics and sound effects have been removed, but what creates this gameplay? Game developers call it the *game mechanics:* the basic rules and interactions that make a game fun to play. Understanding game mechanics is probably the most important part of becoming a good game designer. Sure, creating appealing characters and stories is really important too, but they need to be combined with solid game mechanics to create a good game. Think of game mechanics as the engine of a car and the graphics, characters, and storyline as the bodywork and finishing. A rusty old wreck with a Formula One engine may not win the Grand Prix, but it stands more chance than a Formula One car with a rusty old engine!

Of course, the best games combine great game mechanics with superb graphics, believable characters, spectacular music, and compelling storylines. However, these other aspects are not unique to computer games, and there are plenty of books about filmmaking, storytelling, music, and artwork that cover these topics far better than we could. Therefore, these design chapters will focus on the core skill that distinguishes game designers from designers of other forms of entertainment: game mechanics.

Interactive Challenges

What's the difference between a film, a toy, and a game? It might sound like the start of a bad joke, but it's actually a question that highlights the two main features that make games special as a form of entertainment. The most obvious difference between films and games is that games are *interactive*—players have some control over the outcome of games, but film audiences do not. Toys (like train sets, for example) are also interactive, as players have control over what they want to happen when they play with them. However, toys don't provide *challenges* for the player in the same way that games do. A player can create their own challenges using a toy (like deciding to race trains), but those challenges have to be created by the player and are not part of the toy. A game normally comes with its own set of challenges that the player must overcome in order to win the game.

So you can think of games as being "interactive challenges," therefore it's easy to deduce that both interaction and challenge are key elements of game mechanics. For the remainder of this chapter, we'll look at the various ways these two elements improve the game mechanics of your designs and make them more fun to play.

Game Genres

We often group games into different *genres*, and one way of doing this is to look at the types of interactions and challenges that different kinds of games provide. Games are evolving all the time, so there will never be a final list of genres that everyone agrees on. Nonetheless, we have made our own list of the main genres. As you read each one, try to distinguish the role of the game mechanics from the part that the characters, stories, and graphics play in the experience of that genre.

- **Action games** (e.g., sports, combat, platform, racing) usually involve fast and furious interactions with lots of physical challenges that leave little room for mistakes.

- **Simulator games** (e.g., flight sims, racing sims) usually involve realistic interactions and physical challenges with no room for mistakes at all.

- **Strategy games** (e.g., war games, puzzle games, god games) often involve slow or turn-based interactions with long-term intellectual challenges that involve planning and organization.

- **Adventure games** (e.g., point-and-click) usually let players interact at their own pace, providing short-term puzzle-based challenges and long-term story-led challenges. These challenges are often impossible to fail if you keep trying.

- **Role-playing games** (e.g., online RPGs) usually provide slower interactions with long-term story-led challenges. However, these are often less important to the player than the story and challenges that the player creates for themselves while developing their character.

Of course, most games don't fall neatly into one genre and may combine several kinds of interactions in one game. Nonetheless, a game designer does need to consider players' expectations of a particular genre; a role-playing game that requires lightning reflexes or a turn-based shoot-em-up might not go down too well! It's also worth remembering that new genres are only created when rules and conventions are broken, and the great games of the future are unlikely to follow the same conventions as today.

Challenges

We hope that you can see from the game genre descriptions that different players want different kinds of challenges from the games they play. Despite this, there are some general guidelines that can help you to provide better challenges in your games. We're going to apply these guidelines to the Evil Clutches game from Chapter 2 to see if we can turn it into a better game. All the new versions of the game can be found in the Games/Chapter05 folder on the CD. We've provided these as .exe files because we just want you to play them and notice how the changes are affecting the gameplay. You really don't need to know how they are made, but you can find the corresponding Game Maker project files in the Games/Chapter05/Registered directory on the CD. However, because these versions contain effects that are only available in the registered version of Game Maker, you will need to use the executables to play the game if your copy is still unregistered.

Difficulty

Challenges are important in games, because beating challenges makes players feel good about themselves. For this to happen, a challenge must be easy enough for a player to achieve but hard enough to be worth bothering with. Players give up on games that are too easy, because there is no satisfaction from beating a challenge that you could do blindfolded. However, players give up on games that are too hard because it makes them feel bad about themselves for failing, and they don't feel they are making any progress.

At the moment our Evil Clutches game is far too difficult at the start of the game, but in other ways it's too easy as well. It is too hard because just one touch of a demon will kill the dragon, and the game can be over before the player has worked out the controls! However, it can become too easy later on if players realize that they can always safely hide just offscreen and swoop in to rescue the hatchlings.

Even once these issues have been fixed, the game will still be too difficult for some players and too easy for others. People have different amounts of experience with computer games, but the best games are the ones that players of all levels can get into. We're going to make sure that our game appeals to as many people as possible by adding a difficulty menu at the start of the game, allowing the player to play in easy, medium, or hard mode. So in combination with the other tweaks, these are the changes that we're going to make to the first version of our game:

- Display a health bar for the dragon starting with 100 points of health.

- Make the dragon lose only 10 health points for each collision with a demon.

- Prevent the dragon from leaving the screen.

- Add a difficulty menu at the start of the game for easy, medium, or hard mode.

The file `evil_new1.exe` contains these four changes to the game. Play the new version and see what you think. We've changed the difficulty of the game by adjusting the chance of demons and hatchlings appearing in the different modes. There are now extra demons and fewer hatchlings in the hard mode and fewer demons and extra hatchlings in the easy mode. When you're setting the difficulty of your games, remember that game developers always find their own games easier than anyone else because they play them so much. If you make your own games harder and harder as you get better and better at them, then they will end up too difficult for other players. Always get someone else to test your game to make sure you've got the difficulty levels about right, and if you can't complete the game yourself, then don't expect anyone else to be able to!

Goals

Challenges are created by setting clear goals for players to achieve. If a goal is unclear or forgotten, then it no longer creates a challenge and it loses its power. In the last version of the game, we sneaked in some extra actions that made saving the lives of 50 hatchlings the ultimate goal of the game. However, you won't have felt any more challenged, since you didn't know about this new goal! In fact, even once you know about it, it's difficult to keep track of how many hatchlings you've saved, so any interest in the challenge doesn't last very long. It may sound obvious, but to keep a player challenged you need to make sure that they know what their goals are, and how they are progressing with them. Our game currently has two main goals for the player: saving a set number of hatchlings and beating the top score on the high-score table. We can make sure that these goals challenge the player by clearly displaying information about the player's progression toward these goals on the screen.

When players know what their goals are and how close they are to completing them, it also begins to create the what-if effect when the player loses. The closer a player gets to their goal, the more likely they are to think, "What if I had just been a little bit quicker, or hadn't made that one, stupid mistake?" Of course, this only happens if players get close to their goals—if they don't make it past the first obstacle, then they are more likely to think "As if!" than "What if?" This means that a player who rescues 40 of 50 hatchlings is more likely to have another go than a player who only rescues 10 of 50 hatchlings. We could make our game so easy that everyone can rescue 40 hatchlings, but then the game would become too easy to complete and lose its challenge. Instead, we can be more devious and reduce the chance of hatchlings appearing as more hatchlings are rescued. So if the chance of the first hatchling appearing is 1 in 50 (a 50-sided die), then the second might be 1 in 52, the third 1 in 54, and so forth. That way, by the time the last hatchling appears, the chance of the hatchling appearing has changed to only 1 in 150 (a 150-sided die!). In practice, this just means that hatchlings are released more quickly at the start of the game than at the end. This will make it easier for all players to rescue a good number of hatchlings—and trigger the what-if effect—without making the game too easy overall.

So to incorporate all these improvements to our game's goals, we'll make the following changes to the second version of the game:

- Clearly display how many hatchlings have been rescued and how many need to be rescued in total.

- Clearly display the player's score and the top high score to beat from the high-score table.

- Reduce the chance of hatchlings appearing, based on the number that have already been rescued.

Play the file `evil_new2.exe` containing these three changes. We hope you'll agree that we're already starting to make progress toward a game that is much more fun to play than the original (see Figure 5-2).

Figure 5-2. *Finally we can see our goals and how far away we are from achieving them.*

Rewards

Rewards are extremely important for maintaining a player's interest in a game's challenges. It can take a lot of time and effort to complete a challenge, so a reward makes players feel much better about it. It also makes it much more likely that they'll want to complete other challenges offered by the game. The high-score table already provides a reward system for scores, but we could do with something extra special for reaching the end of the game. So, once all the hatchlings have been rescued, we will:

- Display a congratulatory message.

- Award the player with a large bonus score.

- Show the player an amusing conclusion to the story of the game.

Although it is most important to reward players for completing the game's goals, it also helps to occasionally give them small rewards for no reason at all. Games often do this in the form of health bonuses and other kinds of pickups, which appear at random intervals. The fact that they appear randomly is significant, as it gives players hope that a pickup may come along at any point. This means they are more likely to stick with the game when they're in a desperate situation where they might otherwise give up—and if a bonus does arrive just in time, then the feeling of relief is enormous. It also adds to the power of the what-if effect, as players can now think, "What if I'd had just one more health bonus—maybe I'll be luckier next time?" We're going to add our own random rewards to Evil Clutches by making the following changes:

- Make the boss demon randomly drop health and shield bonuses.

- Randomly add between 5 and 25 percent to the dragon's health when a health bonus is collected.

- Make the dragon immune to taking damage for 15 seconds when a shield bonus is collected.

All of these new rewards are included in the file evil_new3.exe. The animation at the end of the game is an example of the kind of animated rewards you can quickly create in Game Maker with a little bit of imagination. It's not exactly a beautifully rendered cut-scene (see Figure 5-3), but it should make players smile.

Figure 5-3. *If you mess with dragons, then you're bound to get your fingers burned!*

Subgoals

Subgoals can enhance your games by providing short-term or optional challenges for your players to take up. Most games include a long-term goal that must to be met in order to complete the game, but these can often seem very distant and hard to achieve at the start of the game. Subgoals give the player something to aim for in the short term, and good games tend to provide a series of both short- and long-term goals to draw the player through the game. Our game is not very long, but there is certainly room for an additional short-term challenge. We'll challenge the player to shoot demons without taking damage, and reward them by powering up their fireballs as their demon tally increases. To achieve this we will:

- Count and display the number of demons shot in a row and reset the count back to 0 when the dragon takes damage.

- Limit the number of fireballs in the air at once, based on the current demon count. Begin with a limit of 2 and add 1 to this for each 10 demons on the tally.

- Scale the size of the fireball and add smoke effects to make the fireballs look more impressive as the demon tally increases.

Optional subgoals are a good way of providing extra challenges to advanced players, which other players can choose to ignore. These often include collecting particular items to unlock extra options, or hidden levels that less adventurous players are unlikely to find. These are really just a different way of balancing the difficulty of your game, so that players naturally find the right level of challenge for their own abilities. For our game we're going to turn the collection idea on its head and add a subgoal of trying not to accidentally shoot hatchlings! To make this work, we'll include the following changes:

- Each time a hatchling is accidentally shot, subtract one from the total number of hatchlings that have to be rescued (already displayed).

- At the end of the game, award the player bonus points based on the total number of hatchlings they've saved.

Ideally this should have its own special reward at the end of the game, but to keep it simple we've just rewarded the player handsomely in points for each hatchling saved. You can play a version of the game with these new subgoals in the file evil_new4.exe.

Interactivity

As well as challenges, the other main feature of games is their interactivity. Interactivity is about putting the player in control. Good games leave the player feeling in control of the game, while bad games make them feel powerless. As with challenges, players of different game genres often prefer different levels of control, but there are some common ways of helping to maintain a feeling of control in your games.

Choices and Control

To give players a feeling of control, we need to provide them with choices that seem to have a real effect on the outcome of the game. Action games constantly require players to make choices about the physical actions of the game (jumping, shooting, flying, etc.) and so provide an immediate feeling of control. However, games of all genres should ensure that enough choices are available to create this feeling too. Adventure games without enough choices can seem very linear—as if you are being forced through a path that has already been decided for you. Whenever you add choices to your games, think carefully about the difference they really make: is it worth having ten different weapons that all work in the same way? What's the point in allowing the player to choose what to say to a character if it always has the same outcome? Adding these kinds of features won't generally make your game any worse, but changing them so that they make a real difference will give more control to your players and make them more involved in the game.

We're going to add a choice of characters to our game, so that the player can choose to play the mother dragon or the father dragon. To make sure that this is a choice worth making, we're going to give each character a different special ability, which affects the way they play. The mother dragon will be able to call hatchlings to her—causing them to speed up and get out of harm's way more quickly—and the father dragon will be able to blast demons at close quarters with a cloud of steam—sending them crashing back into other demons. To add the new character and include different separate abilities, we will:

- Add the ability to select between playing the mother and father dragons at the start of the game.

- Add the ability for dragons to activate their special abilities using the Ctrl key.

- Make hatchlings at the same vertical level as the mother dragon speed up when she calls them to her.

- Make demons close to the father dragon fly back into other demons when he blasts them with a cloud of steam.

Figure 5-4 shows the character selection screen. You can see the effect of all these new changes by playing the file `evil_new5.exe`.

Control Overload!

Of course, it is possible to have too many choices in a game—particularly if extra choices mean extra controls. Most people can remember between five and nine things at once. If you have more than five controls in your game, some players will have forgotten what the first key does by the time they read what the last key does. In general, it's probably not a good idea to have more than two controls plus the arrow keys to move around. Try to make controls automatically perform different functions depending on the situation: pressing the spacebar might pick up items, open doors, or attack creatures, depending on whether the player was near to an item, a door, or a creature. That way, you can include lots of interesting features without needing extra controls for the player to remember.

Fortunately, this is one area where our Evil Clutches game is okay. Some players may find the special move control a bit too much to cope with at first, but because these moves are optional, we don't need to worry about them too much.

Figure 5-4. *It's one big happy family—and he's the daddy!*

Unfair Punishment

With the right level of control in your games, players will feel that they are the makers of their own fortunes. However, you can still quickly convince them otherwise by punishing them for something that isn't under their control. Such punishments are usually not included intentionally, but friendly characters with suicidal habits and enemies that blow up your objectives are both examples that have accidentally made it into commercial games. Avoiding unfair punishment is usually about making sure your game still works correctly, even when a player isn't playing the game in exactly the way you intended. The best way to find these problems is to get your friends to test your game thoroughly. They'll soon tell you if they think that something is unfair about your game.

Our game occasionally punishes the player unfairly. Fireballs go straight through demons, so it's easy to accidentally kill a hatchling that is flying behind one. The hatchling may not have even appeared until after the player pressed fire, but it is too late for them to do anything about it. When this happens the player may feel frustrated at being punished for something that was out of their control. We'll solve this problem by making the fireballs disappear when they kill a demon. This also has the effect of making the game a bit more fast and frantic, which is not a bad thing for a shoot-em-up.

Audio Feedback

In the final version of Evil Clutches, we're also going to add more sound effects to improve the game mechanics. At first glance, this may seem to go against the idea that mechanics are about rules and mechanisms—not niceties like sound. However, sounds are not just included in games just because they "sound nice," but also because they provide useful feedback to the player about what they are doing. If you go back to the Galactic Squares example from the start of the chapter, you'll notice that it still includes very basic sound effects. These sounds are designed to quickly inform the player about whether their interactions with the game are good or bad. Audio designed in this way can play an important part in helping to naturally steer the player in the right direction, whereas otherwise they might end up confused. Confused players do not feel in control, so audio has a role to play in this too.

Designing sound effects that both inspire the senses and inform the player in this way is not easy, and commercial games have their sound effects designed by professional sound engineers. See Chapter 15 for more information on the kinds of tools that you can use to try to do this for yourself. You'll find our sound effects in the Resources/Chapter05 folder and can hear them in action by playing evil_new6.exe from the Games/Chapter05 folder. This final version of the game includes the following changes to the unfair punishment and audio:

- Make fireballs disappear when they collide with a demon.
- Add audio feedback for shooting fireballs.
- Add audio feedback for when the dragon takes damage.
- Add audio feedback when a hatchling is saved.
- Add audio feedback for pickups.
- Add audio feedback for menus.

Summary

Now that you've played the final version of the game, we hope you found it much more fun than the original from the end of Chapter 2. In this chapter we've learned that challenges and interactivity are a central part of the game mechanics that make games fun to play. We've looked at a number of general principles that can help you to create better interactive challenges and followed them through with the Evil Clutches example. These are certainly not the only principles of good game design, and you are unlikely to design a good game simply by following a set of rules. Nonetheless, here is a summary of the main issues as a starting point for your own Game Maker projects:

- Challenge the player by
    - Providing clear, achievable goals and giving feedback on the player's progress.
    - Including both long and short-term goals.
    - Adding difficulty levels and optional subgoals for players of different abilities.
- Reward the player
    - For achieving goals and subgoals.
    - Randomly.
- Make the player feel in control by
    - Giving them choices that seem to make a real difference to the game.
    - Not confusing them with too many controls.
    - Not punishing them for things out of their control.
    - Giving the player audio feedback about their interactions with the game.

If you apply these principles with a bit of thought and care, then you should find that they can help you to make your own games more fun to play too. That concludes this chapter and the second part of the book—we'll look at some more design principles at the end of the next part, but for now we're joining the creatures of a Japanese coral reef to learn something about parenting . . .

PART 3

■ ■ ■

Level Design

The quality of a game's level design can make or break a game. Your game's popularity will sink like a brick if you don't put enough time into getting it right!

■ ■ ■

CHAPTER 6

Inheriting Events: Mother of Pearl

These days, some of the most inventive games come out of Japan. Japanese designers have a history of taking crazy design scenarios and turning them into brilliantly addictive games (e.g., Puzzle-Bobble, Pikmin, Gitaroo Man). Japanese games also have their own distinctive look derived from manga comics. In this chapter we'll make our own game in this style, based around the classic game of Breakout. In doing so, we'll learn how to use parent objects, one of Game Maker's most powerful features. As always, though, we'll need to start by writing a quick description of our game design.

Designing the Game: Super Rainbow Reef

Titles for Japanese games often start with the word "Super" (Super Monkey Ball, Super Smash Brothers, Super Street Fighter, etc.), so we're calling this game *Super Rainbow Reef* to keep in with the theme. Here's the design:

The monstrous Biglegs have driven the peace-loving creatures of Rainbow Reef from their ancestral homes. Despite their inexperience in the ways of war, Pop and Katch have invented a way of combining their skills to fight back against the Biglegs. For this incredible feat, Pop must bounce from Katch's shell to attack the evil invaders. Katch must then move quickly to save Pop from plummeting into the deep waters below. The cowardly Biglegs often retreat behind coral defenses, so our heroes must be prepared to smash their way through if they are to finally drive the Biglegs from Rainbow Reef!

There will be no direct control over Pop's movement, and he'll bounce freely around a playing area enclosed by walls on all sides except the base. The left and right arrow keys will move Katch horizontally along the base in order to bounce Pop from Katch's shell and stop him from falling out of the level. The collision point along Katch's shell will determine the direction of Pop's bounce, and so allow the player to control his movement. Bounces toward the left will send Pop left and bounces toward the right will send him right. Pop's movement is also affected by gravity, and each time he collides with Katch, he gets slightly faster so that the game becomes increasingly difficult.

The game will have several levels, each containing a number of Biglegs that Pop must collide with in order to complete the level. Most levels will also contain coral block defenses, which must be knocked out of the way in order to reach the Biglegs. Breaking blocks will score extra points and special blocks give the player extra rewards, but they don't have to be destroyed to finish a level. If Pop leaves the screen, the player loses a life and Pop is brought back into play. Once three lives have been lost, the game ends and a high-score table is displayed. A typical level is shown in Figure 6-1.

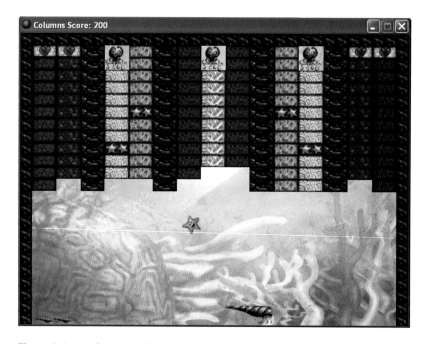

Figure 6-1. *Here's a typical level in Super Rainbow Reef.*

This time we will also make a separate feature list. It consists of all the different kinds of enemies and blocks that are available to create each level:

- Enemies:
    - Large stationary Biglegs
    - Small stationary Biglegs
    - Large Biglegs that move horizontally
    - Small Biglegs that move horizontally
- Blocks:
    - Multicolored blocks that can be destroyed for points
    - Solid blocks that cannot be destroyed
    - Blocks that must be hit twice before they are destroyed
    - Invisible solid blocks that cannot be destroyed
    - Blocks that create two extra copies of Pop when destroyed
    - Blocks that give the player an extra life

This should give enough information to create the game. All resources for this game have already been created for you in the Resources/Chapter06 folder on the CD.

A Game Framework

From now on, we are going to use a standard framework for many of the games we create so that they all have start and end screens that work in the same way. This framework will have the following parts:

- A title screen that displays the name of the game and has buttons to start a new game, load a saved game, show help, display the high-score table, and quit the game. Game developers normally use the term *front-end* to refer to the part of the game that allows the player to make selections like this. This screen will also be responsible for starting the background music and for initializing any other game settings, like the score.

- The actual game.

- The end of game screen that is shown when the game has been completed. This displays a congratulatory message and activates the high-score table, after which the game returns to the front-end.

You should already be familiar with how to do most of this from previous chapters, but this time we're adding button objects so that the player can control what is going on.

The Front-End

We'll begin by creating the front-end. Commercial games often have developers who devote all their time to creating the front-end for a game. Fortunately, ours won't be that complicated; all we need is a background image, a title sprite, several button sprites, and some background music. Let's start by adding these to the game.

Creating the front-end resources for the game:

1. Launch Game Maker if you haven't already and start a new empty game.

2. Create a new sprite called spr_title using Title.bmp from the Resources/Chapter06 folder on the CD (you can use Title.gif instead if you prefer the look of it).

3. Create the five button sprites—spr_button_start, spr_button_load, spr_button_help, spr_button_scores, and spr_button_quit—using the appropriate sprites from the same directory. Disable the **Transparent** option on these sprites.

4. Create a new background called background1 using Background1.bmp from the Resources/Chapter06 folder.

5. Create a new sound resource called snd_music using Music.mp3 from the Resources/Chapter06 folder.

This gives us all the resources we need for creating the front-end, so now we can define the objects for it. We'll start with the object that displays the title sprite, sets the score to 0, and plays the background music (we'll give this object some other functions as well later on). After that we'll create the button objects for the front-end.

Creating the title object resource for the front-end:

1. Create a new object called obj_title and give it the title sprite.

 2. Add a **Create** event to the object and include a **Set Score** action to set **Score** to 0.

 3. Add an **Other, Game Start** event and include a **Play Sound** action (**main1** tab) in it. Select the background music, and set **Loop** to true so that the music plays forever.

4. Click **OK** to close the properties form.

Creating the button objects resources for the front-end:

1. Create a new object called obj_butstart and give it the start button sprite.

 2. Add a **Mouse, Left Pressed** event and include the **Next Room** action (**main1** tab). The **Left Pressed** event happens when the user clicks on an instance's screen position with the left mouse button.

3. Click **OK** to close the Object Properties form.

4. Create a new object called obj_butload and give it the load button sprite.

 5. Add the **Mouse, Left Pressed** event and include the **Load Game** action (**main2** tab). **File Name** must be the same name as the file that we use to save the game to later on, so it's easiest to leave this as the default setting.

6. Click **OK** to close the Object Properties form.

7. Create a new object called obj_buthelp and give it the help button sprite.

 8. Add the **Mouse, Left Pressed** event and include the **Show Info** action (**main2** tab). This action shows the player the text entered under Game Information.

9. Click **OK** to close the Object Properties form.

10. Create a fourth button object called obj_butscores and give it the score button sprite.

 11. Add the **Mouse, Left Pressed** event and include the **Show Highscore** action (**score** tab). Feel free to play around with the settings to make the table look nice.

12. Click **OK** to close the Object Properties form.

13. Create a final object called obj_butquit and give it the quit button sprite.

 14. Add the **Mouse, Left Pressed** event and include the **End Game** action (**main2** tab).

15. Click **OK** to close the Object Properties form.

This gives us all the objects we need. Now we need to create a room to put them in that acts as the front-end itself.

Creating the front-end room resource for the game:

1. Create a new room resource called room_frontend (**settings** tab). Give the room a caption, then scale the room window so that you can see as much of the room as possible (preferably all of it).

2. Switch to the **backgrounds** tab. Click the menu icon to the right of where it says **<no background>** and select the background from the pop-up menu.

3. Next switch to the **objects** tab. Place one instance of each of the button objects along the bottom of the room (or somewhere else if you prefer). A logical order would be Start, Load, Help, Scores, Quit.

4. Select the title object and position it in the center of the room (remember that you can move an instance by holding the Ctrl key). Your room should now look something like Figure 6-2.

▓**Note** When you add an instance on top of an existing instance, the existing instance is deleted. This can be avoided by disabling the **Delete Underlying** option at the bottom left.

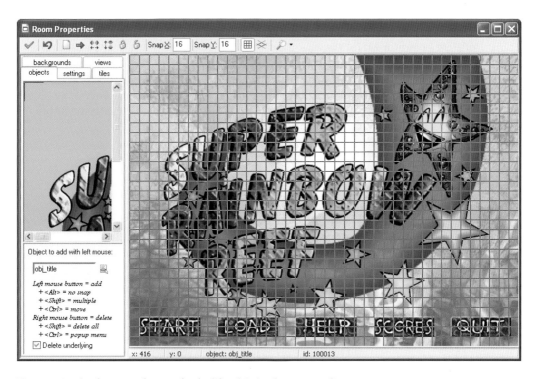

Figure 6-2. *The front-end room looks like this in the room editor.*

Finally, you should write a short help file for the game. You may find this easier once we have finished making the game, but we'll remind you how to do it now anyway.

Adding game information to the game:

1. Double-click on **Game Information** near the bottom of the resource list.

2. Type the name of the game, your name as the creator, a short description of the objectives, and a description of the controls.

3. Click on the green checkmark at the top left to close the editor.

You might want to test the framework now to check that it works correctly. An error message will appear if you click the start button, but that's fine as there are no rooms to go to yet in the game. Likewise, the load button will not do anything as there is no saved game to load, but the help, scores, and quit buttons should all work correctly.

The Completion Screen

We'll create the completion screen in a similar way to the one described in the previous chapter. It will contain one object that displays some text congratulating the player and adds 1,000 points to the player's score. There will then be a short pause and the high-score table will be displayed. After this, the player returns to the opening screen.

To achieve this, we're going to use new kinds of events and actions called *alarms. Alarm actions* work like a countdown for triggering *alarm events.* Alarm actions are given an amount of time to wait, and an alarm event is executed at the moment that time runs out. Like in other places in Game Maker, this time is measured in steps, so for each alarm action you indicate how many steps there should be before the alarm event takes place. Each instance of an object can have up to 12 alarms that can be used to make things happen at set points in the future.

Creating a congratulation object that uses alarm events and actions:

1. Create a new sprite called spr_congrats using the file Congratulation.gif.

2. Create a new object called obj_congrats and give it the congratulation sprite.

3. Add a **Create** event and include the **Set Alarm** action (**main2** tab). Set **Number of Steps** to 120 to create a delay of 4 seconds (as there are 30 steps in a second). Leave **In Alarm No** set to Alarm 0. See Figure 6-3.

4. Include a **Set Score** action below the alarm using a **New Score** of 1000, and enable **Relative** so that the score is added on.

5. Add an **Alarm, Alarm 0** event. This is the event that will now happen four seconds after the alarm action is executed. Include a **Show Highscore** action in this event and give it the same background and font settings as before.

6. Include the **Different Room** action (**main1** tab) and select the front-end room.

7. Click **OK** to close the Object Properties form.

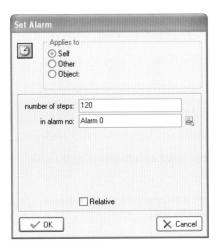

Figure 6-3. *Set an alarm clock to 120 steps, which is equivalent to four seconds.*

Creating a completion room for the game:

1. Create a new room called room_completed (**settings** tab) and give it an appropriate caption.

2. Switch to the **backgrounds** tab. Click the menu icon to the right of where it says **<no background>** and select the background from the pop-up menu.

3. Switch to the **objects** tab. Select the congrats object and position it in the top-left corner of the room.

It is time to test your work and try all the buttons again. Playing the game should now take you straight to the closing screen (you've finished all the levels as there are none!). You can now also add your name to the high-score table and view it again from the front-end. If any of this isn't working correctly, then carefully check that you've followed the instructions correctly. Alternatively, you can load this version from Games/Chapter06/rainbow1.gm6 on the CD.

We'll use this same framework (with different graphics) for many of the remaining games in the book. We won't have the space to explain all the steps again in so much detail, so make sure that you understand it well before continuing. Otherwise, you can either refer back to this chapter, or simply load each game with the framework already made to save yourself some work.

Bouncing Starfish

Now that our framework is complete, let's get started on the fun part: developing our game. In this section, we will create Pop, Katch, and the level boundary so that we can get Pop bouncing around the screen. As usual, we begin by creating the relevant sprites for the game.

Creating new sprite resources for Pop, Katch, and the wall:

1. Create a sprite called `spr_wall` using `Wall.gif` from the `Resources/Chapter06` folder on the CD. Disable the **Transparent** option so that the wall appears completely solid.

2. Create a sprite called `spr_pop` using `Pop.gif`. Click the **Center** button to place the origin of the sprite (where it is "held" from) at its center. Moving Pop from his center will make it easier to work out how far he has landed along Katch's shell when they collide. Also enable the **Smooth Edges** option to make the edges of Pop's legs look neater.

3. Create a sprite called `spr_katch` using `Katch.gif`. Click the **Center** button again and enable the **Smooth Edges** option too.

The next step is to create the corresponding objects. The wall object is extremely easy: it doesn't do much except act as a solid boundary for the playing area.

Creating the wall object resource for the game:

1. Create a new object called `obj_wall` and select the wall sprite.

2. Enable the **Solid** option and click **OK** to close the form.

Next we will add an object for Katch. Although Pop and Katch are both on the player's team, only Katch can be directly controlled by the player. The left and right arrow keys need to move Katch in the appropriate direction when there are no walls in the way. We will check for walls using a **Check Object** action that tells us if another kind of object is nearby. By making this check before moving Katch left or right, we can make sure that we only move her when her path is not blocked.

Creating the Katch object resource for the game:

1. Create a new object called `obj_katch` and give it Katch's sprite.

2. Add a **Keyboard, <Left>** event.

3. Include the **Check Object** conditional action (**control** tab) in this event. Select the wall object, set **X** to `-10` and **Y** to `0`, and enable the **Relative** option. This will check for wall objects 10 pixels to the left of Katch. Also enable the **NOT** option. This reverses the condition so that the next action (to move Katch) will be executed only if there is *not* a wall object in the way. The action should now look like Figure 6-4.

4. Include the **Jump to Position** action (**move** tab). Set the same values for **X** and **Y** (`-10` and `0`) and enable the **Relative** option so that Katch moves into the position that we just checked was free of walls.

5. Add a **Keyboard, <Right>** event.

6. Include the **Check Object** action (**control** tab). Select the wall object, set **X** to `10` and **Y** to `0`, and enable the **Relative** option. Also enable the **NOT** option again. This performs the same check for walls to the right.

7. Include the **Jump to Position** action (**move** tab). Set **X** to `10` and **Y** to `0`, and enable the **Relative** option. This moves Katch to the right if there are no walls blocking the way.

▓Note All conditional actions have a **NOT** field. This is used to indicate that the following actions are executed only if the condition is *not* true.

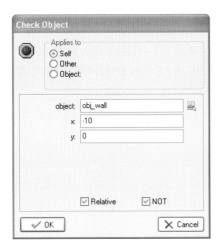

Figure 6-4. *This action checks that there is no wall object to the left of Katch.*

▓Tip When there is just one action that must be executed as a result of a condition, there is no need to put start and end blocks around it.

That completes the Katch object; now we need to create an object for Pop. This will be more complicated as it needs to move around and bounce against the walls. We'll also add some gravity so that Pop moves more realistically, and floats back down toward Katch at the bottom of the screen.

Creating the Pop object resource for the game:

1. Create a new object called obj_pop and give it Pop's sprite. Set its **Depth** to 10 so that it appears behind other objects in the game (this will look better later on).

2. Add a **Create** event and include a **Move Free** action with a **Speed** of 12. We want Pop to start moving upward, but we'll add a little variation by typing random(60)+60 as the **Direction**. The random(60) part will produce a random number between 0 and 60, so by adding 60 to this we will get a value between 60 and 120. This means we will get a direction somewhere between the two green arrows in Figure 6-5.

Note Angles in Game Maker work slightly differently from the way you might be used to. There are still 360 degrees in a full circle, but 0 degrees is horizontally to the right and they increase in an anticlockwise direction (see Figure 6-5).

3. Include a **Set Gravity** action (**move** tab), setting **Direction** to 270 (directly downward, see Figure 6-5) and **Gravity** to 0.2. This means that a downward speed of 0.2 will be added to Pop's current speed in each game step, pulling him slowly toward the bottom of the screen. The form should now look like Figure 6-6.

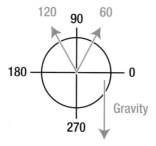

Figure 6-5. *Angles in Game Maker work differently from the way you may be used to.*

Figure 6-6. *This action sets the gravity downward by using an angle of 270 degrees.*

4. Add a **Collision** event with the wall object and include a **Bounce** action. Set the **Precise** option to **precisely** so that it takes into account the exact appearance of the colliding sprites to calculate the result of the collision.

Now we need to create actions to make Pop bounce off Katch's shell. We could use the **Bounce** action again, but then Pop would always bounce in the same way. We want the player to be able to control the direction of the bounce, so we need to alter it according to how far Pop bounces along Katch's shell. A bounce in the center of the shell should send Pop straight up the screen, but a bounce toward the end will send Pop diagonally in that direction (see Figure 6-7). In fact, we're going to send Pop bouncing off at an angle between 50 and 130 degrees, depending on his collision position.

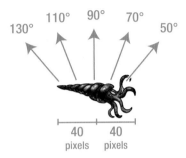

Figure 6-7. *The angle that Pop bounces will depend on how far along Katch's shell he collides.*

To achieve this, we need to compare Pop and Katch's horizontal positions at the moment they collide. Remember that both Pop and Katch's sprites have their origins in the center, so when their horizontal (x) positions are equal, then Pop is exactly in the middle of Katch's shell. When this is the case, we want Pop to rebound with an angle of 90 degrees, straight upward.

However, if Pop's x-position is smaller than Katch's x-position, then Pop has landed on the left side of the shell, which means he should bounce more to the left—with an angle of more than 90 degrees. Similarly, if Pop's x-position is larger than Katch's, then he has landed on the right and we need a direction smaller than 90 degrees. You should remember from previous games that we can get an object's own x-position using the x variable, and the x-position of another object (like Katch) by putting its name in front of it like this: `obj_katch.x`.

So we can work out the difference between Pop's and Katch's horizontal positions by subtracting one from the other: `obj_katch.x-x`. This difference will be a positive number if Pop lands on the left side of Katch and a negative number if he lands on the right (try working it out on paper for a few example positions, if it helps). It will also be exactly zero when Pop is in the middle. So actually, all we need to do is add 90 to this difference (`90+obj_katch.x-x`) and it will give us the range of angles between 50 and 130 degrees we're after (see Figure 6-7). We'll also make the game get harder over time by increasing Pop's speed each time he collides with Katch.

Adding a collision event to the Pop object for colliding with the Katch object:

 1. Add a **Collision** event with the Katch object and include a **Move Free** action in it. Type `90+obj_katch.x-x` in **Direction** and `speed+0.3` in **Speed** (this adds 0.3 to the current speed).

 2. Finally we need to restart the room when Pop falls off the bottom of the screen. Add the **Other, Outside Room** event and include the **Restart Room** action (**main1** tab).

These are all the objects we need to start testing our game, so let's quickly create a test room to do this. This room must be inserted between the front-end room and the completed room in the resource list.

Creating a new test room resource for the game:

1. Right-click on room_completed in the resource list and select **Insert Room** from the pop-up menu that appears. This will insert a new room before room_completed and open the properties window for the new room.

2. Switch to the **settings** tab and call the room room_test.

3. Switch to the **backgrounds** tab and set the background for the room.

4. Our wall sprites are 20 by 20 pixels, so set both **Snap X** and **Snap Y** to 20 in the toolbar at the top of the Room Properties form. The grid in the room will then change accordingly to make it easier to place the walls.

5. Switch to the **objects** tab. Select the wall object and place wall instances all the way along the left, top, and right boundaries of the screen. Remember that you can hold the Shift key to add multiple instances and use the right mouse button to delete them.

6. Select the Katch object and place one instance in the middle at the bottom of the screen. Also add one instance of the Pop object somewhere in the center of the room. The room should now look like Figure 6-8.

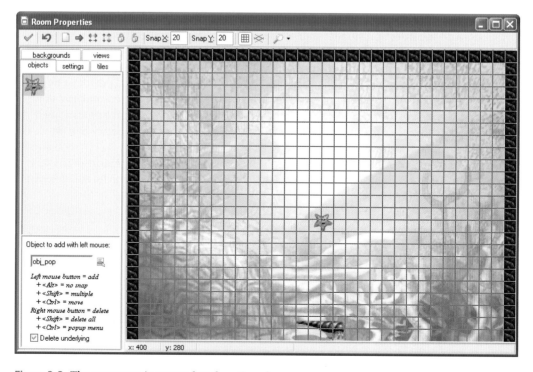

Figure 6-8. *The test room is empty, but functional.*

▐**Note** Sometimes when you close a room form you get a warning message saying that there are instances outside the room. This can happen when you accidentally move the mouse outside the room area while adding objects. You will be asked whether these instances should be removed—simply click the **Yes** button.

Now we can test our game, so save, run, and play the game. Try out the test level and make sure that Pop bounces off the walls and Katch's shell as planned. If there are problems, check your steps or load the current version from Games/Chapter06/rainbow2.gm6 on the CD.

Biglegs

It's about time we put some goals into the game, so we're going to create objects for the Biglegs next. Pop must destroy all of the Biglegs on each level by colliding with them. The level is completed when all the Biglegs have been destroyed, so we're also going to create a *controller object* to check when all the Biglegs have gone. Despite their evil reputation, basic Biglegs will do very little and just destroy themselves when Pop collides with them.

Creating Bigleg object resources for the game:

1. Create a sprite called spr_bigleg using Bigleg.gif from Resources/Chapter06 on the CD.

2. Create an object called obj_bigleg and give it the Bigleg sprite.

3. Add a **Collision** event with Pop and include a **Destroy Instance** action (**main1** tab).

4. Include a **Set Score** action (**score** tab), with **New Score** set to 200 and **Relative** enabled (remember that the **Relative** option will add the value to the current score).

Next we'll create our controller object. Each level of the game (every room except the front-end and completion rooms) will need an instance of the controller object to count the number of Bigleg instances. It will do this in every step, and when it reaches 0 it will pause briefly before advancing to the next room.

Creating a controller object resource for the game:

1. Create an object called obj_controller. No sprite is required.

2. Add the **Step, Step** event and include the **Test Instance Count** action in it (**control** tab). Indicate the Bigleg object as the object to count and leave the default values to check when the number of Biglegs is equal to zero.

3. Include the **Start Block** action to begin a block of actions that depend on the check.

4. Include a **Sleep** action (**main2** tab) with **Milliseconds** set to 1000 (1 second).

5. Include a **Next Room** action (**main1** tab).

6. Finish the current block by including an **End Block** action.

Next we'll add some instances of these objects to a couple of test rooms. We'll make two rooms by copying the first test room; this saves us from having to set the background and place the walls again.

Duplicating test room resources for the game:

1. Reopen the test room by double-clicking on it in the resource list.

2. Put one instance of the controller object into the room. It doesn't matter where, so put it somewhere like the bottom-left corner where it will be out of the way of other instances.

3. Put two instances of the Bigleg object in the top-left and -right corners of the room.

4. Close the properties form for the room.

5. Right-click on the test room in the resource list and choose **Duplicate** from the pop-up menu. This will create a copy of the room and open its properties form.

6. Switch to the **settings** tab and give the room a better name (change the caption too if you like).

7. Switch to the **objects** tab and use the right mouse button to remove the two Bigleg instances.

8. Add a few instances of the Bigleg object in the top center of the room instead. Also add some instances of the wall object below them to make it harder for Pop to reach them. This room should then look something like Figure 6-9.

Figure 6-9. *This test room already provides a challenge.*

Save and test the game at this point to see whether it works correctly.

We now have all the ingredients we need to make a simple game, but it would be nice if there were some variation in the kinds of Biglegs that the player encounters through the game. An obvious candidate is a smaller Bigleg, making it more difficult to hit. To make this, we could repeat all the earlier steps and let the controller object count both the normal objects and the small objects. However, there is a much quicker and easier way to do this: by using *parents*. We'll explain how these work shortly, but for now follow these steps to see how powerful this feature of Game Maker can be.

Creating the small Bigleg object resource:

1. Create a sprite called `spr_bigleg_small` using the file `Bigleg_small.gif`.

2. Create an object called `obj_bigleg_small` and give it the small Bigleg sprite.

3. Click the menu icon next to the **Parent** field (on the left of the new object's properties form) and select `obj_bigleg` as the parent. The left part of the Object Properties form should now look like Figure 6-10.

4. And that's all you need to do! Close the form by clicking the **OK** button.

Figure 6-10. *Set the parent field for the small Bigleg.*

We now have a small Bigleg object that does everything that the normal Bigleg object does. This is because the small Bigleg inherits the behavior (all the events and actions) of the normal Bigleg when we make the normal Bigleg its parent. This means it reacts in the same way to collisions with Pop and will automatically know to increase the player's score by 200 and destroy itself. There's no need to add these events and actions again since they are automatically inherited from the parent. Also, as a child of the Bigleg, the small Bigleg is now considered to be a Bigleg too. This means that the controller object automatically includes it in its count to see how many Biglegs are left in the room.

Try this out by adding some small Biglegs to the test rooms. The small Biglegs are destroyed when Pop hits them, and the level is only completed when all the Biglegs of both types have been removed. We can use this same parenting technique to create a moving Bigleg that inherits all the same behaviors but adds a new behavior of its own as well.

Creating the moving Bigleg object resource:

1. Create an object called obj_bigleg_move and give it the normal Bigleg sprite.

2. Click the menu icon next to **Parent** and select obj_bigleg as the parent. Also set the **Depth** field to 10 so that it appears behind other objects.

3. Add a **Create** event and include the **Move Fixed** action in it. Select both the left and right directions (to make Game Maker choose randomly between them) and set **Speed** to 8.

4. Add a **Collision** event with the wall object and include the **Reverse Horizontal** action in it. Close the form by clicking the **OK** button.

This moving Bigleg automatically inherits the behavior of the normal Bigleg (to destroy itself when Pop collides with it) and adds to that some extra behavior to make it move back and forth. In the same way, we can quickly add a small moving target.

Creating the small moving Bigleg object resource:

1. Create an object called obj_bigleg_move_small and give it the small Bigleg sprite.

2. Click the menu icon next to **Parent** and select obj_bigleg_move as the parent. Also set the **Depth** field to 10 so that it appears behind other objects.

3. Close the form by clicking the **OK** button.

This time were using the moving Bigleg as the parent, which in turn has the normal Bigleg as a parent. This means it inherits the behavior of both the moving Bigleg and the normal Bigleg. Add a few small moving Biglegs to the test levels and carefully check that the game is working correctly. You will find a version of the game so far in Games/Chapter06/rainbow3.gm6 on the CD.

Parent Power

As you have seen, parents are extremely powerful and can save you a lot of time. The Biglegs are quite simple, but parents can save you hours of repeated work for objects with many events and actions. You could just duplicate objects to save time, but any changes you want to make afterward have to be made to both the original and each of the copies you made. However, when you change a parent, the changes automatically apply to the children of that parent too—a very useful feature.

Next we present a number of rules that determine the way that parents work in different situations. We'll describe these now for future reference, but don't worry if they don't make complete sense on your first read. Everything should become a lot clearer once you are working with real examples, so bend down the corner of the page so that you can refer back to them when you're using parents in your own games.

Inheriting Events. A child inherits all the events (and actions) of its parent. A child can have its own events as well, but these only apply to the child and not the parent. When both the child and parent have the same event with different actions, then the actions of the child are used for the child, and the actions of the parent are used for the parent.

We saw this earlier when the moving Biglegs inherited events from normal Biglegs but added their own extra events to make them move as well. Naturally, this did not make the normal Biglegs move as well because parents don't inherit events from children.

Actions on Objects. When an action refers to a parent object, this includes instances of the child object as well. However, when an action refers to the child object, it does not include instances of the parent object.

So when counting the number of instances of normal Biglegs, it automatically included all of the other Bigleg objects that were children of it. The same rule applies to any action that can be applied to an object. However, remember that **Self** and **Other** refer to instances, not objects, so applying an action to them does not affect their parent or child objects.

Collision with Objects. A collision event with a parent object also applies to collisions with children of that object. However a collision event with a child object does not apply to collisions with parents of that object.

This will be useful later on as we want to have many different types of coral blocks that Pop can collide with. By making all of these blocks have the same parent, we only need to define one collision event between Pop and the parent block, and it will also work for all the child blocks.

Parenting Objects. Parents can have parents, which can have parents, etc. However, you must not create cycles of parents, so if P is the parent of C, then C cannot also be the parent of P.

This may sound confusing, but makes perfect sense if you think about it—you couldn't be your own father or grandfather, so it doesn't work in Game Maker either.

Lives

In this kind of game, it is common to give the player a fixed number of lives to try and complete it. Game Maker includes events and actions specifically to handle lives. These allow you to set and display the number of lives as well as testing for when the player has none left. We'll use our controller object to look after the actions that control lives, but first we need to set the number of lives at the start of the game. The best place to do this is in the title object.

Setting the lives in the create event of the title object:

1. Double-click the title object in the resource list to open its properties form.

 2. Select the **Create** event to view its **Actions** list. Include a **Set Lives** action (**score** tab), with a value of 3.

Next we'll make the player lose a life when Pop falls out of the room. However, one of our planned features for the game will make copies of Pop so that there can be several Pops flying around the screen at the same time. So the player should only lose a life when the last surviving Pop falls out of the room. When this happens, we'll reduce the player's lives and create a new Pop in the center of the screen.

Editing the Pop object to add an event for being outside of the room:

1. Double-click the Pop object in the resource list to open its properties form.

 2. Select the **Outside Room** event and remove the **Restart Room** action from it (left-click on the action once and press the delete key, or right-click on the action and select delete). Include a **Destroy Instance** action in its place.

 3. Include the **Test Instance Count** action (**control** tab). Indicate the Pop object as the object to count and leave the default values to check if this is the last Pop leaving the screen.

 4. Include the **Start Block** action to begin a block of actions that depend on the test.

 5. Include a **Set Lives** action with **New Lives** set to -1 and the **Relative** option enabled. This will then subtract one from the number of lives.

 6. Include a **Create Instance** action. Select the Pop object; set **X** to 320 and **Y** to 300.

7. Finally, include an **End Block** action and close the Pop object's properties.

When the player loses their last life, we need to show the high-score table and return to the front-end room. We'll use the controller object to check this using a special event.

Editing the controller object to add an event for having no more lives:

1. Double-click the controller object in the resource list to open its properties form.

 2. Add the **Other, No More Lives** event and include a **Show Highscore** action in it. Use the same **Background** and **Font** as before.

 3. Include the **Different Room** action and indicate the front-end room. Close the controller object's properties form.

Finally, we should display the number of lives on the screen—otherwise, the end of the game could be a bit of a shock to the player! To do this, we're going to use a new event called the **Draw** event, which requires a little explanation. Normally each object automatically draws its own sprite in the correct position on the screen. However, the **Draw** event allows you to draw something else instead, such as several different sprites or colored shapes and text. When the **Draw** event is included, the object's sprite stops being drawn automatically and your own actions in the **Draw** event are executed instead.

We're going to use the **Draw** event of the controller object to show the player's remaining lives as a number of small shells along the bottom of the screen. Game Maker even provides the **Draw Life Images** action to help us do this.

Creating a sprite for the controller object to draw as lives:

1. Create a sprite called spr_katch_small using the file Katch_small.gif.

2. Double-click on the controller object in the resource list to open its properties form.

 3. Add the **Draw** event and include the **Draw Life Images** action (**score** tab). Set **X** to 25 and **Y** to 470, and select the small Katch sprite (as shown in Figure 6-11).

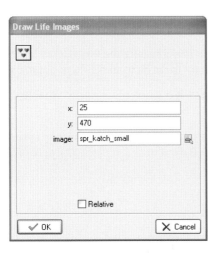

Figure 6-11. *This action will draw the lives as images.*

▓**Note** Adding a **Draw** event to any object stops that object from automatically drawing its own sprite and allows you to include your own draw actions instead. This means that if you want to draw something *in addition* to the object's normal sprite, you need to draw the normal sprite as well. If you always know what sprite this should be, then simply use a **Draw Sprite** action. However, if you want to be able to change the sprite using the **Set Sprite** action, then include an **Execute Code** action (**control** tab) and type draw_sprite(sprite_index, image_index, x, y) into it. This small piece of GML code (see Chapter 12) will then draw the sprite in the usual way *in addition* to any other draw actions in the event.

When you play the game now, there should be three small images of Katch in the bottom left of the screen. One should disappear each time Pop goes off the screen, and the game ends with a high-score table when they're all gone. You'll find a version of the game so far in Games/Chapter06/rainbow4.gm6 on the CD.

Blocks

There are only so many ways of varying a level by placing Biglegs in different places, so we're going to provide them with some defenses to give the level design a bit more scope. We'll start with simple (coral) blocks that deflect Pop but are destroyed in the process. These blocks are just there to get in the way, but later we'll go on to make some special blocks as well.

Normal Blocks

We can use parents to quickly create a number of different-colored blocks. These blocks will all behave in exactly the same way, and the different colors are just to make the Rainbow Reef live up to its name.

Creating block object resources for the game:

1. Create seven sprites called `spr_block1` to `spr_block7` using the files `Block1.gif` to `Block7.gif`. Disable the **Transparent** option on them all to make them appear solid.

2. Create a new object called `obj_block1` and give it the first block sprite. Enable the **Solid** option and close the properties form. That's it for this object.

3. Now create six more objects for the other six blocks using the appropriate sprites. Enable the **Solid** option on each one and set **Parent** to `obj_block1`. They are now all children of the first block.

Editing the Pop object to add a collision event with blocks:

1. Reopen the Pop object's properties form from the resource list.

2. Add a **Collision** event with `obj_block1` and include the **Bounce** action with **Precise** set to **precisely**.

3. Include the **Set Score** action with **New Score** set to 20 and the **Relative** option enabled.

4. Finally, include a **Destroy Instance** action and set **Applies to** to **Other**. This indicates that it is the block rather than Pop that should be destroyed.

This is the only collision event that we need to define between Pop and the seven types of block. This is because all the other blocks are children of the first block, so this event applies to collisions with those blocks as well. Add some of the new blocks to the test levels and play the game to make sure everything works as expected.

Solid Blocks

Next we'll create a solid block that Pop can't destroy. This behaves in the same way as the wall object, so we'll use that as its parent.

Creating a solid block resource for the game:

1. Create a sprite called `spr_block_solid` using `Block_solid1.gif`. Disable the **Transparent** option to make it appear completely solid.

2. Create a new object called `obj_block_solid` and give it the solid block as a sprite. Check the **Solid** option and give it the wall object as a **Parent**.

We do not need to define any collision events between Pop and solid blocks because we've already defined collision events with its parent, the wall. Let's also create an invisible solid block to give the player a surprise in later levels. This is actually probably not such a good idea from a design perspective. Players will just think it's a bug or feel unfairly punished when Pop bounces off in an unexpected direction. However, it illustrates a point about collisions with invisible objects, so we'll make it as an example.

Creating an invisible block resource for the game:

1. Create a new object called `obj_block_solid_inv` and give it the solid block as a sprite. Enable the **Solid** option and give it the wall object as a **Parent**. Also disable the **Visible** option to make the object invisible.

So even though this object is invisible, it still needs a sprite. Game Maker needs a sprite to work out when objects collide with each other, and an object without a sprite will not trigger any collision events.

Special Blocks

Now let's add a few more interesting blocks. This one will require two hits to destroy it.

Creating the double block sprite and object resources:

1. Create a sprite called `spr_block_double` using `Block_double.gif`. Disable the **Transparent** option to make it appear completely solid.

2. Create a new object called `obj_block_double`. Give it the double sprite and enable the **Solid** option. Close the object properties.

Adding a collision event to the Pop object for colliding with the double block:

1. Reopen the Pop object's properties form and add a **Collision** event with the double block object.

 2. Include the **Bounce** action in this event and set **Precise** to **precisely**.

 3. Also include a **Set Score** action with a **New Score** of `20` and the **Relative** option enabled.

 4. Finally, include a **Change Instance** action. Set **Applies to** to **Other** and select `obj_block1` so that the double block changes into a normal block.

5. Close the Object Properties form.

Next we'll add a block that creates two additional instances of Pop, making it look as if he has split into three (like some starfish can do).

Creating the split block sprite and object resources:

1. Create a sprite called `spr_block_split` using `Block_split.gif`. Disable the **Transparent** option to make it appear completely solid.

2. Create a new object called `obj_block_split` and give it this new sprite. Enable the **Solid** option and set the **Parent** field to `obj_block1`.

3. Add a **Collision** event with the Pop object and include a **Create Instance** action. Set **Object** to `obj_pop`, then type `other.x` into **X** and `other.y` into **Y** (see Figure 6-12). This will create the new Pop at the same position as the old Pop.

4. Include another **Create Instance** action exactly the same as in step 3.

Figure 6-12. *Let's create some extra starfish.*

Finally, let's add a block that gives the player an extra life.

Creating the life block sprite and object resources:

1. Create a sprite called `spr_block_life` using `Block_life.gif`. Disable the **Transparent** option to make it appear completely solid.

2. Create a new object called `obj_block_life`. Enable the **Solid** option and set the **Parent** field to `obj_block1`.

3. Add a **Collision** event with the Pop object and include a **Set Lives** action. Set **New Lives** to `1` and enable the **Relative** option.

It is time to test all these blocks by adding them to our test levels. Feel free to experiment and see what incredible combinations of levels you can come up with, or just use ours by loading the file Games/Chapter06/rainbow5.gm6 from the CD.

Polishing the Game

We've already done most of the hard work, so now it's time to put everything together into a playable game.

Sound Effects

All the games we've made so far have benefited from sound effects, and this is no exception. As you saw in the previous chapter, sounds help the player to correctly interpret their interactions with the game. We'll add different sounds for when Pop hits a wall, a block, a Bigleg or Katch's shell, as well as when Pop falls out of the screen.

Creating sound resources and playing them in the appropriate events:

1. Create sounds using the files Sound_wall.wav, Sound_block.wav, Sound_katch.wav, Sound_bigleg.wav, Sound_lost.wav, and Sound_click.wav, and give them appropriate names.

 2. Play the "wall sound" in the Pop object's **Collision** event with the wall object.

3. Play the "block sound" in the Pop object's **Collision** event with the block object and the double block object.

4. Play the "katch sound" in the Pop object's **Collision** event with the Katch object.

5. Play the "lost sound" in the Pop object's **Outside Room** event.

6. Play the "bigleg sound" in the Bigleg object's **Collision** event with the Pop object.

7. Play the "click sound" at the top of the **Left Pressed** event of each of the button objects.

Saving Games and Quitting

If you can remember back to when we were making the framework, we included a button in the front-end to load a saved game. However, in order for this to work, we need to allow the player to save the game at some point using the **Save Game** action. We'll add an event for this on the controller object when the S key is pressed.

▓**Note** Game Maker must be able to write to the filename you provide in the **Save Game** action. This wouldn't normally be a problem, but it does mean you'll get an error message if you run many of the example games directly from the CD-ROM. This is because Game Maker cannot save files to a CD, so copy the game files to your hard disk and run them from there in order to fix the problem.

Adding a save game action to the controller object:

1. Reopen the controller object's properties form from the resource list.

2. Add a **Key Press, Letters, S** event and include the **Save Game** action (**main2** tab). You can leave **File Name** set to the default as it is the same as we used for the **Load Game** action in the front-end.

3. Include the **Display Message** action (**main2** tab) and type "GAME SAVED" into **Message**, so that the user knows the game was saved at this point.

4. Add a line to the **Game Information** describing how the game can be saved.

When you press the Esc key during play, the program ends completely, but it would be better if this returned the player back to the front-end. Adding actions to return to the front-end is simple enough, but this won't work on its own. We also need to disable the default behavior of the Esc key from within the **Global Game Settings**.

Editing the controller object and global game settings to disable the Esc key:

1. Reopen the controller object's properties form from the resource list.

2. Add a **Key Press, Others, <Escape>** event and include the **Different Room** action (**main1** tab). Select the front-end room and close the controller object's properties form.

3. Double-click the **Global Game Settings** at the bottom of the resource list.

4. Switch to the **Other** tab and disable the **Let <Esc> end the game** option.

5. Also disable the **Let <F5> save the game and <F6> load a game** option as we have our own save and load system.

6. Click **OK** to close the form.

There are many other settings that can be changed in the global game settings, but most of these are for advanced use. We will learn more about some of them later in the book.

Caution Beware of disabling the **Let <Esc> end the game** option and forgetting to include your own method for quitting your game (using the **End the Game** action). If this happens, you'll need to press Ctrl+Alt+Delete to bring up the Task Manager and end the task from the Applications list. This will then end the game and return you to Game Maker.

A Slower Start

Currently, Pop starts moving as soon as the level begins, giving the player no time at all to find their bearings. The player may have been at the far side of the screen when Pop last fell out, so it would be fairer to give them a little time to move Katch into a better position. To avoid any complications when new Pop instances are created during play, we're going to make a second, stationary Pop object. This will have an **Alarm Clock** in its **Create** event that changes it into the normal Pop when the time is up. This stationary Pop object will then be the one that gets positioned in each room at the start of the game.

Creating a new stationary Pop object resource:

1. Create a new object called obj_pop_start. Give it the Pop sprite and a **Depth** of 10.

2. Add a **Create** event and include a **Set Alarm** action (**main2** tab) with 30 **Steps** (1 second).

3. Add an **Alarm, Alarm 0** event and include the **Change Instance** action in it. Set **Change Into** to obj_pop and indicate **yes** to **Perform Events** (see Figure 6-13). This will ensure that the new Pop object starts moving in a random direction by performing its **Create** event.

4. Reopen the Pop object's properties form and select the **Outside Room** event. Double-click the **Create Instance** action and change the Pop object to obj_pop_start.

5. Go through each room replacing the Pop objects with the start Pop object.

Figure 6-13. This action changes the stationary Pop into a normal Pop and performs the **Create** *event.*

Creating the Levels

Before we start creating the final levels, we'll add some "cheats" to make it possible to skip through the levels for testing them. We'll use the N key to move to the next level, the P key to go to the previous level, and R key to restart the current level. We'll also add a cheat that adds an extra life when you press the L key.

Editing the controller object to add cheats:

1. Reopen the controller object's properties form from the resource list.

 2. Add a **Key Press, Letters, N** event and include the **Next Room** action.

 3. Add a **Key Press, Letters, P** event and include the **Previous Room** action.

 4. Add a **Key Press, Letters, R** event and include the **Restart Room** action.

 5. Finally, add a **Key Press, Letter, L** event and include the **Set Lives** action. Set **New Lives** to 1 and enable the **Relative** option.

Now it's finally time to create your levels. Let your imagination run wild and see what you can come up with. It will save you time to begin by making a standard room containing only the walls, the controller, the stationary Pop, and Katch. You can then copy this each time and add the Biglegs and blocks for that level. Good level design is crucial for the success of the game and more difficult than you may think. However, you'll learn a lot by just trying it for yourself, and we'll discuss it further in Chapter 8.

Congratulations

Phew—and that's another one done! You'll find the final version of the game in the file Games/ Chapter06/rainbow6.gm6 on the CD. We've designed eight different levels—why not play them and see if they give you any ideas for your own? There's plenty of scope for expanding the features of the game, if you want to. Here are some suggestions:

- Add other types of Biglegs that move in different directions.

- Add blocks that move around.

- Add bonus blocks that give a large number of points to the player's score.

- Add some bad blocks that decrease the score! (Be sure that you make it obvious to the player that this is happening—perhaps by using a new sound effect.)

- Add blocks that increase or decrease the speed of Pop.

- Add blocks that change the size of Pop or Katch.

In this chapter, you have learned about parents and used them in a game for the first time. Parents are very powerful and can save you a lot of work when you are making and changing your games. We strongly encourage you to make sure that you understand them so that you can make full use of them in your own games.

We also introduced our game framework, which we'll use again and refer back to in later chapters. You saw how to deal with lives and how to use draw events and drawing actions. Finally, you used new events and actions introducing gravity, bouncing, and alarm events into your games.

You've already become quite experienced at Game Maker and made some enjoyable games. However, we have a real treat for you in next chapter as we join a cute band of koala bears who just can't help walking into dangerous objects . . .

CHAPTER 7

■ ■ ■

Maze Games: More Cute Things in Peril

Maze games have been popular since the days of Pac-Man, and they're another kind of game that's easy to make in Game Maker. In this chapter, we'll create a puzzle game where the player must help koala bears escape from a maze full of hazardous obstacles. The focus of the game will be on puzzles rather than action, and the levels will be designed to make the player think carefully about the strategies they must use to avoid any unpleasant accidents. (No animals were hurt in the making of this game.)

Designing the Game: Koalabr8

The name *Koalabr8* is a play on the word "Collaborate" with a bit of text-speak thrown in for good measure. This is because the puzzle of the game is based on the idea of controlling many koalas at the same time. So, for example, when you press the up key, all the koalas in your team will move up together. If you imagine trying to steer several koalas through a minefield in this way, then you'll get a sense of the kind of challenge we're aiming for (see Figure 7-1). Anyway, here's the full description of the game:

A colony of koala bears have been captured by the evil Dr. Bruce for use in his abominable experiments. The koalas manage to escape from their cages only to find that the doctor has implanted some kind of mind control device in their brains. The only way they can overpower the controlling effect is to combine their thoughts and all perform the same actions at once. The koalas must work together to find their way past the many dangers in the doctor's laboratory and escape to freedom.

The arrow keys will simultaneously move all of the bears on a level, except bears whose paths are blocked by a wall or another bear. Each level will be a hazardous maze that is completed by getting all of the koalas to an exit. However, if a koala touches a dangerous hazard on the way, then he dies and the level must be replayed. The game will contain a number of fatal and nonfatal hazards shown in the following feature list:

- *Fatal hazards*

  - *Explosive TNT*

  - *Moving circular saws*

- *Nonfatal hazards*
  - *Red exits—Allow any number of koalas to exit the level*
  - *Blue exits—Allow a single koala to exit the level*
  - *Locks—Block the path of koalas (red, blue, and green)*
  - *Switches—Open locked passageways (normal, timed, and pressure)*
  - *Boulders—Can be pushed by koalas and destroy other hazards*

Figure 7-1. *Here's a typical level in the Koalabr8 game.*

As always, you'll find all the resources for this game in the Resources/Chapter07 folder on the CD.

The Basic Maze

We'll start by making a basic maze and getting a koala to walk around it. This same technique can be used for making any kind of maze game, so feel free to copy it for your own projects.

The Game Framework

This game will use the same basic framework as we made in the previous chapter. This consists of a front-end with buttons to start a new game, load a saved game, show help, and quit the game, as well as a completion screen that congratulates the player. However, there is no score in this game so there will be no high-score table. The instructions that follow will show you how to create the front-end for this game, although you might want to refer back to Chapter 6 for a more detailed explanation. Alternatively, you can just load the completed framework from Games/Chapter07/koala1.gm6 on the CD and skip to the next section, "A Moving Character."

Creating the front-end:

1. Launch Game Maker and start a new game from the **File** menu.

2. Create sprites using the following files from the Resources/Chapter07 folder on the CD: Title.gif, Button_start.gif, Button_load.gif, Button_help.gif, and Button_quit.gif. Remember to name them appropriately.

3. Create a background using the file Background.bmp.

4. Create sounds using the files Music.mp3 and Click.wav.

5. Create a title object using the title sprite. Add an **Other, Game Start** event and include a **Play Sound** action. Select the background music and set **Loop** to true.

6. Create a start button object using the start sprite. Add a **Mouse, Left Pressed** mouse event and include an action to play the click sound followed by an action to move to the next room.

7. Create a load button object using the load sprite. Add a **Mouse, Left Pressed** mouse event and include an action to play the click sound followed by an action to load the game (use the default file name).

8. Create a help button object using the help sprite. Add a **Mouse, Left Pressed** mouse event and include an action to play the click sound followed by an action to show the game information.

9. Create a quit button object using the quit sprite. Add a **Mouse, Left Pressed** mouse event and include an action to play the click sound followed by an action to end the game.

10. Create a room using the background, and place the title and four button objects in it so that it looks like Figure 7-2.

Figure 7-2. *The finished front-end for Koalabr8 should look something like this.*

Now follow these instructions to create the completion screen. Refer to Chapter 6 for a more detailed explanation.

Creating the completion screen:

1. Create a sprite using the file Congratulation.gif.

2. Create a new object using this sprite. Add a **Create** event and include a **Set Alarm** action to set **Alarm 0** using 120 **Steps**.

3. Add an **Alarm, Alarm 0** event and include an action to move to the front-end room.

4. Create a completion room using the background and place an instance of the congratulations object in it.

We also need to create the game information and change some of Game Maker's default settings for the game.

Changing the game settings:

1. Double-click **Game Information** near the bottom of the resource list and create a short help text based on the game's description.

2. Double-click **Global Game Settings** at the bottom of the resource list.

3. Switch to the **Other** tab and disable the two options **Let <Esc> end the game** and **Let <F5> save the game and <F6> load a game** as we handle this ourselves.

That completes our game framework for Koalabr8, which can also be loaded from the file Games/Chapter07/koala1.gm6 on the CD.

■**Caution** Beware of disabling the **Let <Esc> end the game** option and forgetting to include your own method for quitting your game (using the **End the Game** action). If this happens, you'll need to press Ctrl+Alt+Delete to bring up the Task Manager and end the task from the Applications list. This will end the game and return you to Game Maker.

A Moving Character

The basis of every maze game is a character that moves around walled corridors, so we will begin by creating a wall object.

Creating the wall object:

1. Create a sprite called spr_wall using the file Wall.gif. Disable the **Transparent** option, as our wall is just one large solid block.

2. Create a new object called obj_wall using this sprite and enable the **Solid** option.

You might be wondering why we are using an ugly black square for our walls. Don't worry; we'll transform it into something that looks much nicer when we learn how to use *tiles* later on in the chapter.

Next we need to create a character, which in this case is a koala bear. We'll use five different sprites for the koala: four animations for walking in each of the four directions and another sprite for when koalas are standing still.

Creating the koala sprites:

1. Create a sprite called spr_koala_left using the file koala_left.gif and enable the **Smooth edges** option.

2. Create sprites in the same way using the files koala_right.gif, koala_up.gif, koala_down.gif, and koala_stand.gif.

Now we can create our koala object and give it actions that allow the player to move it around the screen. You can probably work out how to do this yourself by now, using either **Jump** or **Move** actions in a similar way to one of the previous games. You may even like to have a try for yourself before continuing, but you'll actually find that it's very tricky to move a character through a maze using just these actions. This is because the sprites of both the walls and koalas are exactly 40×40 pixels, so all the corridors are only just big enough for the koalas to walk down. You'll see the problem if you imagine running through a maze with your arms fully stretched out, where the width of the corridors is exactly the same as your arm span! Bumping into walls and struggling to change direction in corridors soon removes all feeling of control and the game stops being fun.

Fortunately, Game Maker comes to the rescue with the **Check Grid** action. This conditional action allows us to test for when a koala is exactly lined up with the corridors. This means we can ignore the player's badly timed key presses (that normally cause the koala to walk into walls) and wait until Game Maker knows the koala is in exactly the right place. Only then do we let the player stop or turn their character, so that the koalas end up gliding gracefully along the corridors with no fuss at all.

In addition to checking that koalas are aligned correctly, we will check that there is nothing blocking their way before even starting to move. This results in a reliable control system that feels slick to the player and is a solid basis for any kind of maze game you might be making. Follow these steps and you'll see what we mean.

Creating the koala object:

1. Create a new object called `obj_koala` using the standing koala sprite. Set the object's **Parent** to be the wall object—this may sound odd, but all will be explained in the following steps.

2. Add a **Keyboard, <Left>** event and include the **Check Grid** action (**control** tab). Set both **Snap hor** (horizontal snap) and **Snap vert** (vertical snap) to 40 to indicate a grid size of 40×40 pixels. Also enable the **NOT** option so that the event checks for koalas not being aligned with the grid. The form should look like Figure 7-3.

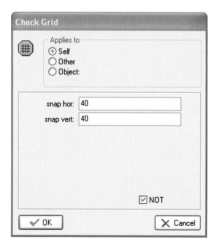

Figure 7-3. Check whether the instance is not aligned with the grid.

3. Include the **Exit Event** action. This action stops any more actions from being performed in the **Actions** list. We have put it underneath our **Check Grid** condition so that none of the following actions are performed when the koala is *not* aligned with the grid.

4. Include the **Check Object** action. Indicate the wall object and enable the **NOT** option. Set **X** to -40 and **Y** to 0 and then enable the **Relative** option so that it checks that there are no wall objects one grid square to the left of the koala.

5. Include the **Start Block** action followed by the **Move Fixed** action. Select the left arrow and set **Speed** to 5 (this speed must divide exactly into the grid size of 40; otherwise the koalas will not stop on each grid square).

6. Include the **Change Sprite** action and indicate the left-facing koala sprite. Set **Subimage** to -1 so that the animation keeps playing despite the sprite being changed.

7. Those are all the actions we need to move the koala, so include an **End Block** action.

8. However, if there is a wall in the way, then we must stop the koala from moving. We've already checked for walls *not* being present using the **Check Object** action, so including an **Else** action will allow us to define what should happen when a wall *is* present. Include the **Else** followed by a new **Start Block** action.

9. Include the **Move Fixed** action, select the middle square, and set **Speed** to 0.

10. Include the **Change Sprite** action using the standing sprite with a **Subimage** of -1.

11. Finally, include the **End Block** action. The actions should now look like Figure 7-4.

12. Now repeat steps 2–11 to create similar rules for the Right, Up, and Down arrow keys. Make sure you choose the correct direction for each **Move Fixed** action, the correct sprite for each **Change Sprite** action, and the correct **X** and **Y** values for each **Check Object** action. When you're making the up and down rules, remember that y increases as you move down the screen.

*Figure 7-4. These are the actions for moving the koala to the left. Note that the first condition has its **NOT** property set, so it checks for when the instance is not aligned with the grid.*

Before continuing, check through your actions and make sure that you can logically follow what they do.

The **Keyboard** actions start the bear moving if there isn't a wall in the way, but we haven't added any actions to stop the bear yet. This will happen automatically if the player keeps their finger on one of the arrow keys, as the actions in the **Keyboard** events will eventually detect a wall and stop. However, the bear also needs to come to a halt if the player stops pressing any arrow keys. If you're thinking that we need a **<No Key>** event, then you're on the right track, but if we stopped bears moving in a **<No Key>** event, then what would happen if the player was pressing another key such as the spacebar? The spacebar isn't used in this game, but it's still a key—so the **<No Key>** event would never be called and the koala would never stop!

Instead of using a **<No Key>** event, we're going to use a **Begin Step** event. This will keep checking if the bear has reached the next grid square, and stop it when it does. We need to use a **Begin Step** rather than any other kind of **Step** event, because the **Begin** part means that the actions will be called at the beginning of each step—before the **Keyboard** events. Therefore, we can stop the bear moving in **Begin Step** and start it again in **<Left>** if the player is pressing the Left key. If we used a **Step** or **End Step**, then these events would happen the other way around: **<Left>** would start the bear moving and **Step** would stop it again—canceling the effect of the pressing the key. Once you've added the actions that follow, try changing the **Begin Step** event to a **<No Key>** or a normal **Step** event and seeing what effect it has on the game.

Adding a Begin Step event to the koala object:

1. Add a **Step, Begin Step** event to the koala object and include the **Check Grid** action. Set **Snap hor** to 40 and **Snap vert** to 40, but this time leave **NOT** disabled.

2. Include a **Start Block** action followed by a **Move Fixed** action. Set **Speed** to 0 and select the center square to stop the koala moving.

3. Include a **Change Sprite** action, indicating the standing koala sprite with **Subimage** set to -1.

4. Include an **End Block** action and close the koala object's properties.

▍Caution When setting a **Move Fixed** action with a speed of 0, you must also select the center square of the direction grid. If no direction square is selected at all, then the action is ignored!

Okay, hopefully that makes sense so far, but we still haven't explained why we made the wall object a parent of the koala. While this may be against the laws of nature, it's not against the laws of Game Maker, and it's actually saved us a lot of work. Koalas need to stop for both walls and other koalas so we *could* add extra actions to check for koalas in the same way we did earlier. However, this happens automatically when we make walls a parent of koalas, as Game Maker now treats koalas as a special kind of wall!

Before we can test our work, there is something we need to fix. When we were making the front-end we indicated that pressing the Esc key should not automatically end the game. However, we need *some* way of quitting a level once it is running, so we'll use a controller object to take us back to the front-end when the Esc key is pressed.

Creating the controller object:

1. Create a new object called `obj_controller` and leave the sprite as **<no sprite>**.

2. Add a **Key Press, Others, <Escape>** key event. Include the **Different Room** action and indicate the front-end room.

To test our basic maze game system, we'll need to create a test level by adding a new room between the front-end and closing rooms.

Creating a test room:

1. Right-click the completion room in the resource list and select **Insert Room** from the pop-up menu. This will insert the new room between the two existing rooms.

2. Switch to the **settings** tab and give the room an appropriate name and caption.

3. Switch to the **backgrounds** tab and give the room the background.

4. Set the **Snap X** and **Snap Y** on the toolbar to the correct cell size of 40 pixels.

5. Select the **objects** tab and create a maze out of instances of the wall object. Leave the top row free, as we'll need this space for displaying other game information later on. Place three or four instances of the koala object in the maze and put one instance of the controller object in the top-left corner of the room. The room should then look something like Figure 7-5.

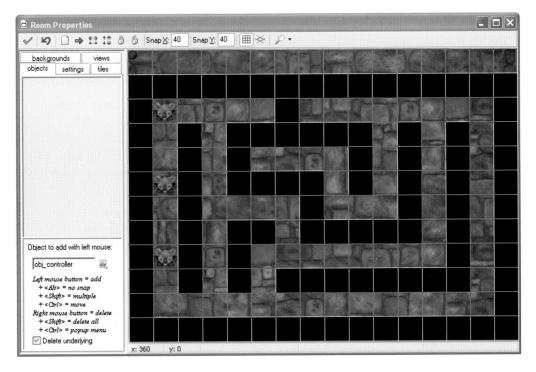

Figure 7-5. *Here's our first maze.*

Save your work and run the game to test it. Check that the koalas don't get stuck walking around and that the animations play correctly. Also notice how the koalas react when they bump into each another. If you need it, you'll find this version of the game in the file Games/Chapter07/koala2.gm6 on the CD.

Save the Koala

Most of what we have done so far could be used for any kind of maze game, but now we'll begin adding features specific to the Koalabr8 game design. The aim of each level is to get all the koalas out alive, so in this section we'll add exits and check whether all koalas have been rescued before moving on to the next level.

We'll begin by creating objects for the two different kinds of exits: one that can be used by any number of koalas to escape, and one that is destroyed after being used by just a single koala. When a koala collides with an exit, we know it has escaped the level and so we can destroy the koala instance. We'll use Game Maker's built-in mechanism for controlling the player's lives to indicate how many koalas have been saved in each level.

Creating the exit objects:

1. Create sprites called spr_exit1 and spr_exit2 using Exit1.gif and Exit2.gif and enable the **Smooth edges** option for them both.

 2. Create an object called obj_exit1, and give it the first exit sprite and a **Depth** of 10. We only want the koala to disappear when it's completely on top of the exit, so add a **Collision** event with the koala object and include a **Check Grid** conditional action. Select **Other** from **Applies to** (the koala) and set **Snap hor** and **Snap vert** to 40.

 3. Include a **Start Block** action.

 4. Include a **Destroy Instance** action and select **Other** from **Applies to** (the koala).

 5. Include a **Set Lives** action with **New Lives** set to 1 and the **Relative** option enabled.

 6. Finally, include an **End Block** action and close the properties form.

7. Now create another exit object in exactly the same way using the sprite for exit2. The only difference is that you need to include an additional **Destroy Instance** action after step 4 with **Applies to** set to **Self** (the exit).

We'll use the controller object to check when all koalas have been rescued. It will also display the rescued koalas along the top of the screen using the **Draw Lives** action.

Adding events to handle rescued koalas in the controller object:

1. Create a sprite called spr_rescued using Rescued.gif and enable the **Smooth edges** option.

2. Reopen the properties form for the controller object by double-clicking it in the resource list.

3. Add a **Create** event and include the **Set Lives** action with **New Lives** set to 0. We're using lives to represent rescued koalas—so the lives need to start at 0.

4. Add a new **Step, Step** event and include the **Test Instance Count** action. Set **Object** to the koala object and **Number** to 0. When there are no koala instances left, then the player must have completed the level.

5. Include the **Start Block** action followed by the **Sleep** action. Set **Milliseconds** to 2000 (2 seconds).

6. Include the **Next Room** action and set **Transition** to **Create from center** (or any other one that takes your fancy).

7. Include the **End Block** action to complete the actions for this event.

8. Add a new **Draw** event. Switch to the **draw** tab and include the **Draw Sprite** action. Set **Sprite** to the rescued sprite, **X** to 10, and **Y** to 0. Leave the **Relative** option disabled, as we want this sprite to be drawn in the top left of the screen.

9. Include the **Draw Life Images** action with **Image** set to the standing koala sprite, **X** to 150, and **Y** to 0. This will draw the sprite once for each of the player's lives (saved koalas).

▌**Caution** **Draw** actions all have a light yellow background and can only be used in **Draw** events. If you put them in a different event, then they are ignored.

Now add some exits to your test room and give it a quick play to make sure they are working correctly. You might also want to add a second test room (remember that you can duplicate rooms). You'll find the current version in Games/Chapter07/koala3.gm6 on the CD.

Creating Hazards

Our maze is rather dull at the moment, so it's time to create some challenges by making it a lot more dangerous for the koalas. We'll start by adding TNT that blows koalas off the level if they touch it and restarts the level. This may sound like an easy hazard to avoid, but carefully positioned TNT can present quite a challenge when you're controlling several koalas at once!

We'll begin by creating a dead koala (how often do you get to say that?). Dead koalas will fly off the screen in an amusing fashion—nothing too gory, as we want to keep this a family game. We'll do this using Game Maker's gravity action, as that will do most of the work for us and make the movement look realistic.

Creating the dead koala object:

1. Create a sprite called spr_koala_dead using Koala_dead.gif and enable **Smooth edges**.

2. Create a new object called obj_koala_dead using this sprite. Give it a **Depth** of -10 to make sure it appears in front of all other objects.

 3. Add a **Create** event and include the **Move Free** action. Set **Direction** to 80 and **Speed** to 15.

 4. Include the **Set Gravity** action with **Direction** set to 270 (downward) and **Gravity** set to 2.

 5. Add an **Other, Outside room** event and include the **Sleep** action. Set **Milliseconds** to 1000.

 6. Include the **Restart Room** action with **Transition** left as **<no effect>**. It would soon annoy the player to have to wait for a transition to restart the level each time.

Next we'll create our TNT object. It is a very simple object that just sits there and turns koalas into dead koalas when they collide with it.

Creating the TNT object:

1. Create a sprite called spr_TNT using TNT.gif and enable **Smooth edges**.

2. Create a new object called obj_TNT using this sprite.

 3. Add a **Collision** event with the koala object. Include the **Change Instance** action and select **Other** from **Applies to**, in order to change the koala. Set **Change into** to the dead koala object and set **Perform events** to **yes**.

We've now actually created a bug (an unintentional error) in our game. Remember that the controller object moves to the next room when there are no koalas left on the level—assuming that the player must have rescued them all. However, if the last koala is killed by TNT, then there will also be no koalas left on the level—but the player has failed! Consequently, we must alter the controller object so that it also checks that there are no dead koalas before moving to the next level.

Editing the controller object to fix the dead koala bug:

1. Double-click the controller object in the resource list and select the **Step** event.

 2. At the top of the action list, include another **Test Instance Count** action and set **Object** to the dead koala. As this appears directly above the old check for koalas, the block of actions will only be performed if both conditions are true.

Test this out by adding some TNT to your levels. It's actually possible to build very difficult levels just using TNT. The level, shown in Figure 7-6, looks almost impossible to solve, but it is solvable once you work out how to use the extra wall piece on the left. It's designing puzzles like this that will make this game interesting.

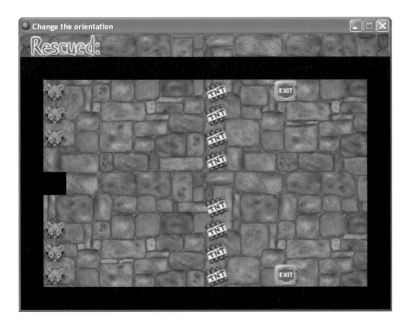

Figure 7-6. *This is a surprisingly difficult maze level.*

TNT is fun, but moving hazards should add an even greater challenge, so we're going to create two kinds of circular saws. One will move vertically and the other will move horizontally, but both will leave koalas wishing they had stayed in bed!

Creating the saw objects:

1. Create sprites called spr_saw_horizontal and spr_saw_vertical using Saw_horizontal.gif and Saw_vertical.gif. Enable the **Smooth edges** option for both.

2. Create an object called obj_saw_horizontal and give it the horizontal sprite. Add a **Create** event and include the **Move Fixed** action. Select the right arrow and set **Speed** to 4. This is slightly slower than the speed of the koala to give the player a chance to escape.

3. Add a **Collision** event with the wall object and include the **Reverse Horizontal** action.

4. Add a **Collision** event with the koala object. Include the **Change Instance** action and select **Other** from **Applies to**, in order to change the koala. Set **Change into** to the dead koala object and set **Perform events** to **yes**.

5. Create an object called obj_saw_vertical and give it the vertical sprite. Add a **Create** event and include the **Move Fixed** action. Select the down arrow and set **Speed** to 4.

6. Add a **Collision** event with the wall and include the **Reverse Vertical** action.

7. Finally add a **Collision** event with the koala object. Include the **Change Instance** action and select **Other** from **Applies to**. Set **Change into** to the dead koala object and set **Perform events** to **yes**.

At this point, you might be wondering why having the wall as a parent doesn't mess things up for the koala's collisions with saws. After all, if koalas are a "special kind of wall," then why don't the saws just turn themselves around when they collide with koalas? Fortunately Game Maker automatically chooses the most specific collision event and ignores the other (a koala is a koala first and only a wall second). However, if you remove the collision event between the saw and the koala, then saws will start treating koalas as if they were walls again!

Create some new levels using the moving saws. You might also want to add a cheat in the controller object, so that pressing the N key moves you to the next room and pressing the P key moves you to the previous room. You should know how to do this by now. You'll find the current version in Games/Chapter07/koala4.gm6 on the CD.

Tiles

The walls of our maze need brightening up a bit, and we're going to do this by using *tiles*. Tiles work by creating a new background resource that consists of a number of small, identically sized images (40×40 pixels in our case). This is called a *tile set*, and we've created one that contains all the various combinations of wall connections that are needed to draw a maze (see Figure 7-7).

Figure 7-7. *This tile set contains 16 wall segments.*

Creating the tile set:

1. Create a new background called back_tiles using the file Wall_tiles.bmp. Enable the **Transparent** option so that the green areas appear transparent.

2. Enable the **Use as tile set** option. The properties form will then become larger to display all the properties of a tile set.

3. Set **Tile width** and **Tile height** to 40 and leave the other values as 0. The image will now show an exploded view of the tiles, as shown in Figure 7-8.

4. Close the properties form.

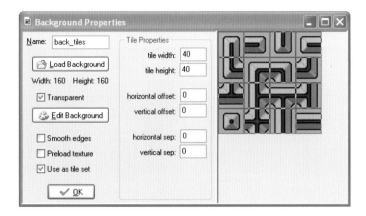

Figure 7-8. *Add the tile set to the game.*

Now we can begin adding these tiles to the rooms. You might have noticed that there is a special tab in the room properties form for this. This allows us to add tiles to the background image of the room. However, these tiles have no behavior and instances won't react to them, so how do we stop the koalas from moving through the walls? The answer is that we use the wall object we've already created and place instances of this object on top of the tiles. Once this is done, we make the wall object invisible, so that the player doesn't see the ugly walls in the game. When the koalas walk around, they will still be blocked by the invisible wall instances, but the player only sees the nice-looking tiles.

Adding tiles to your rooms:

1. Double-click the first room in the resource list and use the right mouse button to delete all of the wall instances in the room.

2. Click the **tiles** tab. Use the menu halfway down on the left to select the background with the tiles. Once this is done, the tiles will be displayed in the left top.

3. Click on one of the tile images to select a particular tile, and it will become outlined. Now you can place and remove copies of that tile using the left and right mouse buttons in the same way as for instances. You can also hold the Shift key to add multiple copies.

4. Select and place tiles in order to create a maze that looks like the one in Figure 7-9.

5. Select the **objects** tab and carefully place instances of the wall object on top of the wall tiles.

6. Repeat the process for the other rooms.

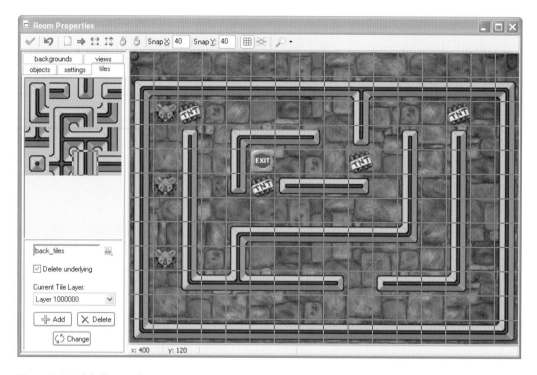

Figure 7-9. *Add tiles to the room.*

▓**Tip** When creating levels, you may find it helpful to hide tiles or objects using the magnifying glass menu in the toolbar. This allows you to temporarily hide all the tiles or objects in the room. However, you cannot hide objects while the **objects** tab is selected or hide tiles while the **tiles** tab is selected.

Finally we must make the wall object invisible so that the tiles can be seen instead.

Making the wall object invisible:

1. Double-click the wall object in the resource list to open the properties form.

2. Disable the **Visible** option to make it invisible.

Test the game again to make sure that the tiles are displayed correctly and koalas cannot walk through walls. You'll find the current version in the file Games/Chapter07/koala5.gm6 on the CD.

Adding Additional Hazards

You can already build some interesting levels using just the TNT and the saws, but we're going to add a couple of other features to add a bit more variation.

Locks and Switches

Locks block the path of koalas in the maze and open only when the corresponding switch is pressed. We'll create three different types of locks: the blue lock will disappear forever once its switch is activated, the yellow lock will reappear 5 seconds later, and the red lock will only stay open while the switch continues to be pressed. So in this final case one koala must keep the lock open for another one to pass.

We'll begin with the blue switch since this is the simplest to do. We'll use two objects: one for the lock, and one for the switch. The switch sprite will contain two subimages showing the switch in closed and open positions, and we'll use actions in the switch object to display the correct one.

Creating the blue lock and switch objects:

1. Create sprites called spr_lock_blue and spr_switch_blue using Lock_blue.gif and Switch_blue.gif. Enable the **Smooth edges** option for them both. Notice how the switch sprite has two frames of animation showing the switch in different positions.

2. Create a new object called obj_lock_blue and give it the blue lock sprite. Enable the **Solid** option. Set **Parent** to the wall object so that it behaves like a wall (blocking koalas).

3. Create a new object called obj_switch_blue and give it the blue switch sprite. Set **Depth** to 10 to make sure that it appears behind other objects.

4. Add a **Create** event and include a **Change Sprite** action. Select the blue switch sprite and set both **Subimage** and **Speed** to 0. This will display the first subimage and will stop the sprite from animating.

5. Add a **Collision** event with the koala object and include the **Destroy Instance** action. Select **Object** from **Applies to** and select obj_lock_blue from the menu.

6. Include the **Change Sprite** action, selecting spr_switch_blue with a **Subimage** of 1 and a **Speed** of 0.

The other switches are a bit more complicated as they both involve temporarily removing the locks. The trick here is to move the lock to a place just outside the room and set an alarm clock. When the time is up, we can use the **Jump to Start** action to bring the lock back into play. However, we will need to make sure that there is nothing in the way when we bring it back and set the alarm clock to try again later if there is.

Creating the yellow and red lock and switch objects:

1. Create sprites called spr_lock_yellow and spr_switch_yellow using Lock_yellow.gif and Switch_yellow.gif. Enable the **Smooth edges** option for them both.

2. Create a new object called obj_lock_yellow and give it the yellow lock sprite. Enable the **Solid** option. Set **Parent** to the wall object.

 3. Add an **Alarm, Alarm 0** event and include the **Check Empty** action. Set **X** to xstart, **Y** to ystart, and **Objects** to **all**. Using the variables xstart and ystart will check that there are no collisions at the start position of the lock.

 4. Switch to the **move** tab and include the **Jump to Start** action.

 5. Include the **Else** action followed by a **Set Alarm** action. Set **Number of Steps** to 2 so that the lock tries again quite quickly.

 6. Create a new object called obj_switch_yellow and give it the yellow switch sprite. Set **Depth** to 10 to make sure that it appears behind other objects.

 7. Add a **Create** event and include a **Change Sprite** action. Select spr_switch_yellow and set **Subimage** and **Speed** to 0.

 8. Add a **Collision** event with the koala object and include the **Jump to Position** action. Select **Object** from **Applies to** and select obj_lock_yellow from the menu. Set **X** to 1000 and **Y** to 0 to make it move way off the screen.

 9. Add a **Set Alarm** action with 150 **Steps** (5 seconds). Select **Object** from **Applies to** and select obj_lock_yellow from the menu.

 10. Finally add the **Change Sprite** action, selecting spr_switch_yellow with a **Subimage** of 1 and a **Speed** of 0.

11. Reopen the properties form for the yellow lock and select the **Alarm 0** event. Include a **Change Sprite** action at the top of the list of actions. Select **Object** from **Applies to** and select obj_switch_yellow from the menu. Select spr_switch_yellow and set **Subimage** and **Speed** to 0. This will return the switch to the normal position.

12. Create the red lock and the red switch in the same way. However, this time set the alarm to only 2 **Steps** so that it resets as soon as the koala moves away from the switch.

If you try using them in your rooms, you'll see that you can use switches to create some very interesting and tricky levels.

A Detonator

This one's going to be very easy. The detonator object will blow up all the TNT on a level—making the koala's life much easier. As with the switches, we'll use a sprite that consists of two subimages to show the detonator before and after the explosions.

Creating the detonator object:

1. Create a sprite called spr_detonator using Detonator.gif and enable the **Smooth edges** option.

2. Create a new object called obj_detonator and give it the detonator sprite. Set the **Depth** to 10.

3. Add a **Create** event and include the **Change Sprite** action. Select the detonator sprite and set **Subimage** and **Speed** to 0.

4. Add a **Collision** event with the koala object and include a **Destroy Instance** action. Select **Object** from **Applies to** and select obj_TNT from the menu.

5. Include a **Change Sprite** action. Select spr_detonator, and then set **Subimage** to 1 and **Speed** to 0.

Detonators can potentially make your levels very easy, so make sure you put them in locations that are very difficult to reach!

Rocks

Rocks can be pushed around by koalas, as long as there is free space to push them into. Rocks will block moving saws and cause TNT to explode when they are pushed onto it—harmlessly destroying both the rock and TNT. When a rock is pushed onto a switch or detonator, it will also be destroyed, allowing the player to remove switches without pressing them.

Creating the basic rock object:

1. Create a sprite called spr_rock using Rock.gif and enable the **Smooth edges** option.

2. Create a new object called obj_rock and give it the rock sprite. Enable the **Solid** option and set **Depth** to -5 so that it appears in front of most objects but behind the dead koala object.

To push the rock in the right direction, we need to know which direction the koala was moving in when it collided with the rock. We can find this out using the variables hspeed (the current horizontal speed of an instance) and vspeed (the vertical speed of an instance). The koala will be the *other* object involved in the collision, so its speed is indicated by other.hspeed and other.vspeed. The koala moves with a speed of 5 and the cell size is 40, so multiplying the koalas' horizontal speed by 8 will give us the rock's new x-position (5 × 8 = 40). Likewise, multiplying the koala's vertical position by 8 will give us the rock's new y-position. Therefore, we can use this calculation to verify that there is nothing in the way of the new position and move there.

Adding actions to the rock object to allow koalas to push it around:

1. Add a **Collision** event with the koala object.

2. Include the **Check Object** action and indicate the wall object. Set **X** to 8*other.hspeed and **Y** to 8*other.vspeed. Enable both the **Relative** and **NOT** options.

3. Add a similar **Check Object** action for the rock object using all the same settings.

4. Add two more similar **Check Object** actions for the horizontal and vertical saw objects using all the same settings.

5. Finally, include a **Jump to Position** action. Set **X** to 8*other.hspeed and **Y** to 8*other.vspeed, and enable the **Relative** option.

This will do the trick. You might want to add some rocks to your levels and push them around to check that they work correctly. Next we need to make the rock destroy TNT, switches, and the detonator.

Adding actions to the rock object to make it destroy things:

1. Add a **Collision** event with the TNT object and include the **Destroy Instance** action with default settings (to destroy the rock). Include another **Destroy Instance** action and select **Other** (to destroy the TNT) from the **Applies to** option.

2. Add a **Collision** event with the detonator object and include the **Destroy Instance** action. Select **Other** from the **Applies to** option (to destroy the detonator).

3. In the same way, add **Collision** events with the three switches and include **Destroy Instance** actions that apply to the switches.

We also need to make sure that the saws do not move through rocks.

Adding events to the saw objects to make them turn for rocks:

1. Double-click the horizontal saw object in the resource list to open its properties form.

2. Add a **Collision** event with the rock object and include the **Reverse Horizontal** action.

3. Close the properties form.

4. Double-click the vertical saw object in the resource list to open its properties form.

5. Add a **Collision** event with the rock object and include the **Reverse Vertical** action.

6. Close the properties form.

Now go ahead and make levels using every combination of locks, switches, detonators, and rocks you can think of. You can create an almost endless combination of different challenges. For example, Figure 7-10 shows a level in which the koalas must move the rocks around very carefully if they are to reach the exit (it is solvable). You can find the current version in the file Games/Chapter07/koala6.gm6 on the CD.

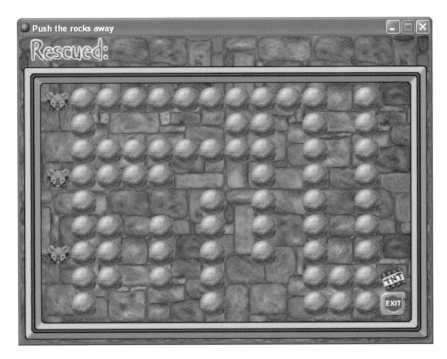

Figure 7-10. *You can make quite difficult levels just using rocks.*

Finishing the Game

That's just about it, but as always there are some loose ends we can tie up to make the game a bit more presentable and user-friendly.

Now that we have so many features, it is possible to get into a situation on a level where the level can no longer be completed. Consequently, we need to give the player a way to restart the level when this happens. We'll add a button to do this in each room and allow them to use the R key as a shortcut for restarting the level as well.

Creating a restart button object:

1. Create a sprite called spr_restart using Restart.gif.

2. Create a new object called obj_restart and give it the restart sprite. Add a new **Mouse, Left Pressed** event. Include the **Play Sound** action using the click sound and follow it with the **Restart Room** action.

3. Add a **Key Press, Letters, R** event and include the **Restart Room** action.

4. Add an instance of this new object into the top-right corner of every level room.

Next we'll add a mechanism to save the game. Rather than letting the player do this, we'll get the controller object to automatically save the game at the start of each level.

Save the game in the controller object:

1. Double-click the controller object in the resource list to open its properties form.

2. Add an **Other**, **Room Start** event and include the **Save Game** action to save the game.

Finally, we should add some sound effects. You should be able to do this by yourself, so here is a list of the ones that are required.

Adding sound effect to objects:

1. Explosion.wav needs to play in the **Collision** event between the TNT and the koala and the **Destroy** event of the TNT.

2. Saw.wav needs to play in the **Collision** events between both the saws and the koala.

3. Saved.wav needs to play in the **Collision** event between the two exit objects and the koala. Put it inside the block, so that it is only played when the koala is removed.

4. Rock.wav needs to play in the **Collision** event between the rock objects and the koala. However, you only want to play it when the rock actually moves, so add **Start Block** and **End Block** around the **Jump to Position** action and include the **Play Sound** action within it.

You might also want to attempt to add a sound for pressing the switches and opening locks. However, this is a lot more difficult than it seems because **Collision** events happen constantly while the koala stands on a switch. So if you play a sound in this event, it will also play continuously in a very annoying way! There are several (complex) ways of working around this, and we have provided a sound effect if you fancy the challenge.

Finally, you might want to update the game information to include details about the different hazards—although you might want to let the players find out for themselves!

Congratulations

We hope you enjoyed creating Koalabr8 and that you've had fun designing challenging levels. You may get some more ideas by playing ours from Games/Chapter06/koala7.gm6 on the CD. The great thing about puzzle games is that the possibilities are endless, and we look forward to seeing what you come up with.

The two Game Maker concepts that we have introduced in this chapter are **Grid** actions and tiles. Both **Grid** actions and tiles are very useful for making this kind of game. There is actually a lot more to learn about tiles, such as creating different layers. You can use layers to let characters walk in front of certain tiles and behind others, giving a feeling of depth. If you want to know more, then take a look at the Game Maker documentation on tiles.

Anyway, we hope you like koalas, because you haven't seen the last of them yet! In the next chapter we'll be using Koalabr8 as an example of how designing good levels and features can make your game more fun to play. So time to take a rest from programming for a while and start thinking of some new ways of keeping koalas "entertained."

CHAPTER 8

Game Design: Levels and Features

Even the most captivating game ideas will eventually become dull if the challenges never change. Good level design is about providing players with new and interesting challenges as they progress through the game. Usually this requires a steady flow of fresh features that introduce new equipment, opponents, enemies, or obstacles into the gameplay. Creating the right kind of features is as important to good level design as the way those features are used in the levels themselves. In this chapter, we'll take a look at the issues surrounding level design and try to give you some pointers for designing your own games.

Selecting Features

So you've created a game prototype with a solid core mechanic and carefully tweaked the gameplay with the help of your friends. Everyone thinks it could be really good and you just need another 25 levels to turn it into a finished game. Sitting down with your designer's notebook, you begin to make a list of all the extra features you want to include—but where do you start, and how do you tell a good feature from a bad one?

The good news is that coming up with plenty of ideas is not usually a problem at this stage. If you start running dry, try showing your game to some of your game-playing friends. Providing your basic mechanics work okay, they'll usually start pouring forth their own suggestions for how you could expand upon it. The bad news is that even a game with amazing potential can end up being dreadful if you don't get the levels and features right. Learning to distinguish a feature idea with potential from a "nonstarter" is an essential skill for a designer to develop, so in this section we'll pass on a few tips.

Features can be divided into two groups: those that change the abilities available for the player to use, and those that change the level obstacles that the player has to overcome. Here's a list of some different types of features that you might consider including:

- New features for the player(s) to use:

    - Abilities (e.g., attack moves, swimming, flying)

    - Equipment (e.g., weapons, armor, vehicles)

    - Characters (e.g., engineer, wizard, medic)

    - Buildings (e.g., garage, barracks, armory)

- New level features for the player(s) to overcome:

  - Opponents (e.g., with new abilities, buildings, or equipment)

  - Obstacles (e.g., traps, puzzles, terrain)

  - Environments (e.g., battlefields, racing tracks, climate)

A game doesn't need to include all the types of features listed here, and the first step is to decide which types you want to include in your game. We're going to use the Koalabr8 game from the previous chapter as an example. This game only includes obstacle-based features, but there's no real reason why it couldn't include new player abilities, equipment, or characters as well. However, we decided to stick to obstacles and save these other options for a sequel. Making these kinds of choices from the start can help to focus your game design and give it a clearer identity. If you try to include too many different types of features, you run the risk of creating a mishmash of ideas with no identifiable strengths.

So before you begin thinking of feature ideas, give some serious thought to the kind of progression you want to see running through your game. Is it about developing the equipment and abilities of a single character or building up a specialist team? Will levels force the player to apply their skills in different kinds of environments, or just pit them against increasingly challenging obstacles? Once you've made some of these kinds of decisions, then you're ready to sit down with some friends and start brainstorming ideas.

Pie in the Sky

So the koala picks up this jetpack, right, and everything goes 3D and you have to start flying it through the maze at like 1,000 miles an hour . . .

Whenever you ask people to brainstorm for you, you can guarantee that many ideas will fall into this category. Faced with such a creative opportunity, it's easy to let enthusiasm get the better of us—especially if we're not the one who has to do all the work! However, as the game's designer and programmer, it should be easier for you to spot ideas that are impossible or just too much work. Be gentle with your collaborators and try to bring them down to earth without too much of a bump. If you reject all their ideas before they finish their sentence, they'll quickly stop contributing! Explain how the same idea might be turned into something more feasible, and don't dismiss any ideas until you've finished the brainstorming process. It's worth keeping everyone brainstorming, as it's often the case that people who have the craziest ideas eventually come up with a brilliant idea that no one else would have thought of.

Do You Have That in Blue?

Yeah—on some levels we could have like, plastic explosives! Awesome! They'd be like the TNT, but sort of plastic looking . . .

Equivalent features are another kind of idea that designers need to be wary of. These are features that may look different, but actually perform a very similar function to an existing feature. There's nothing wrong with including equivalent features, as long as you don't try to pretend that they're anything more than that. For example, imagine that halfway through the Koalabr8 levels we introduced plastic explosives alongside TNT. As with any new feature, the player would approach them cautiously and try to figure out how they work. One way or another, they would eventually discover that they're exactly the same as TNT and feel slightly stupid and cheated by the whole experience.

Instead, imagine that we decided to theme the game so that half the levels were set in the doctor's workshop and half the levels were set in his laboratory. Every obstacle in the workshop could then have an equivalent high-tech feature in the laboratory setting: the TNT becomes plastic explosives, the rotating saw becomes a laser, the padlocks become electronic doors, and so forth. This approach would make the equivalence more obvious to the player and reduce the chances of their expectations being falsely raised. This way, they can appreciate the visual variation as something they have gained rather than something they have lost because they were expecting more from it.

Starting an Arms Race

Of course, once the koalas get into their nuclear tanks, then the TNT and circular saws can't hurt them any more . . .

If you plan to improve the player's equipment or abilities, then you need to consider the escalating effect this can have on the rest of the game. Everybody loves the idea of über weapons and, if you're aware of the pitfalls, there's no reason why they can't be a great addition to your game. However, problems can arise because über weapons have a tendency to make all previous features redundant. Having a nuclear tank that's invulnerable to TNT and saws would be a lot of fun for one level, but where do we go from there? We need something to challenge the player on the next level, so we invent equivalent features that work against tanks (perhaps land mines and robot drills). Of course, land mines and robot drills will be no use against the koala's alien flying saucers on the following level . . .

Hopefully, you can see that it's possible to end up in an arms race between the player and the game in which the features get increasingly powerful but the gameplay doesn't actually progress at all! The player faces exactly the same challenges with a tank and a land mine as they do with a koala and TNT.

You may think that taking the tank away from the player will solve everything, but this is like giving a child a new toy only to snatch it away again moments later. A better way is to create features that are less powerful in the first place by including a trade-off in their design. We'll discuss the idea of trade-offs more in the next design chapter, but we could achieve this by making the tank just *resistant* to TNT (perhaps it could survive three hits) as well as only moving at half the speed of the koala. Now the tank becomes a tool that can be helpful in certain situations (clearing paths), rather than something that the player wants to use all the time. More important, it's now a feature that varies the challenges of the game and provides a new angle on the gameplay—rather than just repackaging an old one.

One-Trick Ponies

On this one level, the doctor's pet psycho-whale swallows all the koalas and they have to escape from his intestines before they get digested!

As a game developer, you should start measuring every potential feature in terms of the quantity and quality of gameplay it creates. It's easy to end up with many more ideas than it's possible to create, so you must carefully choose the features that provide the greatest return. In particular it's often a good idea to avoid "one-trick ponies"—features that would undoubtedly be cool on one level but couldn't be used on any others. You may actually decide that the psycho-whale level is such a quality idea that you don't mind only using it once (as a final level, for example). However, be aware that you might be able to create a number of features in the same time that can be used on several different levels. In general, such ideas can be a bonus to a game that is already brimming with features, but are probably best avoided until then.

Emerging with More Than You Expected

No—you're not supposed to use it like that . . . oh—cool!

Game designers like to talk about *emergence* as it's one of the most exciting (and potentially dangerous) aspects of game design. Emergence is what happens when the rules of a game interact with each other so that the player can do something the designer hadn't predicted. Emergence can either be an uplifting surprise or terrible shock, depending on the situation. It's difficult to know whether a game contains emergence, unless you know what its designers intended, so we'll use examples from a PlayStation game called Hogs of War, about which we have insider knowledge.

Hogs was a comical war game where players took turns taking potshots at each other's squad until one side was wiped out (see Figure 8-1). There were plenty of crazy weapons to choose from, and surviving pigs could be promoted to specialist roles within their teams. The final level of the single-player game pits the player against the unstoppable "Team Lard" in the ultimate battle for control of the "swill mines." At the start of this level, the battlefield appears to be defended by a single enemy pig hauled up in a pillbox, but major reinforcements soon arrive on the scene. We designed this level to provide the player's biggest challenge yet, requiring them to use all their skill and knowledge to win the battle. However, in practice we also got two different emergent solutions that we never expected.

The first of these was an example of "good emergence," where the player used their ingenuity and lateral thinking to win the game fair and square. Rather than face the enemy in a straight firefight, they turned to the landscape to help them gain an advantage. The player's weakest pigs were quickly wiped out on this level, but they could be sacrificed to knock enemy pigs into pools of poisonous grime that surrounded the mines. The player could then use pigs trained in espionage to hide from the enemy until they all died from the effects of poison. Okay, so it wasn't the most valiant solution, but it was a clever one and it emerged from the interaction between the poison and hide features in the game.

The other emergent solution was an example of "bad emergence" as it exploits an interaction between oversights in the game's programming in order to complete the level. It was possible to use a jetpack to land a commando pig on the roof of the enemy pillbox in the very first turn of the game. The game's programming wouldn't normally allow its pigs to leave the safety of a pillbox, but another pig standing on its head (so to speak) confused it into coming out and attacking the commando. Out in the open, the player could use their best attacks to quickly kill it—before the reinforcements arrived. Since there were now no enemy pigs left on the battlefield, the game's programming concluded that the player had won the battle and finished the game. Using this method, the final level could be completed in two turns and without the player's team ever having to fight the reinforcements!

Of course, the problem with emergence is that you can't deliberately design it into a game; otherwise it wouldn't be emergent! Nonetheless, you can create features that encourage interplay with other game features and hope that good things come out of it. At the same time, you need to make doubly sure that this interplay doesn't reveal oversights in your programming that create the "bad" rather than the "good" kind of emergence. Fortunately, there's another kind of emergence between the programmer and level designer that's much easier to control, and we'll discuss it more in the section "Emerging Springs," later in this chapter.

Figure 8-1. *A Commando pig encourages an enemy Grunt to take a plunge in Hogs of War (reproduced by kind permission of ZOO Digital Publishing Ltd.).*

Designing Levels

Okay, so you've whittled your feature ideas down to a manageable shortlist of those with the most potential. Now before you immediately rush off and start programming, you first need to consider how you're going to use these features to structure your levels. It might be that all the best-sounding features are too hard for introductory levels, so you need to swap a few ideas for simpler ones. Levels and features will always continue to evolve as you work on them, but it certainly helps to make an overall plan from the start. In this section, we'll discuss some of the skills that a designer can use to help them think about this process and come up with a well-structured level plan.

The Game Maker's Apprentice

The title of this book conjures up images of a young apprentice learning a mysterious craft from a slightly crazy old professor. However, if you were thinking of yourself as the apprentice in this scenario, then think again. "The Game Maker's Apprentice" is actually a reference to the *game player*, which makes you (as the Game Maker) the crazy professor! Being a good game designer has a lot in common with being a good teacher—and just realizing this can improve your approach to game design. Inexperienced designers often see players as their opponents, and try to trick or outwit them by creating impossible challenges. As Phil Wilson discovered from his own first game designs (in this book's foreword), this does not help to make games fun! A successful game designer needs to treat players like their apprentices, balancing the game's theatrical threat of failure with a true desire to train the player to master the game. Once you accept this as your goal, you'll get a lot more satisfaction from players completing the challenges you set for them, as it proves that you're a successful game designer rather than a poor opponent!

In the last design chapter, we learned that games shouldn't be too hard or too easy to complete. This is not as straightforward as it seems because players have different levels of ability, but including difficulty modes and optional subgoals can help (as we saw in the Evil Clutches example). However, level designers also need to consider how players' abilities develop as their experience with the game grows. A task that was quite challenging for the player on level 1 may have become quite easy by the time they reach level 20. Knowing something about the way that people learn really can help a designer to create levels that pitch the difficulty correctly as players progress through the game.

Learning Curves

In general, the more time we spend on a task, the better we become at doing it. Once you've mastered the basics of a new skill, it's easy to improve by spending more time practicing it. However, the more you improve, the harder it becomes to make further progress, until eventually you seem to stop improving altogether. Figure 8-2 shows a model of how this process works for something like learning to juggle. We've taken the number of successful throws and catches that a learner makes in a minute as a measure of their juggling skill. You can see from the graph (or if you've ever tried it) that it takes quite a lot of effort to first grasp the technique for juggling, and it may be a long time before a beginner can make even a dozen successful catches in a single minute. Nonetheless, sooner or later they will get the hang of it and their catches per minute will start to increase rapidly for a while. However, once they reach the stage where they rarely drop balls, it becomes a lot harder to make further improvements. Their skill will still increase as they refine their precision and technique, but these improvements will get smaller and it will take longer to increase their catches per minute by the same amount.

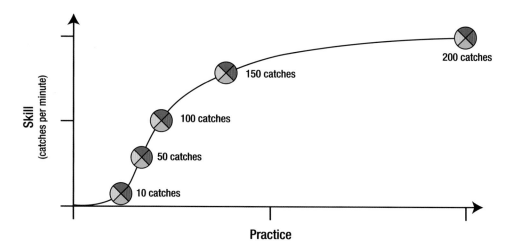

Figure 8-2. *A learning curve shows how a learner's performance changes with practice.*

Learning curves apply to computer games, too, and taking this pattern into account can improve a game's level designs. To understand how this information can help a designer, it's useful to think of learning curves as having the three different stages shown in Figure 8-3. These stages separate the emotional states that a player often goes through when they face the kind of challenge that a new computer game presents:

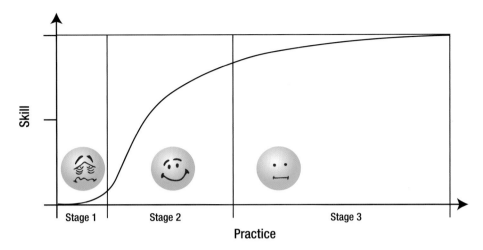

Figure 8-3. *The three stages of a learning curve tell us about the player's likely emotional state.*

Stage One: At the start of a completely new challenge, players have to absorb and process a lot of information at the same time. This means their progress is slow and there is a big risk of frustration as a result. People are often afraid of failure, too, so if the challenge appears too great, they may decide to give up rather than risk feeling humiliated. Therefore, a game design should give the player plenty of support during this period, perhaps by guiding players using a training mode or making them invulnerable until they have grasped the basic elements of the new challenge.

Stage Two: At this stage the player has found their feet and their skill is increasing at a rapid rate. As the player becomes aware of their success, any feelings of frustration will fade away and they'll become happily engrossed in the challenge. This is the ideal state for the player to be in, and it is the designer's job to try and make it last for as long as possible.

Stage Three: This stage represents the player's mastery of the challenge. This doesn't mean they couldn't improve any further, but a flat slope means playing for a long time to make even a little more progress—for example, trying to knock another few seconds off your best lap time after you've already come first in every race. If the goals stop challenging the player or it just seems like too much effort to improve, then it is only a matter of time before players will get bored. A designer must try and make sure that this doesn't happen too early in the game. If players feel they have mastered all the available challenges before they reach the end of a game, there's not much chance that they will bother completing it.

Difficulty Curves

The learning curve provides a good representation of how a player might come to grips with a game like Evil Clutches, where the game's challenges never change. However, games like this have a limited lifespan because players soon get bored when they reach stage three. The aim of good level design is to slowly introduce new challenges and features into the game at a rate that keeps the player in stage two of the learning curve. Introducing new features and challenges also plays a key part in determining the difficulty of a game. Difficulty curves are related to learning curves but represent how the game's difficulty changes over time rather than the player's skill level. If you think of the player's journey through the game as a bit like climbing a mountain slope, then it should look something like the one shown in Figure 8-4.

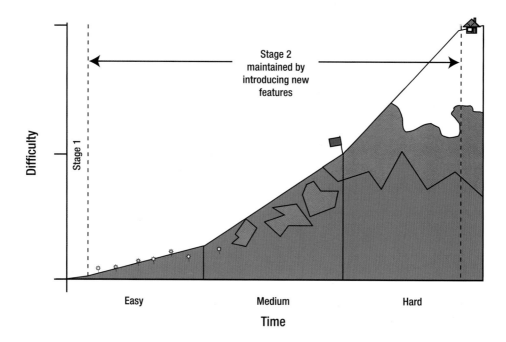

Figure 8-4. *The difficulty curve of a computer game is represented here as a mountain.*

The mountain starts with a shallow slope, in order to support players during the hardest stage of their own learning curves, but gradually increases as the game progresses. As the player's skill grows and they approach the top of their learning curve (see Figure 8-3), the game introduces new, harder challenges to bring them back down the curve and keep them in stage two. In this way, the player's positive emotional state is maintained while the difficulty of the game gradually rises as a result of the extra challenges. By the time the player reaches the steepest section of the slope, they should be well prepared for the game's greatest challenges. At this stage, knowing that they have a lot more distance behind them than in front also helps to drive players on to complete the game.

The slope of a game's difficulty curve has a big effect on the playability of the game. If you make it too steep at the start, then players give up, but if it gets too shallow at any point, players will get bored. Unfortunately, the only way to guarantee that you've got the difficulty curve right is to test and tweak your game with lots of different players. Once you've designed a few games, you'll begin to develop your own ideas and strategies for doing this, but here's one suggested approach that may help you find your way:

1. Decide how many levels you want in your game.

2. Divide this total into three equal groups for EASY, MEDIUM, and HARD levels.

3. Design each level and decide which group it belongs to:

   • All players should be able to complete EASY levels. Design these for players who have never played a game of the same genre before.

   • Most players should be able to complete MEDIUM levels. Design these for casual game-players of this genre.

   • Good players should be able to complete HARD levels. Design these for yourself and your friends who play these kinds of games.

4. If you end up with too many levels in one group, then redesign some of them to make them harder or easier for another group.

5. Play all of the levels again yourself and arrange them in order of difficulty.

6. Test your levels on different players:

   • Friends or family members who dislike games of this genre should be able to complete the EASY levels without help (although bribery may be required!)

   • As the game's designer, you should be able to complete all of the MEDIUM levels without ever having to restart a level.

   • Your friends who like games of this genre should eventually be able to complete all of the HARD levels without any help from you.

7. Tweak or reorder your levels according to the outcome of your tests.

Probably the most important tip here is that a game should only start to challenge its designer about two thirds of the way through the game (where the red flag is on the mountain). We've said it before, but the easiest trap for a designer to fall into is to make your games too hard because you find your own game so easy. And remember—even your final level shouldn't be so hard that you can't complete it yourself!

▓**Note** It's easy to get difficulty and learning curves confused, and people often do. If we want to suggest that something is hard, we will sometimes say it has a "steep learning curve," but as we have seen, a steep learning curve is more likely to suggest that something is easy!

Saving the Day

Giving the player the opportunity to save their progress can also make a big difference to the difficulty of a game. Players these days don't expect to have to go right back to the start of a game every time they fail to complete it, and may quickly lose interest if they do. Save points are considered a natural part of playing longer games, but a designer needs to be wary of the effect that saving can have on the way that a game is played. Providing the player with the ability to save at any point is a gift that many players will not be able to resist abusing—even when it begins to ruin their own playing experience! Saving the game every 30 seconds breaks up the flow of a game and can make its challenges much easier than they were designed to be. Even worse, a designer may be tempted to take it into account and create challenges that require the player to save all the time in order to succeed. This is not a good path to go down and is best avoided by creating automatic save points (such as at the end of each level) or rationing their use, so that the player has to find some kind of token before they can save their progress.

Applying It All

We've covered a lot of theory in this chapter, but we haven't been applying it to our example game as we went along. This had been a deliberately different approach to the first game design chapter because we wanted to emphasize that level design involves planning. Designing as you go along can be a good way to come up with your game's core game mechanics, but if you approach level and feature design in the same way, you're unlikely to end up with a well-structured game. However, now that we have the theory under our belt we can use this to finish off Koalabr8 and turn it into a complete playable game. You'll find a new version of the game containing all the changes we make in this section in Games/Chapter08/new_koala.gm6 on the CD.

Features

The features we already have for Koalabr8 avoid all the undesirable issues we mentioned at the start of this chapter. There are no equivalent features, one-trick ponies, or arms race issues in any of these, so we already have eight good features to use in our levels. Furthermore, one of the features (boulders) also has the potential for emergent behavior, because it's designed to encourage interactions between features (by allowing the player to destroy them!). This already gives us the following features to structure our level designs around:

- Explosive TNT

- Moving circular saws

- Red exits—Allow any number of koalas to exit the level

- Blue exits—Allow a single koala to exit the level

- Blue locks/switches—Permanently open locked passageways

- Yellow locks/switches—Open locked passageways for a limited time

- Red locks/switches—Open locked passageways only whilst pressed

- Boulders—Can be pushed by koalas and destroy other hazards

We're going to create 18 game levels and two training levels in total, so we already have enough features for a new one nearly every two levels. However, we think there's room for just one more feature, so we'll try to create another that encourages emergence by creating more potential for interactions between features.

Emerging Springs

Earlier in the chapter we mentioned that there were "good" and "bad" kinds of emergence. Unfortunately, the structured nature of puzzle games means that emergence often ends up being the bad kind. If the player discovers how to use a feature in a way the designer didn't expect, it's often more likely to prevent the player from solving the puzzle than helping them to complete it! There's already a good example of this if the player uses a boulder to crush a switch. This interaction has actually been used to create an interesting level, but you can probably see how it could potentially cause problems in the wrong situation.

Fortunately, there is another kind of "good" emergence that can take place between a programmer and level designer. This is where the level designer is able to utilize interactions between features in ways that the programmer hadn't expected. It happens as a result of the same kinds of interactions between features that we discussed before, and can trigger a really constructive evolution of ideas in a game's design. It also has the advantage that any "emergent bugs" that the designer finds can be fixed before the game is finished. With the right kind of relationship between the programmer and level designer, this kind of emergence can have a really positive effect on the gameplay. It's well worth trying to recruit your friends as level designers for this very reason!

We're going to create springs as a new feature that has the potential to create emergence. Springs will send koalas flying in a straight line at twice their normal speed until they hit a solid object. Flying koalas are vulnerable to dangerous obstacles in the same way, but will automatically operate switches and detonators along the way. Traveling at speed immediately creates interplay between other objects that involve speed, like timed switches and circular saws. Making switches operate as koalas fly over them creates more interplay, and we can enhance this a bit by making it possible to turn blue switches back on again after they have been turned off. Therefore, the following are the changes we've made to the features of the game:

- Add springs that turn koalas into flying koalas.

- Make flying koalas travel at double speed.

- Make blue switches alternately switch between on and off.

Training Missions

To help the player through the early stages of their learning curve at the start of the game, we're going to create two training levels. These levels will introduce the player to the main features of the game (TNT, saws, and switches) with a bit of helpful prompting on the screen (see Figure 8-5). However, the main challenge of this game is controlling more than one character at once, so the training levels will give the player a chance to get used to this, too. They will complete the training level first with just one koala, and then try the same level again with two. In this way, we should be able to make sure that the difficulty curve isn't so steep that it puts players off before they have a chance to get into the game.

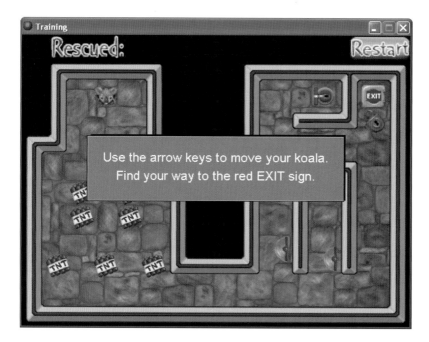

Figure 8-5. *The new Koalabr8 training level contains helpful prompts.*

Dividing Levels

Our finished game will have 20 levels, including the two training levels, so that's six in each of the easy, medium, and hard difficulty brackets (18 in total). To help us make sure that the easy levels live up to their name, we'll try to avoid using features that involve timing on these levels (saws and yellow switches). Timing adds extra pressure for the player, so we'll save these until they're a bit more comfortable with the game. Instead, the easy levels will attempt to teach the player how to control more than one koala at once.

The medium levels will try to build on the player's skills by making them control their koalas under pressure. We'll introduce saws and switches and provide situations in which the whole team has to be moved in synchronization in order to avoid obstacles. The hard levels will develop these skills even more and add cryptic elements to the puzzles that involve counterintuitive or inventive interactions between the features.

To give the player a sense of progression, we're also going to make the easy levels slightly smaller than the medium levels and only use the whole screen for the hard levels. We'll also give the player a little extra breathing space when new features are introduced by putting those features in situations where they can be explored without too much danger. So after a lot of designing, testing, and tweaking we eventually came up with the 18 levels that you'll find in the latest version of the game (see Figure 8-6).

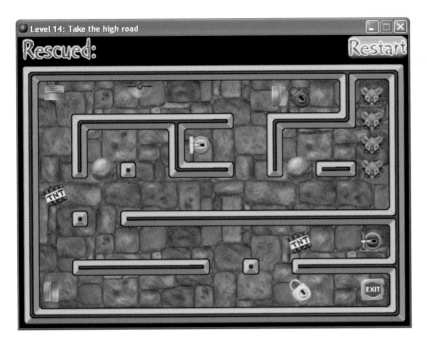

Figure 8-6. *A finished Koalabr8 level contains the new spring feature.*

Summary

And that's it! We hope you enjoy playing our new version of Koalabr8 and that it will inspire you to have a go at creating more levels and features for the game. Perhaps you'll even find some emergent solutions to the levels that we hadn't spotted! In this chapter you've learned that there is more to level design that churning out the first ideas that come into your head. We've looked at a number of principles that can help you to design better levels and followed them through with the Koalabr8 example. The main issues for level and feature design were:

- Choose features by
  - Brainstorming with your friends.
  - Being wary of equivalent features.
  - Avoiding starting an arms race.
  - Avoiding one-trick ponies.
  - Encouraging emergence through features that interact.
- Structure your level designs by
  - Including training levels to support the player when they most need it.
  - Carefully controlling the difficulty curve of your game.
  - Tweaking your level designs based on how hard *others* find your game.

However, perhaps the most important thing to remember from this chapter is that the player is *your apprentice* and a good game designer uses their level designs to teach the player how to master their game. That concludes this chapter and the third part of the book. In Part 4, we'll be looking at multiplayer games, and what better way could there be to learn about them than by shooting at your friends with a great big tank?

PART 4

■■■

Multiplayer Games

Spread a little happiness by bringing a friend along for the ride. Then demonstrate your complete superiority by kicking their butt.

■■■

CHAPTER 9

Cooperative Games: Flying Planes

Up to now we've only created single-player games, but for the next two chapters we'll be creating games that are played with a friend. This chapter's game will require players to cooperate in order to succeed, while the next will make players compete against one another for ultimate supremacy. Cooperative multiplayer games challenge players to work together and sometimes even make sacrifices for each other in order to succeed in their common goals.

In this chapter we'll also use a number of new Game Maker features: we'll take an in-depth look at the use of variables and learn about using *time lines*.

Designing the Game: Wingman Sam

We're calling this game *Wingman Sam* as it sets American and British fighter planes alongside each other in World War II. Here is a description of the game:

At the end of World War II you and your wingman are part of an allied squadron with secret orders to intercept the dangerous General von Strauss. Unfortunately, your mission turns out to be less secret than you thought and you are soon engaged by wave after wave of enemy fighters. You'll need to work together to survive the onslaught and destroy the general's plane, so the mission will be aborted if either of your planes is destroyed.

One player will control their plane with the arrow keys and fire bullets with the Enter/Return key. The other player will control their plane with the A, S, D, and W keys, and will fire bullets with the spacebar. Enemy planes will appear from the front, the sides, and behind. Some will just try to ram you while others will shoot at you. Both of the player's planes can only take a limited amount of damage before they are destroyed.

The game consists of just one level that takes place over an ocean scene. It will present you with increasingly difficult waves of planes and end with a battle against the infamous general himself. The game is won only if both players survive this final battle. See Figure 9-1 for a screenshot.

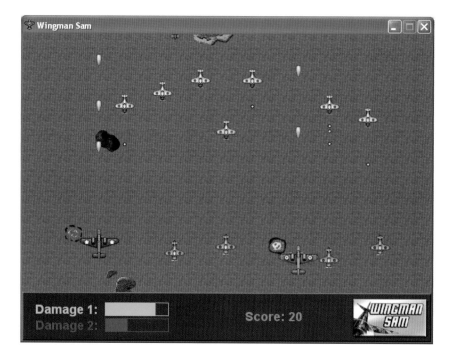

Figure 9-1. *This is how the Wingman Sam game will look in action.*

All resources for this game have already been created for you in the Resources/Chapter09 folder on the CD.

Variables and Properties

Before we begin creating the Wingman Sam game, let's take a moment to consolidate our understanding of variables in Game Maker. This simple concept can provide a very powerful mechanism for creating more interesting gameplay. We've already used them in several games, but what actually is a variable? Essentially, a variable is just a place for storing some kind of information, such as a number or some text. Most variables you will use in Game Maker store information about a numeric property of an instance. There are certain properties we can set when we define an object, such as whether it is visible or solid. Other properties store information that is different for each individual instance, such as its x- and y-position in the room. There are also a number of global properties, like the score, that are not related to individual instances. Each variable has its own unique name, which we can use to retrieve or change the value of that variable in Game Maker. Here are some important variables that every instance has—some of them should look familiar, as we have already used them before:

- x is the x-coordinate of the instance in the room.

- y is the y-coordinate of the instance in the room.

- hspeed is the horizontal speed of the instance (in pixels per step).

- `vspeed` is the vertical speed of the instance (in pixels per step).

- `direction` is the instance's current direction of motion in degrees (0–360 anticlockwise; 0 is horizontally to the right).

- `speed` is the instance's current speed in the `direction`.

- `visible` determines whether the object is visible or invisible (1=visible, 0=invisible).

- `solid` determines whether the object is solid or not solid (1=solid, 0=not solid).

▪Note Different variables employ different conventions for the meaning of the information that they store. A common convention for variables that either have a property or don't have a property is to use the values `0` and `1`. So if an instance is visible then its `visible` property will be set to `1`, whereas if it is invisible then its visible property will be set to `0`. This convention is so common that you can use the keyword `true` in place of the value `1` and the keyword `false` in place of the value `0`.

And here are some important global variables:

- `score` is the current value of the score.

- `lives` is the current number of lives.

- `mouse_x` is the x-position of the mouse.

- `mouse_y` is the y-position of the mouse.

- `room_caption` is the caption shown in the window title.

- `room_width` is the width of the room in pixels.

- `room_height` is the height of the room in pixels.

You can refer to an instance's variables from within its own actions by entering the names in their basic form shown here. Retrieving or changing an instance's variables in this way will only affect the instance concerned. To refer to variables in other instances, you need to use an object name followed by a dot (period/full stop) and then the variable name, such as `object_specialmoon.x` (the x-coordinate of the special moon object). When you use the name of an object to retrieve a variable in this way, Game Maker will give you the value of the first special moon instance's variable—ignoring any other instances there might be in the game. However, if you change the variable `object_specialmoon.x`, then it will change the x-coordinate of *all* special moon instances in the game! Game Maker also includes some special object names that you can use to refer to different instances in the game:

- `self` is an object that refers to the current instance. It is usually optional as `self.x` means the same as just `x`.

- `other` is an object that refers to the other instance involved in a collision event.

- `all` is an object that refers to all instances, so setting `all.visible` to `0` would make all instances of all objects invisible.

- `global` is an object used to refer to global variables that you create yourself.

Note You should only use the global object to refer to global variables that you create yourself. You do not use the global object to refer to built-in global variables, like score and lives. So `global.score` is not the same as `score` and would refer to a different variable. Global variables are particularly useful when you want to refer to the same variable in different instances or in different rooms, as they keep their values between rooms.

There are many, many more global and local instance variables, all of which can be found in the Game Maker documentation. There are actions to test the values of variables as well as manipulating them directly. You can even define variables for your own purposes as well. For example, the planes in Wingman Sam can only survive a certain amount of enemy fire, so each needs its own property to record the amount of damage it has taken. We'll create a new variable for this property called `damage`. The plane's **Create** event will set this variable to 0, and we'll increase it when the plane is hit. Once the damage is greater than 100, the plane will be destroyed.

Caution A variable's name can only consist of letters and the underscore symbol. Variable name are case-sensitive, so `Damage` and `damage` are treated as different variables. It is also important to make sure that your variable names are different from the names of the resources; otherwise Game Maker will become confused.

Two important actions that deal with variables directly are found in the **control** tab:

The **Set Variable** action changes the value of any variable, by specifying the **Variable** name and its new **Value**. Setting a variable using a name that does not exist will create a new variable with that name and value. Enabling the **Relative** option will add the value you provide to the current value of the variable (a negative value will subtract). However, the **Relative** option can only be used in this way if the variable already has a value assigned to it! You can also type an *expression* into the **Value**. For example, to double the score you could enter the **Variable** `score` and a **Value** of `2*score`.

The **Test Variable** action tests the value of any variable against selected criteria and then only executes the next action or block of actions if the test is true. The test criteria can be whether a variable is *equal to, smaller than*, or *larger than* a given value.

Don't worry if this seems like a lot of information to take in at once—we'll make use of many of these concepts creating the Wingman Sam game, so you'll have a chance to see how it all works in practice.

The Illusion of Motion

The style of game we are creating in this chapter is often referred to as a *Scrolling Shooter*. This style takes its name from the way that the game world scrolls horizontally or vertically across the screen as the game progresses. Although the player's position on the screen remains fairly static, the scrolling creates the illusion of continuous movement through a larger world.

Game Maker allows us to create scrolling backgrounds by using a tiling background image that moves through the room.

Creating a room with a scrolling background:

1. Start up Game Maker and begin a new empty game.

2. Create a background resource called background using the file Background.bmp from the Resources/Chapter09 folder on the CD.

3. Create a new room called room_first and give it an appropriate caption.

4. Switch to the **backgrounds** tab and select the new background from the menu icon, halfway down on the left.

5. At the bottom of the tab set **Vert Speed** to 2 to make the background scroll slowly downward.

Run the game, and you'll see that the background continually scrolls downward. To enhance the look and feel, we're going to add a few islands in the ocean. An easy way to do this would be to create a larger background image and add the island images to this background. The disadvantage of this approach would be that the islands would appear in a regular pattern, which would soon become obvious to the player. Consequently, we'll choose a slightly more complicated approach: using island objects that move down the screen at the same speed as the background. When they fall off the bottom, they'll jump to a random position across the top of the screen again so that they look like a new island in a different position.

Creating looping island objects:

1. Create sprites called spr_island1, spr_island2, and spr_island3 using Island1.gif, Island2.gif, and Island3.gif from the Resources/Chapter09 folder on the CD.

2. Create a new object called obj_island1 using the first island sprite. Set **Depth** to 10000 to make sure that it appears behind all other objects.

3. Add a **Create** event and include the **Move Fixed** action with a downward direction and a **Speed** of 2. This will make it move at exactly the same speed as the background.

4. Add an **Other, Outside room** event and include a **Test Variable** action. Set **Variable** to y, **Value** to room_height, and **Operation** to **larger than**. room_height is a global variable that stores the height of the room in pixels. Therefore, this will test for when the island has fallen off the bottom of the screen by checking whether the vertical position of the island is larger than this value (see Figure 9-2).

5. Add a **Jump to Position** action with **X** set to `random(room_width)` and **Y** set to `-70`. Using the global variable `room_width` with the `random()` command will provide a random number that does not exceed the width of the room. This will move the island to a random horizontal position just above the top of the room where it is out of sight.

6. Create objects for the other two islands and set the first island to be their parent.

7. Add one instance of each of the island objects to `room_first` at different vertical positions in the room.

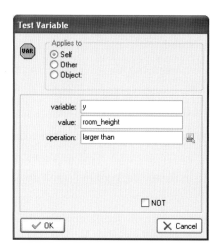

Figure 9-2. *This action tests whether the island is below the visible edge of the room.*

Now test the game. The scrolling sea should contain three islands, which reappear back at the top of the screen after disappearing off the bottom. Because the island instances move at exactly the same speed as the background, they appear as if they are part of it.

Flying Planes

Our scrolling background is complete, so it's time to create the planes that the players will control. These planes will have nearly the same behavior as each other, but there will need to be a few differences, such as the controls. To avoid duplicated work, we'll use the parent mechanism and three different plane objects. `obj_plane_parent` will contain all the behavior common to both planes, `obj_plane1` will be player one's plane, and `obj_plane2` will be player two's plane. Both of these last two objects will have `obj_plane_parent` as their parent so that they can inherit its behavior. Let's create the basic structure for these objects.

Creating the plane objects:

1. Create sprites called `spr_plane1` and `spr_plane2` using `Plane1.gif` and `Plane2.gif` from the `Resources/Chapter09` folder on the CD. Set the **Origin** of both sprites to **Center**. This is important for creating bullets and explosions later on.

2. Create a new object called `obj_plane_parent`. It doesn't need a sprite, and we'll come back to create events and actions for it later.

3. Create another object called `obj_plane1` and give it the first plane sprite. Set **Depth** to `-100` to make sure that it appears above other objects and set its **Parent** to be the `obj_plane_parent`.

4. Create a similar object called `obj_plane2` using the second plane sprite. Set **Depth** to `-99` to make sure that it appears above other objects (apart from the first plane). Also set its **Parent** to be `obj_plane_parent`.

The players will be able to move their planes around most of the screen using their own movement keys, but should be prevented from going outside of the visible area. When the player isn't pressing any keys, the plane will not move, but will still appear to be cruising along because of the scrolling background. We'll control the position of the planes manually (rather than setting their speed) so that we can easily prevent them from leaving the boundaries of the room.

Adding movement keyboard events to player one's plane object:

1. Reopen the properties form for `obj_plane1` by double-clicking on it in the resource list.

2. Add a **Keyboard, <Left>** event and include the **Test Variable** action. Set **Variable** to `x`, **Value** to `40`, and **Operation** to **larger than**. Include a **Jump to Position** action. Set **X** to `-4` and **Y** to `0`, and enable the **Relative** option. This will now only move the plane to the left if its x-position is greater than 40, which means it must be well inside the left boundary of the screen.

3. Add a **Keyboard, <Right>** event and include the **Test Variable** action. Set **Variable** to `x`, **Value** to `room_width-40`, and **Operation** to **smaller than**. Include a **Jump to Position** action. Set **X** to `4` and **Y** to `0`, and enable the **Relative** option. This will only move the plane right if its x-position is well inside the right boundary of the screen.

4. Add a **Keyboard, <Up>** event key and include the **Test Variable** action. Set **Variable** to `y`, **Value** to `40`, and **Operation** to **larger than**. Include a **Jump to Position** action. Set **X** to `0` and **Y** to `-2`, and enable the **Relative** option. This will only move the plane up if its y-position is well inside the upper boundary of the screen.

5. Add a **Keyboard, <Down>** event and include the **Test Variable** action. Set **Variable** to `y`, **Value** to `room_height-120`, and **Operation** to **smaller than**. Include a **Jump to Position** action. Set **X** to `0` and **Y** to `2`, and enable the **Relative** option. This will only move the plane down if its y-position is well inside the lower boundary of the screen.

Note that we only move the planes 2 pixels vertically in each step. Any more than this would make them move faster than the background, and it would look like the planes were flying backward! Also note that we have left a large area at the bottom of the screen where the planes cannot fly. We'll use this space later for displaying a status panel, but first we need to add similar events and actions to control the second plane.

Adding movement keyboard events to player two's plane object:

1. Reopen the properties form for obj_plane2 by double-clicking on it in the resource list.

2. Add similar events with the same actions as before but this time using the A key for left, the D key for right, the W key for up, and the S key for down.

Your planes are now ready to fly! Place one instance of each of the planes in room_first and run the game. You should have control of both planes, within the bounds of the room, and get the illusion of passing over the sea beneath you. In case your game isn't working, you'll find a version of the game so far in the file Games/Chapter09/plane1.gm6 on the CD.

Enemies and Weapons

Well, there seems to be plenty of scrolling going on in our scrolling shooter, but not a lot of shooting yet! Let's rectify this by adding events and actions to make the planes fire bullets and create some enemies for them to shoot at while we're at it. We'll start by creating the bullet object.

Creating the bullet object:

1. Create a new sprite called spr_bullet using Bullet.gif from the Resources/Chapter09 folder on the CD. Set the sprite's **Origin** to the **Center** of the sprite.

2. Create a new object called obj_bullet and give it the bullet sprite.

 3. Add a **Create** event and include the **Move Fixed** action. Select the up arrow and set the **Speed** to 8.

 4. Add the **Other, Outside room** event and include the **Destroy Instance** action.

Deciding when to create a bullet instance is a little more complicated. In this game we want it to be possible for the player to keep the fire key pressed and create a continuous stream of bullets. Nonetheless, creating a new bullet every step would create way too many bullets (30 every second!). To limit the rate at which bullets appear we'll create a new variable called can_shoot. We'll only allow the player to shoot when can_shoot has a value larger than 0, and once a shot has been made we'll set can_shoot to -15. We'll then increase the value of can_shoot by 1 in each step so that it will be 15 steps (half a second), before the player can shoot again. As this behavior needs to be largely the same for both planes, we'll put most of it in the parent plane object.

Adding shooting keyboard events to the plane objects:

1. Reopen the properties form for obj_plane_parent by double-clicking on it in the resource list.

2. Add a **Create** event and include the **Set Variable** action (**control** tab). Set **Variable** to can_shoot and **Value** to 1. Using **Set Variable** for the first time with a new variable name creates that new variable. Subsequent **Set Variable** actions may then use the **Relative** option to add and subtract from it.

3. Add a **Step, Step** event and include the **Set Variable** action with **Variable** set to can_shoot, **Value** set to 1, and the **Relative** option enabled.

4. Now reopen the properties form for obj_plane1. Add a **Keyboard, <Enter>** event and include the **Test Variable** action. Set **Variable** to can_shoot, **Value** to 0, and **Operation** to **larger than**. Include the **Start Block** action to make all the following actions depend on this condition.

5. Include the **Create Instance** action and select the bullet object. Set **X** to 0 and **Y** to −16, and enable the **Relative** option to create the bullet relative to the plane's position. Include the **Set Variable** action, with **Variable** set to can_shoot and **Value** set to -15.

6. Finally, include the **End Block** action. The event should look like Figure 9-3.

7. Repeat steps 4–6 for obj_plane2, this time using the **Keyboard, <Space>** event for the fire key.

Figure 9-3. *These are the actions required for shooting a bullet.*

To make the gameplay a bit more interesting, we'll also allow the player to shoot bullets more quickly if they repeatedly press the fire button. So when the player releases the fire button, we'll add 5 to the can_shoot variable.

Adding key release events to the plane objects:

1. Reopen the properties form for obj_plane1. Add a **Key Release, <Enter>** event and include the **Set Variable** action. Set **Variable** to can_shoot and **Value** to 5, and enable the **Relative** option.

2. Reopen the properties form for obj_plane2. Add a **Key Release, <Space>** event and include the **Set Variable** action. Set **Variable** to can_shoot and **Value** to 5, and enable the **Relative** option.

It might be wise to run the game now and make sure that this all works correctly before proceeding. Carefully check through your steps if there is a problem.

Now it's time to create our first enemy. This will be a small plane that simply flies down the screen and ends the game if it collides with one of the players (we'll add health bars later). The player's bullets will destroy the enemy and increase the player's score.

Creating an enemy plane object along with its sprites and explosions:

1. Create sprites called spr_enemy_basic, spr_explosion1, and spr_explosion2 using Enemy_basic.gif, Explosion1.gif, and Explosion2.gif from the Resources/Chapter09 folder on the CD. Set the **Origin** of all the sprites to the **Center**.

2. Create sounds called snd_explosion1 and snd_explosion2 using the files Explosion1.wav and Explosion2.wav from the Resources/Chapter09 folder on the CD.

3. Create an object called obj_explosion1 and give it the first explosion sprite. Add a **Create** event and include the **Play Sound** action to play the first explosion sound.

4. Add the **Other, Animation end** event and include the **Destroy Instance** action.

5. Create an object called obj_explosion2 and give it the second explosion sprite. Add a **Create** event and include a **Play Sound** action to play the second explosion sound.

6. Add an **Other, Animation end** event and include the **Sleep** action. Set **Milliseconds** to 1000 and set **Redraw** to **false**. Include the **Restart Game** action directly afterward.

7. Create an object called obj_enemy_basic and give it the basic enemy sprite. Add a **Create** event and include the **Move Fixed** action with a downward direction and a **Speed** of 4.

8. Add an **Other, Outside room** event and include the **Test Variable** action. Use it to test whether y is **larger than** room_height and include a **Destroy Instance** action after it. This will destroy the enemy plane when it reaches the bottom of the room.

9. Add a **Collision** event with the bullet object and include a **Set Score** action with a **Value** of 10 and the **Relative** option enabled. Include a **Destroy Instance** action to make the enemy object destroy itself.

10. Now include the **Create Instance** action. Set **Object** to obj_explosion1 and enable the **Relative** option so that it is created at the enemy's position. Finally for this event, add a **Destroy Instance** action to destroy the bullet (the **Other** object in this collision).

11. Add a **Collision** event with the parent plane object and include a **Destroy Instance** action to make the enemy object destroy itself. Include a **Create Instance** action with **Object** set to obj_explosion1 and the **Relative** option enabled.

12. Include a **Destroy Instance** action to destroy the player's plane object (the **Other** object). Finally, include a **Create Instance** action with **Object** set to obj_explosion2 and the **Relative** option enabled. Also select **Other** for **Applies to** so that the explosion is created at the position of the player's plane—not the enemy's.

This gives us a working enemy plane object, but we still need a mechanism to create enemy planes in the first place. To begin with, we'll do this in a controller object and randomly generate enemy planes about every 20 steps.

Creating a controller object:

1. Create a new object called obj_controller. It doesn't need a sprite.

2. Add a **Step, Step** event and include a **Test Chance** action with **Sides** set to 20. Follow this with a **Create Instance** action, with **Object** set to obj_enemy_basic. Set **X** to random(room_width) and **Y** to -40. This will create an enemy plane instance at a random position just above the top of the room.

3. Add one instance of this controller object to the room.

This gives us the first playable version of our game. Recruit a willing volunteer to play with and check that everything is working okay so far. You can also find this version in the file Games/Chapter09/plane2.gm6 on the CD.

■**Note** You can easily change this into a single-player game by removing the second plane from the room.

Dealing with Damage

The current version of the game ends as soon as one of the player's planes is hit by the enemy. We saw from the versions of Evil Clutches in Chapter 5 that this works better if we use a health bar that can absorb several hits instead. If you were curious enough to look and see how this was done, then you will have noticed that Game Maker provides simple actions to control and display the player's health. However, these actions only work for recording and displaying the health of one player, and in Wingman Sam we have two. Consequently, we'll create a new variable called damage for each player, and use this to record and display the status of their health independently. As the name suggests, each plane's damage will be set to 0 at the start of the game and increase slightly for each collision with enemy planes or bullets. If a plane's health gets larger than 100, then it explodes and the game is over. We'll update the damage variable in the parent plane object, because it will work the same for both players.

Adding a damage variable to the parent plane object:

1. Reopen the properties form for obj_plane_parent and select the **Create** event. Include a **Set Variable** action, setting **Variable** to damage and **Value** to 0.

2. Select the **Step** event and include a **Test Variable** action. Set **Variable** to damage, **Value** to 100, and **Operation** to **larger than**. Follow this with a **Start Block** action to begin a block of events.

3. Next include a **Destroy Instance** action to destroy the player's plane. Also include a **Create Instance** action that creates an instance of obj_explosion2 **Relative** to the position of the plane.

4. Finally, include an **End Block** action.

5. Reopen the properties form for obj_enemy_basic and select the **Collision** event with obj_plane_parent. Remove the last two actions that deal with destroying the plane and creating the second explosion.

6. Include a **Set Variable** action with **Variable** set to damage, **Value** set to 10, and the **Relative** option enabled. Also select the **Other** object from **Applies to** so that it increases the player's damage variable (rather than the enemy's, which doesn't exist!).

If you try running the game now, each plane should take about 10 hits before it explodes and the game ends (it actually takes 11—can you think why?). Nonetheless, this is a little hard to keep track of in your head, so clearly we need to display each player's current damage for them to see. To this end we're going to add a panel at the bottom of the screen and draw over the top of it. The controller object will be responsible for showing the panel, which will look something like Figure 9-4. We'll use a number of Game Maker's drawing actions to draw the panel, damage bars, and the score over the top.

Figure 9-4. *The information panel will display the damage of each plane and the combined score.*

Creating the panel sprite and object:

1. Create a sprite called spr_panel using Panel.gif from the Resources/Chapter09 folder on the CD.

2. Create a font resource called fnt_panel for displaying the panel text (just like you would any other resource). Set **Font** to **Arial** and **Size** to 14, and enable the **Bold** option, or choose a completely different font if you prefer.

3. Reopen the properties form for the controller object and set its **Depth** to -100. This will make the panel appear in front of enemy planes.

4. Add a **Draw** event and include the **Draw Sprite** action (**draw** tab). Set **Sprite** to spr_panel, **X** to 0, and **Y** to 404. This will draw the panel at the bottom of the screen.

5. Include the **Set Font** action and set **Font** to fnt_panel. Actions that draw text will now use this font.

6. Include a **Set Color** action and choose a green color, as this is the color of the first player's plane. Actions that draw graphics or text will now do so in this color.

7. Include a **Draw Text** action, setting **Text** to Damage 1:, **X** to 20, and **Y** to 420.

8. Include a **Draw Rectangle** action. **X1** and **Y1** refer to the top-left corner of the rectangle and **X2** and **Y2** refer to the bottom-right corner. Working down the form in order, set these to 130, 420, 230, and 440. Also set **Filled** to **outline**. This will draw a green box around the edge of the damage bar for player one.

9. Before we use each plane object's damage variable, we need to check that it hasn't already died and been deleted; this would mean Game Maker couldn't access the variable and would produce an error. Include a **Test Instance Count** action. Set **Object** to obj_plane1, **Number** to 0, and **Operation** to **larger than**. The next action will now only be executed if the first plane exists.

10. Include a **Draw Rectangle** action. Set **X1** to 130, **Y1** to 420, **X2** to 130+obj_plane1.damage, and **Y2** to 440, and set **Filled** to **filled**. This will draw a filled rectangle with a length equal to the damage variable of obj_plane1.

11. Now we'll do the same for the second plane. Include the **Set Color** action and choose a reddish color. Include a **Draw Text** action, setting **Text** to Damage 2:, **X** to 20, and **Y** to 445.

12. Include the **Draw Rectangle** action. Set **X1**, **Y1**, **X2**, and **Y2** to 130, 445, 230 and 465, respectively, and set **Filled** to **outline**.

13. Include the **Test Instance Count** action, setting **Object** to obj_plane2, **Number** to 0, and **Operation** to **larger than**. Follow this with a **Draw Rectangle** action, setting **X1** to 130, **Y2** to 445, **X2** to 130+obj_plane2.damage, and **Y2** to 465. Also set **Filled** to **filled**.

We'll also use the panel, rather than the window caption, to display the player's score, and get the controller object to show a high-score table when the game is over.

Displaying the score and high-score table:

1. Add a new background called background_score using the file Score.bmp from the Resources/Chapter09 folder on the CD.

2. Reopen the properties form for the controller object and select the **Draw** event.

3. Include a **Set Color** action at the end of the list of actions and select a bluish color. Include a **Draw Score** action (**score** tab), setting **X** to 350 and **Y** to 430.

4. Add a **Create** event and include the **Score Caption** action (**score** tab). Change **Show Score** to **don't show** to stop Game Maker from displaying the score in the window caption.

5. Reopen the properties form for obj_explosion2 and select the **Animation end** event.

6. Include the **Show Highscore** action between the **Sleep** and **Restart Game** actions. Set **Background** to background_score, set **Other Color** to yellow, and choose a nice font.

Now test the game to check that the damage and score are shown correctly on the new panel. This version can also be found in the file Games/Chapter09/plane3.gm6 on the CD.

Time Lines

So far all the enemy planes have been generated randomly, but this doesn't tend to create interesting gameplay. Therefore, we will use Game Maker's time line resource to create waves of enemy formations that start off easy and gradually grow more difficult through the level. A time line allows actions to be executed at preset points in time, so we can use them here to determine when enemy planes are created.

We'll begin with a very simple example of a time line. We'll need to create a new time line resource and indicate when we want actions to be performed. This should feel familiar as a time line resource has a list of **Moments** and their **Actions** similar to an object resource's list of **Events** and their **Actions** (see Figure 9-5). Then we'll need to set the time line running by using the **Set Time Line** action.

Creating a new time line resource and starting it running:

1. From the **Resources** menu choose **Create Time Line**. A properties form will appear like the one shown in Figure 9-5. The buttons on the left allow moments to be added and removed from the **Moments** list in the middle of the form. Each moment can have its own list of actions, which can be added in the usual way from the tabbed pages of action icons on the right. Call the new time line time_level1.

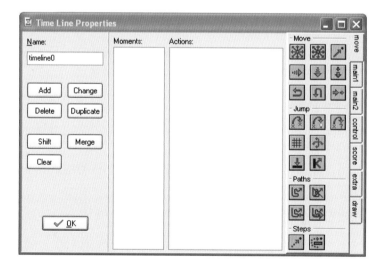

Figure 9-5. A time line has a list of moments and actions.

2. Click the **Add** button to add a new moment. Type 60 in the prompt that appears and click **OK**. Moments are measured in steps, so this creates a moment that happens after 2 seconds and adds it to the **Moments** list.

3. Include the **Create Instance** action (**main1** tab) in the **Actions** list for this moment. Set **Object** to obj_enemy_basic, **X** to 80, and **Y** to -40. This is the first of many new instances we will create in the time line, so from now on we will refer to their **X** and **Y** positions using the shorthand form: (**X**, **Y**), which would be (80, -40) in this case.

4. Add similar actions in the same moment to create enemy planes at the following positions: (200, -40), (320, -40), (440, -40), and (560, -40). This will create a horizontal row of five planes at the top of the screen, two seconds into the level.

5. Reopen the properties form for the controller object and select the **Create** event. Include a **Set Time Line** action from the **main2** tab and set **Time Line** to the one we just created. Leave **Position** set to 0 so that the time line starts at the beginning. The action should now look like Figure 9-6.

6. Select the **Step** event and remove the two actions, as we no longer want to generate random enemies.

■**Note** Each instance in the game can only have one time line set on it at a time. Setting a new time line replaces the old one and setting a time line to **no time line** stops the execution of the current time line.

Figure 9-6. *The **Set Time Line** action is used to start a time line.*

Now run the game, and you should find that a row of enemy planes appears after about two seconds. These are the only enemies that ever appear, so clearly we need to add a lot more moments to the time line to make an interesting level! By giving planes different movement directions, we can also make formations that fly horizontally or diagonally. But before we can do that we'll have to create some more types of enemy planes.

More Enemies

In this section we'll create several types of enemy planes with varying behaviors. First, we'll create enemy planes that come from the left, right, and bottom of the screen. These are harder to avoid and more difficult to shoot.

Creating new enemy plane objects:

1. Create sprites for the new enemies using Enemy_right.gif, Enemy_left.gif, and Enemy_up.gif from the Resources/Chapter09 folder on the CD. Set the **Origin** of each sprite to the **Center**.

2. Right-click on obj_enemy_basic in the resource list and select **Duplicate**. Call the duplicate object obj_enemy_right and give it the right-facing enemy sprite.

3. Select the **Create** event for the new object and double-click on the **Move Fixed** action in the **Actions** list. Select the right movement arrow instead of the down arrow and close the action properties again. Select the **Outside room** event and double-click on the **Test Variable** action in the **Actions** list. Change **Variable** to x and **Value** to room_width, to test for when the plane is off the right edge of the screen.

4. Repeat steps 2 and 3 to create obj_enemy_left, which moves left and tests for x being **smaller than** 0.

5. Repeat steps 2 and 3 to create obj_enemy_up, which moves up and tests for y being **smaller than** 0.

Add some new moments and actions to the time line to test these new enemy planes. Leave an appropriate pause between waves so that the step for each moment is between 100 and 200 steps more than the last. You'll need to create instances of obj_enemy_right just to the left of the room (**X** less than 0 and **Y** between 0 and 360), obj_enemy_left just to the right of the room (**X** greater than 640 and **Y** between 0 and 360) and obj_enemy_up just below the room (**X** between 0 and 640 and **Y** greater than 360). As you will see, this last type of plane is particularly nasty and difficult to avoid.

The two other enemy planes that we're going to create will shoot bullets. One will shoot bullets in a straight line, while the other will direct bullets toward the player's planes. We'll start by creating three types of bullets: one that moves downward and two others that move toward each of the player's planes.

Creating new enemy bullet objects:

1. Create a new sprite called spr_enemy_bullet using Enemy_bullet.gif and set the **Origin** to the **Center**. Create an object called obj_enemy_bullet and give it the enemy bullet sprite.

2. Add an **Other, Outside room** event and include a **Destroy Instance** action to destroy the bullet.

3. Add a **Collision** event with the parent plane object and include a **Destroy Instance** action followed by a **Play Sound** action to play snd_explosion1.

4. Include a **Set Variable** action and select **Other** for **Applies to** (the plane object). Set **Variable** to damage and **Value** to 5, and enable the **Relative** option.

5. Create an object called obj_enemy_aim1 and give it the same bullet sprite. Set the **Parent** to obj_enemy_bullet. This bullet will move toward player one's plane, so we need to check that it exists as we did in the control panel.

6. Add a **Create** event and include the **Test Instance Count** action. Set **Object** to obj_plane1, **Number** to 0, and **Operation** to **larger than**. Follow this with the **Move Towards** action (**move** tab) so that it is only executed if player one's plane exists. Set **X** to obj_plane1.x, **Y** to obj_plane1.y, and **Speed** to 8 so that it targets player one's plane.

7. Include an **Else** action followed by a **Move Fixed** action with a downward direction and a **Speed** of 6. This will make the bullet move straight down if the player's object doesn't exist.

8. Finally, duplicate the obj_enemy_aim1 object and call it obj_enemy_aim2. Select the **Create** event and edit the **Test Instance Count** action to set **Object** to obj_plane2. Click on the **Move Towards** action and change the references to obj_plane1.x and obj_plane1.y to obj_plane2.x and obj_plane2.y. This bullet will now target player two's plane instead.

The aiming bullets check to see if their target exists and start moving toward that plane's current position if they do. If it doesn't exist, then they start moving straight downward. Now we need to create the enemies that will shoot these bullets. Note that we haven't yet given the normal enemy bullet a direction and speed because we're going to do this when we create instances of it.

Creating enemy plane objects that shoot:

1. Create sprites called spr_enemy_shoot and spr_enemy_target using the sprites Enemy_shoot.gif and Enemy_target.gif. Set the **Origin** of both sprites to the **Center**.

2. Create a new object called obj_enemy_shoot and give it the shooting enemy sprite. Set **Parent** to obj_enemy_basic as its behavior is almost the same.

3. Add a **Step, Step** event and include a **Test Chance** action with 40 **Sides**. Include a **Create Moving** action with **Object** set to obj_enemy_bullet, **X** set to 0, and **Y** set to 16. Enable the **Relative** option, and set **Speed** to 6 and **Direction** to 270 (downward).

4. Create an object called obj_enemy_target and give it the correct sprite and obj_enemy_basic as its **Parent**.

5. Add a **Step, Step** event and include a **Test Chance** action with 100 **Sides**. Include a **Create Instance** action with **Object** set to obj_enemy_aim1, **X** set to 0, **Y** set to 16, and the **Relative** option enabled.

6. In a similar way, include an equal chance of creating instances of obj_enemy_aim2.

Add some additional moments to the time line in order to test the new enemy types. Note that you can duplicate moments. This makes it easier to repeat the same formation many times. A version of the game containing all the enemies and a simple time line to test them can also be found in the file Games/Chapter09/plane4.gm6 on the CD.

End Boss

Games of this type usually finish with some kind of end of level boss. This boss is often an extra strong enemy with its own damage counter and additional weapons. Our game only has one level, so defeating the boss is also the ultimate goal of the game. Our boss will be General von Strauss's plane—a large plane flying in the same direction as the players as they slowly catch up to it. It will let loose a barrage of bullets in different directions and must be hit 50 times to be destroyed. If the players survive this onslaught, then the general's plane will explode in a satisfying way and the game will end.

Creating the boss plane object:

1. Create a new sprite called spr_boss using Boss1.gif and set the **Origin** to the **Center**.

2. Create a new object called obj_boss and give it the boss sprite. Set its **Depth** to -10 so that it appears above other planes and bullets.

3. Add a **Create** event and include a **Move Fixed** action with a downward direction and a **Speed** of 1. Also include a **Set Alarm** action to set **Alarm 0** to 200 steps.

4. Add an **Alarm, Alarm 0** event and include the **Move Fixed** action with the middle square selected and a **Speed** of 0 (to make the boss stop moving).

5. Reopen the time line and add another moment at the end of the list. Include a **Create Instance** event to create obj_boss at (320, -80).

Quickly run the game and check that the boss plane moves into sight and stops in the middle of the screen. Next we'll include a hit counter that indicates how many times the boss has been hit. We'll use a variable called hits to record the number of hits and destroy the boss when this reaches 50.

Adding a hit counter to the boss object:

1. Select the **Create** event for the boss object and include a **Set Variable** action. Set **Variable** to hits and **Value** to 0.

2. Add a **Collision** event with the obj_bullet and include a **Set Score** action with a **Value** of 2 and the **Relative** option enabled.

3. Add a **Create Instance** action and select the **Other** object from **Applies to** (the bullet). Set **Object** to obj_explosion1 and enable the **Relative** option. Next include a **Destroy Instance** action and select the **Other** object from **Applies to** (the bullet).

4. Include a **Set Variable** action. Set **Variable** to hits and **Value** to 1, and enable the **Relative** option.

5. Include a **Test Variable** action. Set **Variable** to hits, **Value** to 50, and **Operation** to **equal to**. Include a **Start Block** action so that the next block of actions will be only executed once the boss has taken 50 hits.

6. Include a **Destroy Instance** action to destroy the boss object. Include a **Set Score** action with a **Value** of 400 and the **Relative** option enabled (to reward the players).

7. Next include five **Create Instance** actions to create instances of obj_explosion2, at the following **Relative** positions: (-30, 0), (30, 0), (0, 0), (0, -30), and (0, 10).

8. Finally, include an **End Block** action.

While this does the job, the player has no way of knowing how many shots they have landed on the boss plane, or how close it is to destruction. Adding a bar to show this will help to make the player's goal and progress toward it much clearer.

Adding a bar to display the boss's hit counter:

1. Add a **Draw** event to the boss object and include a **Draw Sprite** action. Remember that object's sprite stops being drawn automatically if we add a **Draw** event, so we need to do this for ourselves. Set **Sprite** to spr_boss and **Subimage** to -1 (which means keep the current subimage), and enable the **Relative** option.

2. Include a **Set Color** action and choose a dark red color. We will use this color to draw a bar that decreases in length by 4 pixels for each hit that the boss object takes. As it takes 50 hits to destroy it, we will need the bar to be 200 pixels wide to start with (50 * 4 = 200). This can be achieved by including a **Draw Rectangle** action with **X1** set to 10, **Y1** set to 5, **X2** set to 210-(4*hits), and **Y2** set to 15.

Now it's time to make the boss fight back. Colliding with the boss should instantly kill players, and the boss itself should fire bullets in all directions. After a while we'll even make it send smaller ships out to target the player—just to make things interesting!

Making the boss object more challenging:

1. Add a **Collision** event with the parent plane object and include a **Set Variable** action. Set **Variable** to damage and **Value** to 101, and select the **Other** object from **Applies to**. This will immediately destroy the plane and end the game.

2. Select the **Create** event and include a **Set Alarm** action for **Alarm 1** with 100 steps.

3. Add an **Alarm, Alarm 1** event and include the **Repeat** action (**control** tab). This will repeat the next action (or block of actions) a specified number of times. Set **Times** to 10 to repeat the next action 10 times.

4. Include the **Create Moving** action and set **Object** to obj_enemy_bullet. Set **Speed** to 6 and **Direction** to random(360), and enable the **Relative** option.

5. Finally, include a **Set Alarm** action for **Alarm 1** with 30 steps. This makes the boss fire again in 1 second's time.

6. Select the **Create** event and include a **Set Alarm** action for **Alarm 2** with 250 steps.

7. Add an **Alarm, Alarm 2** event and include a **Create Instance** action. Create an instance of obj_enemy_target just below the boss's left wing by providing a **Relative** position of (-40, -10). Include another **Create Instance** action to create a second instance of obj_enemy_target just below the boss's right wing using a **Relative** position of (40, -10).

8. Finally, include a **Set Alarm** action for **Alarm 2** with 40 steps.

And that concludes the boss object! You should now be able to create a varied and interesting time line with many different waves of enemy planes. These should gradually get more and more challenging before the boss plane eventually appears on the scene for the final battle. If you want to play our version, then you'll find it on the CD in the file Games/Chapter09/plane5.gm6.

Finishing Touches

All that remains is to add the final bells and whistles that turn this into a finished game. First, let's add some background music played by the controller object.

Playing background music in the controller object:

1. Create a new sound resource called snd_music using Music.mp3 from the Resources/Chapter09 folder on the CD.

2. Reopen the controller object and select the **Create** event. Include a **Play Sound** action, with **Sound** set to snd_music and **Loop** set to **true**.

Now we're going to change some of the global game settings. You might have noticed that all games created so far use the standard Game Maker loading image and the same red ball icon when you create an executable. However, both of these can be changed very easily to create a more individual feel for your game. We can also make the game automatically start in full-screen mode and disable the cursor in the game.

Editing the global game settings to change the loading image and game icon:

1. Double-click on **Global Game Settings** at the bottom of the resource list and select the **loading** tab.

2. Enable the **Show your own image while loading** option and click the **Change Image** button. Select the Loading.gif from the Resources/Chapter09 folder on the CD.

3. Select the **No loading progress bar** option, as there is not much point in a loading bar for a game that loads so quickly.

4. Click the **Change Icon** button and select Icon.ico from the Resources/Chapter09 folder on the CD.

5. Select the **graphics** tab and enable the **Start in full-screen mode** option.

6. Disable the **Display the cursor** option.

7. Click the **OK** button to close the **Global Game Settings**.

Test these changes by choosing **Create Executable** from the **File** menu. Save the executable on your desktop and you'll notice that it now has the plane icon. When you run the game, you should also see the new loading image and the game should start in full-screen mode.

There are many more useful options in the global game settings. You might want to take a look at the different tabbed pages and consult the Game Maker documentation on them. Before you finish, remember to add some help text (including the controls) in the **Game Information** section.

Congratulations

We hope you've enjoyed creating a game that can be played with a friend. You'll find the final version on the CD in the file Games/Chapter09/plane6.gm6. It only has one level, so why not add some more of your own? You could create several more levels just by using the enemy planes we've already created, but obviously you can create new enemies too. You could create planes that fly diagonally, shoot more bullets, go faster, and so forth. You could also create some new end-of-level bosses as well. You might also want to add a title screen using Title.bmp provided for you in the resources directory. Finally, you could add some bonus objects that repair the damage of the plane or provide additional firing power.

Most of the graphics for this game come from Ari Feldman's collection, which you'll find on the CD. There is one big image called all_as_strip.bmp that contains many different images. In the **File** menu of the Sprite Editor, there is a command called **Create from Strip**, which can be used to grab subimages out of the big image (search for "Strips" in the Game Maker help for more details). The big image also contains a boat and a submarine that you can use to create ground targets.

The main new concept that you learned in this chapter was the use of time lines. Time lines are very useful for controlling the order of different events over the course of a game. We used just one time line to control the flow of enemy planes, but you can use many different time lines simultaneously (on different objects). For example, we could have used a second time line to control the attacking behavior of the boss plane. You can even use them to create little movies using Game Maker.

Wingman Sam is an example of a game in which two players must cooperate to achieve a common goal. However, multiplayer games aren't always this amicable, and in the next chapter we'll create a game in which two players must compete with each other by trying to blow up each other's tanks!

CHAPTER 10

■ ■ ■

Competitive Games: Playing Fair with Tanks

Combat arenas are a popular theme in multiplayer games, because they create extremely compelling gameplay from very simple ingredients. This can often just be an environment filled with weapons that the players can use to wipe each other out. The game that we're going to create in this chapter is exactly that, with futuristic battle tanks. Although games like this are relatively easy to make, care must be taken in their design to ensure that both players feel they are being treated fairly. We'll discuss this more in Chapter 11.

This game will also introduce *views* in Game Maker to help create a larger combat arena. We will also use views to create a split-screen mode, where each player can only see the part of the arena around their own tank.

Designing the Game: Tank War

We're calling this game *Tank War* for obvious reasons. Both players pilot a tank within a large battle arena and the winner is the last one standing. Here's a more detailed description of the game:

> *Tank War is a futuristic tank combat game for two players. Each player drives his or her own tank through the walled battle arena with the aim of obliterating the other's tank. Once a tank is destroyed, both tanks are respawned at their start position, and a point is awarded to the surviving player. Most walls provide permanent cover, but some can be temporarily demolished to create a way through. There is no ultimate goal to the game, and players simply play until one player concedes defeat.*
>
> *Each tank has a primary weapon that it can fire indefinitely. Pickups provide a limited amount of ammunition for a secondary weapon, or repair some of the tank's damage:*

- *Homing rockets: Always move in the direction of your opponent*

- *Bouncing bombs: Bounce against walls, and can be used to fire around corners*

- *Shields: Are activated to provide a temporary protective shield*

- *Toolbox: Repairs part of the tank's damage*

The game uses a split-screen view divided in two parts (see Figure 10-1). The left part is centered on player one's tank and the right part is centered on player two's tank. There is also a mini-map at the bottom of the screen for locating pickups and the other player.

Player one will move their tank with the A, D, W, and S keys and fire with the spacebar (primary) and Ctrl key (secondary). Player two will control their tank with the arrow keys, and fire with the Enter key (primary) and Delete key (secondary).

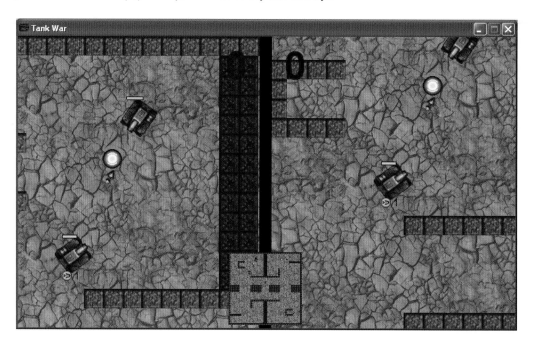

Figure 10-1. *Tank War has a split-screen with a little mini-map at the bottom.*

All resources for this game have already been created for you in the Resources/Chapter10 folder on the CD.

Playing with Tanks

Our first task is to create the battle arena. This will be a simple environment with two types of walls that will stop tanks and their shells. The first type of wall will be permanent, whereas the second type can be demolished by tank fire but will reappear again after a while.

Creating the arena background and walls:

1. Launch Game Maker and start a new empty game.

2. Create a background resource called background using Background.bmp from the Resources/Chapter10 folder on the CD.

3. Create two sprites called spr_wall1 and spr_wall2 using Wall1.gif and Wall2.gif. Disable the **Transparent** property for both sprites.

4. Create a new object called obj_wall1 and give it the first wall sprite. Enable the **Solid** property and close the object properties. No further behavior is needed.

5. Create a new object called obj_wall2 and give it the second wall sprite. Enable the **Solid** property and set **Parent** to obj_wall1.

Like most of the previous games, this game will have a controller object. For the time being, this will only play the background music but later it will also be responsible for displaying the score.

Creating the controller object and the room:

1. Create a sound resource called snd_music using Music.mp3 from the Resources/Chapter10 folder on the CD.

2. Create a new object called obj_controller, with no sprite. Set **Depth** to -100 to make sure that the drawing actions we will give it later on are drawn in front of other objects. Add an **Other**, **Game Start** event and include the **Play Sound** action. Set **Sound** to snd_music and set **Loop** to **true**.

3. Create a new room and switch to the **settings** tab. Call the room room_main and give it an appropriate caption.

4. Switch to the **backgrounds** tab and select the background you created earlier.

5. Switch to the **objects** tab. In the toolbar, set **Snap X** and **Snap Y** to 32, as this is the size of the wall objects.

6. Create a continuous wall of obj_wall1 objects around the edge of the room. Also add walls of both types to the interior so that they create obstacles for the tanks (remember that you can hold the Shift key to add multiple instances of an object).

7. Add one instance of the controller object into the room.

Now we'll create our tanks. We'll need different tank objects for each of the two players, but most of their behavior will be identical so we'll create a parent tank object that contains all the common events and actions. In this game we're going to control the tank instances by directly changing their local direction and speed variables. Remember that the direction variable indicates the direction of movement in degrees (0–360 anticlockwise; 0 is horizontally to the right). The speed variable indicates the speed of movement in this direction, so a negative value represents a backward movement.

Creating the parent tank object:

1. Create a new object called obj_tank_parent, with no sprite.

2. Add a **Create** event and include a **Set Friction** action with **Friction** set to 0.5. This will cause the tanks to naturally slow down and come to rest when the player is not pressing the acceleration key.

3. Add a **Collision** event with `obj_wall1` and include a **Set Variable** action. Set **Variable** to `speed` and **Value** to `-speed`. This will reverse the tank's movement direction when it collides with a wall.

 4. Likewise, add a **Collision** event with `obj_tank_parent` and include a **Set Variable** action. Set **Variable** to `speed` and **Value** to `-speed` (you could also right-click on the previous collision event and select **Duplicate Event** to achieve this).

Creating the two players' tank objects:

1. Create two sprites called `spr_tank1` and `spr_tank2` using `Tank1.gif` and `Tank2.gif`. Set the **Origin** of both sprites to **Center**. Note that these sprites have 60 subimages corresponding to different facing directions for the tanks.

2. Create a new object called `obj_tank1` and give it the first tank sprite. Set **Parent** to `obj_tank_parent` and enable the **Solid** option. Set **Depth** to `-5` to make sure it appears in front of other objects, such as shells, later on.

 3. Add a **Keyboard, Letters, A** event and include a **Set Variable** action. Set **Variable** to `direction` and **Value** to `6`, and enable the **Relative** option. This will rotate the tank anticlockwise.

 4. Add a **Keyboard, Letters, D** event and include a **Set Variable** action. Set **Variable** to `direction` and **Value** to `-6`, and enable the **Relative** option. This will rotate the tank clockwise.

 5. Add a **Keyboard, Letters, W** event and include a **Test Variable** action. Set **Variable** to `speed`, **Value** to `8`, and **Operation** to **smaller than**. Include a **Set Variable** action, setting **Variable** to `speed` and **Value** to `1` and enabling the **Relative** option. This will then only increase the speed if it is smaller than 8.

 6. Add a **Keyboard, Letters, S** event and include a **Test Variable** action. Set **Variable** to `speed`, **Value** to `-8`, and **Operation** to **larger than**. Include a **Set Variable** action, setting **Variable** to `speed` and **Value** to `-1` and enabling the **Relative** option. This will only reduce the speed (reverse) if the speed is greater than -8 (full speed backward).

 7. Add a **Step, End Step** event. In this event we must set the subimage of the sprite that corresponds to the direction the tank is facing. Include the **Change Sprite** action, setting **Sprite** to `spr_tank1`, **Subimage** to `direction/6` and **Speed** to `0`. As in Galactic Mail, `direction/6` converts the angle the object is facing (between 0 and 360) to the range of images in the sprite (between 0 and 60).

 8. We will draw the tank ourselves because later we want to draw more than just the sprite. Add a **Draw** event. Include the **Draw Sprite** action, setting **Sprite** to `spr_tank1` and **Subimage** to `-1` and enabling the **Relative** option.

9. Repeat steps 2–8 (or duplicate `obj_tank1` and edit it) to create `obj_tank2`. This time you should use the arrow key events to control its movement (**Keyboard, Left**, etc.)

10. Reopen the room and put one instance of each tank into it.

Now test the game to make sure everything is working correctly. In case something is wrong, you'll find a version of the game so far in the file Games/Chapter10/tank1.gm6 on the CD.

Firing Shells

Now the fun begins. In this section we'll create shells for the tanks to shoot at each other, but first we need a mechanism to record the tank's damage and scores. As in Chapter 9, we'll give each tank a variable called damage to record the amount of damage it has taken. It will start with a value of 0, and once it reaches 100 the tank is destroyed. We'll also use two global variables called global.score1 and global.score2 to record how many kills each tank has made. The controller object will initialize these variables and display their values.

Recording the player's score in the controller object:

1. Create a font called fnt_score and select a font like Arial with a **Size** of 48 and the **Bold** option enabled. We only need to use the numerical digits for the score, so you can click the **Digits** button to leave out the other characters in the font. This will save storage space and reduce the size of your .gm6 and executable game files.

2. Reopen the controller object and select the **Game Start** event. Include a **Set Variable** action with **Variable** set to global.score1 and **Value** set to 0. Include another **Set Variable** action with **Variable** set to global.score2 and **Value** also set to 0. This creates and initializes the global score variables that will store the player's score.

3. Add a **Draw** event and include a **Set Font** action. Set **Font** to fnt_score and **Align** to **right**. Include a **Set Color** action and choose a dark red color.

4. Include a **Draw Variable** action from the **control** tab. Set **Variable** to global.score1, **X** to 300, and **Y** to 10.

5. Include another **Set Font** action with **Font** set to fnt_score, but this time set **Align** to **left**. Include a **Set Color** action and choose a dark blue color.

6. Include a **Draw Variable** action with **Variable** set to global.score2, **X** set to 340, and **Y** set to 10.

If you run the game now, you should begin with a large 0–0 score displayed on the screen. Next we're going to create two explosions: a large one for when a tank is destroyed, and a small one for when a shell hits something.

Creating the large explosion object:

1. Create a sprite called spr_explosion_large using Explosion_large.gif and **Center** the **Origin**.

2. Create a sound called snd_explosion_large using Explosion_large.wav.

3. Create a new object called `obj_explosion_large`. Give it the large explosion sprite and set **Depth** to `-10`. Add a **Create** event and include a **Play Sound** action, with **Sound** set to `snd_explosion_large` and **Loop** set to **false**.

4. Add an **Other, Animation End** event and include the **Restart Room** action.

Creating the small explosion object:

1. Create a sprite called `spr_explosion_small` using `Explosion_small.gif` and **Center** the **Origin**.

2. Create a sound called `snd_explosion_small` using the file `Explosion_small.wav`.

3. Create an object called `obj_explosion_small`. Give it the small explosion sprite and set **Depth** to `-10`. Add a **Create** event and include the **Play Sound** action, with **Sound** set to `snd_explosion_small` and **Loop** set to **false**.

4. Add the **Other, Animation End** event and include the **Destroy Instance** action.

Explosions in hand, we're now ready to create the damage mechanism. The parent tank object will be responsible for initializing the `damage` variable, checking the damage, and drawing the tank's health bar on the screen. It will also be responsible for blowing up the tank when its damage reaches 100, which is why we needed the explosion objects first.

This is all pretty straightforward, and putting this code in the parent tank object will save us some time. However, when the tank blows up we also need to increase the correct player's score—so how do we know which player's tank has died if we are working with the parent object? Fortunately, every instance has a variable called `object_index` that records a number corresponding to the type of object it is. Every object has its own unique number, which can be accessed by using the object name as if it was a variable (in this case `obj_tank1` and `obj_tank2`). So by comparing `object_index` and `obj_tank1` we can tell if the instance is an instance of player one's tank or an instance of player two's.

We'll check the tank's damage in the **Step** event of the parent tank object and increase the appropriate score if it is larger than 100. Then we'll create a large explosion and destroy the tank. The large explosion object will automatically restart the room once the animation is finished.

Adding a damage mechanism to the parent tank object:

1. Reopen `obj_tank_parent` and select the **Create** event. Include a **Set Variable** action with **Variable** set to `damage` and **Value** set to `0`.

2. Add a **Step, Step** event and include a **Test Variable** action. Set **Variable** to `damage`, **Value** to `100`, and **Operation** to **smaller than**. Include an **Exit Event** action so that no further actions are executed if the damage is smaller than 100.

3. Now we need to find out what type of tank we are dealing with. Include a **Test Variable** action with **Variable** set to `object_index`, **Value** set to `obj_tank1`, and **Operation** set to **equal to**. Include a **Set Variable** action with **Variable** set to `global.score2`, **Value** set to `1`, and the **Relative** option enabled. This will then increase player two's score if this instance is player one's tank.

4. Include an **Else** action followed by a **Set Variable** action. Set **Variable** to global.score1 and **Value** to 1, and enable the **Relative** option. This will increase player one's score if this instance is player two's tank.

5. Include a **Create Instance** action with **Object** set to obj_explosion_large and the **Relative** option enabled.

6. Finally, include a **Destroy Instance** action.

Obviously, we need to draw some kind of health bar so that the players can see how well they are doing. It would be easiest to use the **Draw** event of the parent tank object to do this, but there is a problem. The two tank objects already have their own **Draw** events so they won't normally execute the **Draw** event of the parent object because their own takes priority. Fortunately, we can use the **Call Parent Event** action in the two tanks' own **Draw** events to make sure that the parent's **Draw** event is called as well.

Adding a draw event to the parent tank object to draw the health bars:

1. Add a **Draw** event for the parent tank object.

2. Include a **Set Health** action (**score** tab) and set **Value** to 100-damage. Damage is the opposite concept to health, so subtracting it from 100 makes this conversion (e.g., 80 percent damage converts to 100 – 80 = 20 percent health).

3. Add a **Draw Health** action. Set **X1** to -20, **Y1** to -35, **X2** to 20, and **Y2** to -30. Enable the **Relative** option, but leave the other parameters as they are. This will draw a small health bar above the tank. It may seem strange to be using the health functions here as they only work with one health value and we have two players. However, this technique works because we set the health in step 2 using the instance's own damage variable, just before we draw the health bar.

4. Reopen obj_tank1 and select the **Draw** event. Include the **Call Parent Event** action (**control** tab) at the end of the list of actions for this event. This will make sure that the **Draw** event of the parent tank object is also executed.

5. Reopen obj_tank2 and select the **Draw** event. Include the **Call Parent Event** action (**control** tab) at the end of the list of actions for this event.

With the damage and scoring mechanism in place, we can now create the tank shells. We only want the player's shells to damage their opponent's tank, so we will create a separate shell object for each tank and put common behavior in a shell parent object. We'll also use an alarm clock to give shells a limited life span (and therefore a limited range). Alarm clocks will also help us to temporarily demolish the second wall type when they are hit by shells. We'll move the walls outside the room and use an alarm event to bring them back to their original position after a period of time.

Creating the parent shell object:

1. Create a sprite called spr_shell using Shell.gif and **Center** the **Origin**. Note that like the tank sprite, this contains 60 images showing the shell pointing in different directions.

2. Create a new object called obj_shell_parent and leave it without a sprite (you can set it, but it isn't necessary for the parent as it never appears in the game).

3. Add a **Create** event and include the **Set Alarm** action. Set the **Number of Steps** to 30 and select **Alarm 0**.

4. Add an **Alarm, Alarm 0** event and include the **Destroy Instance** action.

5. Add a **Step, End Step** event and include the **Change Sprite** action. Set **Sprite** to spr_shell, **Subimage** to direction/6, and **Speed** to 0 (to stop it from animating).

6. Add a **Collision** event with obj_wall1 and include a **Create Instance** action. Set **Object** to obj_explosion_small and enable the **Relative** option. Also include a **Destroy Instance** action to destroy the shell.

7. Add a **Collision** event with obj_wall2. This object must be temporarily removed. Include a **Create Instance** action with **Object** set to obj_explosion_small and the **Relative** option enabled. Include a **Jump to Position** action with **X** and **Y** set to 100000. Also select the **Other** object for **Applies to** so that the wall is moved rather than the shell.

8. Include a **Set Alarm** action and select the **Other** object for **Applies to** so that it sets an alarm for the wall. Select **Alarm 0** and set **Number of Steps** to 300. Finally, include a **Destroy Instance** action to destroy the shell.

9. Add a **Collision** event with obj_shell_parent and include a **Create Instance** action. Set **Object** to obj_explosion_small and enable the **Relative** option. Also include a **Destroy Instance** action to destroy the shell.

We now need to make sure that any removed obj_wall2 instances are returned to their original position when the alarm clock runs out. We will also need to check that the original position is empty first, as we did for the locks in Koalabr8.

Editing the destructible wall object to make it reappear:

1. Reopen the obj_wall2 object and add an **Alarm, Alarm 0** event. Include a **Check Empty** action with **X** set to xstart, **Y** set to ystart, and **Objects** set to **All**. Include a **Jump to Start** action.

2. Next include an **Else** action followed by a **Set Alarm** action. Select **Alarm 0** and set **Number of Steps** to 5. That way, when the position is not empty it will wait five more steps and then try again.

We can now create the actual shell objects.

Creating the players' shell objects:

1. Create a new object called `obj_shell1`. Give it the shell sprite and set its **Parent** to `obj_shell_parent`.

2. Add a **Collision** event with `obj_tank2` and include a **Set Variable** action. Set **Variable** to `damage` and **Value** to 10, and enable the **Relative** option. Also select the **Other** object for **Applies to** so that the tank's `damage` variable is changed.

3. Include a **Create Instance** action with **Object** set to `obj_explosion_small` and enable the **Relative** option. Also include a **Destroy Instance** action to destroy the shell.

4. Repeat steps 1–3 to create `obj_shell2` using a **Collision** event with `obj_tank1` rather than `obj_tank2`.

Finally, we'll add the actions to make the tanks fire shells. Player one's tanks will shoot shells of type `obj_shell1` when the spacebar is pressed, and player two's tank will shoot shells of type `obj_shell2` when the Enter key is pressed. As in the Wingman Sam game, we'll limit the speed with which the player can fire shells using a `can_shoot` variable. To create bullets that face in the same direction as the tank, we will use the **Create Moving** action and pass in the tank's own `direction` variable.

Adding events to make the tank objects fire shells:

1. Reopen the parent tank object and select the **Create** event. Include a **Set Variable** action with **Variable** set to `can_shoot` and **Value** set to 0.

2. Select the **Step** event and include a **Set Variable** action at the beginning of the list of actions. Set **Variable** to `can_shoot` and **Value** to 1, and enable the **Relative** option.

3. Reopen `obj_tank1` and add a **Key Press, <Space>** event. Include the **Test Variable** action, with **Variable** set to `can_shoot`, **Value** set to 0, and **Operation** set to **smaller than**. Next include the **Exit Event** action so that the remaining actions are only executed when `can_shoot` is larger or equal to 0.

4. Include a **Create Moving** action. Set **Object** to `obj_shell1`, **Speed** to 16, and **Direction** to `direction`, and enable the **Relative** option. Also include a **Set Variable** action with **Variable** set to `can_shoot` and **Value** set to -10.

5. Repeat steps 3–4 for the `obj_tank2`, this time using a **Key Press, <Enter>** event for the key and `obj_shell2` for the **Create Moving** action.

That completes the shells. Test the game carefully and check yours against the one in the file `Games/Chapter10/tank2.gm6` on the CD if you have any problems.

Secondary Weapons

We're going to include secondary weapons and pickups to increase the appeal of the game. Pickups will appear randomly in the battle arena and can be collected by driving into them. Each tank can only have one secondary weapon active at once, so picking up a new weapon will remove the current one. Toolboxes can also be collected to repair some of the tank's damage, but these will remove any secondary weapons too. All the secondary weapons will have limited ammunition, so the players must take care to make the most of them.

We'll use just one object for all these different kinds of pickups and change its appearance depending on the type of pickup. We'll use a variable called kind to record what sort of pickup it is by setting its value to 0, 1, 2, or 3. The value 0 will stand for the homing rocket, 1 for the bouncing bomb, 2 for the shield, and 3 for the toolbox. We can then choose a pickup type at random by using the choose() function. To make things more interesting, the pickup will change its kind from time to time and jump to a new position. It will also jump to a new position when it is collected by a tank.

Creating the pickup object:

1. Create a sprite called spr_pickup using Pickup.gif. Note that it consists of four completely different subimages, representing each different kind of pickup.

2. Create a new object called obj_pickup and give it the pickup sprite.

 3. Add a **Create** event and include the **Set Variable** action. Set **Variable** to kind and **Value** to choose(0,1,2,3). This will choose randomly between the numbers in brackets that are separated by commas.

 4. Include the **Set Alarm** action for **Alarm 0** and set **Number of Steps** to 100+random(500). This will give a random time between 100 and 600 steps or about 3 and 20 seconds. Finally, include a **Jump to Random** action with the default parameters. This will move the instance to a random empty position.

 5. Add an **Alarm, Alarm 0** event and include the **Set Variable** action. Set **Variable** to kind and **Value** to choose(0,1,2,3).

 6. Include the **Set Alarm** action for **Alarm 0** with **Number of Steps** set to 100+random(500). Finally, include a **Jump to Random** action.

 7. Add a **Collision** event with obj_tank_parent and include a **Jump to Random** action.

 8. Add a **Draw** event and include the **Draw Sprite** action. Set **Sprite** to spr_pickup, **Subimage** to kind and enable the **Relative** option.

Now reopen the room and add a few instances of the pickup object to it. Test the game to make sure that the pickups have different images and that they change their type and position from time to time. Also check out what happens when you drive over one with your tank.

We'll also need to record the kind of pickup that has been collected by the tank so that it can change its secondary weapon. We'll use the variable weapon for this, where a value of -1 corresponds to no weapon. The variable ammunition will indicate how many shots the tank has left of this weapon type. Once ammunition reaches 0, weapon will be set to -1 to disable the secondary weapon from then on. We'll check the value of the pickup object's kind variable in the collision event, and use it to set the tank's weapon accordingly.

Editing the parent tank object to record pickups:

1. Reopen obj_tank_parent and select the **Create** event.

2. Include a **Set Variable** action with **Variable** set to weapon and **Value** set to -1. Include a second **Set Variable** action with **Variable** set to ammunition and **Value** set to 0.

3. Add a **Collision** event with obj_pickup and include a **Test Variable** action. Set **Variable** to other.kind, **Value** to 3, and **Operation** to **equal to**. A value of 3 corresponds to the toolbox. This needs to repair the tank's damage, so include a **Start Block** action to begin the block of actions that do this.

4. Include a **Set Variable** action with **Variable** set to weapon and **Value** set to -1. Include a second **Set Variable** action with **Variable** set to damage and **Value** set to max(0,damage-50). The function max decides which is the largest of the two values you give it (more about functions in Chapter 12). Therefore, this sets the new damage to the largest out of damage-50 and 0. In effect, this subtracts 50 from damage but makes sure it does not become smaller than 0. Include an **End Block** action.

5. Include an **Else** action, followed by a **Start Block** action to group the actions that are used if this is not a toolbox pickup.

6. Include a **Set Variable** action with **Variable** set to weapon and **Value** set to other.kind. Include another **Set Variable** action with **Variable** set to ammunition and **Value** set to 10.

7. Finally, include an **End Block** action.

Obviously, it will help players to be able to see the type of secondary weapon they've collected and the ammunition they have remaining for it. We'll display this below each tank using a small image of the pickup. These images have been combined into one sprite again, so we'll need to test the value of weapon and draw the corresponding subimage if it is equal to 0, 1, or 2. We can then also draw the value of the variable ammunition next to it.

Displaying the secondary weapon in the parent tank object:

1. Create a new sprite called spr_weapon using Weapon.gif. Note that it consists of three subimages (no image is required for the toolbox).

2. Create a font called fnt_ammunition and keep the default settings for it.

3. Select the **Draw** event in obj_tank_parent and include a **Test Variable** action. Set **Variable** to weapon, **Value** to -1, and **Operation** to **larger than**. This will ensure that we only draw something when there is a secondary weapon. Include a **Start Block** action to group the drawing actions.

4. Include the **Draw Sprite** action and select spr_weapon. Set **X** to -20, **Y** to 25, and **Subimage** to weapon. Also enable the **Relative** option.

5. Include a **Set Color** action and choose black. Then include a **Set Font** action, selecting fnt_ammunition and setting **Align** to **left**.

6. Next include a **Draw Variable** action with **Variable** set to ammunition, **X** set to 0, **Y** set to 24, and the **Relative** option enabled.

 7. Finally, include an **End Block** action to conclude the actions that draw the weapon information.

Test the game to check that the weapon icons are displayed correctly when you collect the different weapon pickups. However, so far only the repair kit actually does anything for the player, so let's start by sorting out the rocket. It will behave in much the same way as the shell but automatically starts moving in the direction of the enemy tank. We'll use the same structure of objects as we did for the shell, with common behavior contained in a parent rocket object (obj_rocket_parent) and separate rocket objects that home in on the different tanks (obj_rocket1 and obj_rocket2). We'll also make obj_shell_parent the parent of obj_rocket_parent so that it inherits obj_shell_parent's **Collision** and **Alarm** events. However, we don't want obj_rocket_parent to have the same **Create** and **End Step** events as obj_shell_parent so we'll give it new versions of these events that give the rocket a longer lifetime and draw the correct sprite.

Creating the parent rocket object:

1. Create a sprite called spr_rocket using Rocket.gif and **Center** the **Origin**.

2. Create a new object called obj_rocket_parent and set **Parent** to obj_shell_parent.

 3. Add a **Create** event and include the **Set Alarm** action. Set **Number of Steps** to 60 and select **Alarm 0**.

 4. Add a **Step, End Step** event and include a **Change Sprite** action. Select the rocket sprite, then set **Subimage** to direction/6 and **Speed** to 0.

Next we create the two actual rocket objects.

Creating the actual rocket objects:

1. Create a new object called it obj_rocket1 and give it the rocket sprite. Set **Parent** to obj_rocket_parent.

 2. Add a **Create** event and include the **Move Towards** action. Set **X** to obj_tank2.x, **Y** to obj_tank2.y, and **Speed** to 8.

 3. Add a **Collision** event with obj_tank2 and include a **Set Variable** action. Select **Other** from **Applies to** (the tank), set **Variable** to damage and **Value** to 10, and enable the **Relative** option.

 4. Include a **Create Instance** action, selecting obj_explosion_small and enabling the **Relative** option. Also include a **Destroy Instance** action.

5. Create obj_rocket2 in the same way, but move toward obj_tank1 in the **Create** event, and add a **Collision** event with obj_tank1 for the actions in steps 3 and 4.

Finally, we need to make it possible for the tanks to fire rockets. We'll check whether they have the weapon and ammo in the **Key Press** event of the sceondary fire key. If they do, then we'll create the rocket and decrease the ammunition. When it reaches 0, we'll set weapon to –1 to disable it.

Adding events to shoot rockets for the tank object:

1. Reopen the first tank object and add a **Key Press, <Ctrl>** event. Include a **Test Variable** action, with **Variable** set to can_shoot, **Value** set to 0, and **Operation** set to **smaller than**. Next include the **Exit Event** action so that the remaining actions are only executed when can_shoot is larger than or equal to 0.

2. Include the **Test Variable** action, with **Variable** set to weapon, **Value** set to 0, and **Operation** set to **equal to**. Next include a **Test Instance Count** action with **Object** set to obj_tank2, **Number** set to 0 and **Operation** set to **larger than**. Follow this with a **Create Instance** action for obj_rocket1, and enable the **Relative** option. This creates a rocket only when it is the current secondary weapon and the other tank exists (this avoids a rare error when the other tank has just been destroyed).

3. Next we need to decrease the ammunition. Include a **Set Variable** action with **Variable** set to ammunition, **Value** set to –1, and the **Relative** option enabled. Include a **Test Variable** action with **Variable** set to ammunition, **Value** set to 1, and **Operation** set to **smaller than**. Follow this with a **Set Variable** action with **Variable** set to weapon and **Value** set to -1.

4. Finally, include a **Set Variable** action with **Variable** set to can_shoot and **Value** set to -10.

5. Repeat steps 1–4 for obj_tank2, using a **Key Press, Others, <Delete>** event and creating obj_rocket2.

Now we'll create the bouncing bomb secondary weapon in a similar fashion. It behaves in the same way as the shell except that it bounces against walls.

Creating the bouncing bomb objects:

1. Create a sprite called spr_bouncing using Bouncing.gif and **Center** the **Origin**.

2. Create a new object called obj_bouncing_parent and set its **Parent** to obj_shell_parent.

3. Add a **Collision** event with obj_wall1 and include the **Bounce** action. Select **precisely** and set **Against** to **solid objects**.

4. Add a similar **Collision** event with obj_wall2.

5. Add a **Step, End Step** event and include a **Change Sprite** action. Select spr_bouncing, set **Subimage** to direction/6, and set **Speed** to 0.

6. Create a new object called obj_bouncing1 and give it the bouncing bomb sprite. Set its **Parent** to obj_bouncing_parent.

7. Add a **Collision** event with obj_tank2 and include a **Set Variable** action. Select **Other** from **Applies to**, set **Variable** to damage, set **Value** to 10, and enable the **Relative** option. Include a **Create Instance** action for obj_explosion_small and enable the **Relative** option.

8. Include a **Destroy Instance** action.

9. Repeat steps 6 and 7 to create obj_bouncing2 using a **Collision** event with obj_tank1.

Before we add actions to make the tank objects shoot bouncing bombs, we'll create the final special weapon: the shield. This is a bit more complicated as it allows the player to temporarily make their tank invincible. Activating the shield will set a new variable called shield to 40, and display a shield sprite. The value of shield will be reduced by 1 in each step until it falls below 0 and the shield is disabled again. We'll check the value of shield each time the tank is hit and only increase its damage when shield is less than 0.

Editing the parent tank object to support shields:

1. Create sprites called spr_shield1 and spr_shield2 using Shield1.gif and Shield2.gif and **Center** their **Origins**.

2. Reopen the parent tank object and select the **Create** event. Include a **Set Variable** action with **Variable** set to shield and **Value** set to 0.

3. Select the **Step** event and include a **Set Variable** action at the start of the list. Set **Variable** to shield, set **Value** to -1, and enable the **Relative** option.

4. Reopen obj_shell1 and select the **Collision** event with obj_tank2. Include a **Test Variable** action directly above the **Set Variable** that increases the damage. Select **Other** from **Applies to**, then set **Variable** to shield, **Value** to 0, and **Operation** to **smaller than**. Now the damage will only be increased when the tank has no shield.

5. Repeat step 4 for objects obj_shell2, obj_rocket1, obj_rocket2, obj_bouncing1, and obj_bounding2.

6. Reopen obj_tank1 and select the **Draw** event. Include a **Test Variable** action at the start of the action list. Set **Variable** to shield, **Value** to 0, and **Operation** to **larger than**. Follow this with a **Draw Sprite** action for spr_shield1 with the **Relative** option enabled.

7. Repeat step 6 for obj_tank2, this time drawing spr_shield2.

Now all that remains is to adapt the tanks so that both the bouncing bombs and the shields can be used.

Editing tank objects to shoot bombs and use shields:

1. Reopen obj_tank1 and select the **Key Press, <Ctrl>** event.

2. Include a **Test Variable** action below the **Create Instance** action that creates obj_rocket1. Set **Variable** to weapon, **Value** to 1, and **Operation** to **equal to**. Follow this with a **Create Moving** action for obj_bouncing1, setting **Speed** to 16 and **Direction** to direction, and enabling the **Relative** option.

3. Include another **Test Variable** action below this, with **Variable** set to weapon, **Value** set to 2, and **Operation** set to **equal to**. Follow this with by a **Set Variable** action with **Variable** set to shield and **Value** set to 40.

4. Repeat steps 1–3 for obj_tank2, adapting the **Key Press, <Delete>** event and creating obj_bouncing2.

This completes all the secondary weapons and the game should now be fully playable. We encourage you to play it a lot with your friends, to make sure everything is working as it should. You'll find the current version on the CD in the file Games/Chapter10/tank3.gm6.

Views

Currently, our playing area is quite small and both players can see all of it at once. However, we can create more interesting gameplay by giving each player a limited "window" into a much larger playing area. This can easily be achieved in Game Maker using *views*. We'll use two views to create a split screen, in which the left half of the screen shows the area around the first tank and the right half shows the area around the second tank. Later we use a third view to display a little mini-map as well.

To understand the concept of views, you need to appreciate that there is a distinction between a room and the window that provides a view of that room on the screen. Up to now, rooms have always been the same size as the window and the window has always showed the entire contents of the room. However, rooms can be any size you like, and views can be used to indicate the specific area of the room that should appear in the window. We're going to create a room that's twice the width of a normal room with an equal height (see Figure 10-2). The green rectangle shows the size of a normal room, and the red and blue squares show the size of the views we will give to each player in the room. To create these views, we will need to specify the following information on the **views** tab in the room properties:

- **View in room**: This is an area of the room that needs to be displayed in the view. The **X** and **Y** positions define the top-left corner of this area and **W** and **H** specify the width and height of it.

- **Port on screen**: This is the position on the window where the view should be shown. The **X** and **Y** positions define the top-left corner of this area and **W** and **H** specify the width and height of it. If the width and height are different from the size of the view area, then the view will be automatically scaled to fit. Game Maker will also automatically adapt the size of the window so that all ports fit into it.

- **Object following**: Specifying an object here will make the view track that object as it moves around the room. **Hbor** and **Vbor** specify the size of the horizontal and vertical borders that you want to keep around the object. The view will not move until the edge of the screen is closer than this distance from the object. Setting **Hbor** to half the width of the view and **Vbor** to half the height of the view will therefore maintain the object in the center. Finally, **Hsp** and **Vsp** allow you to limit the speed with which the view moves (–1 means no limit).

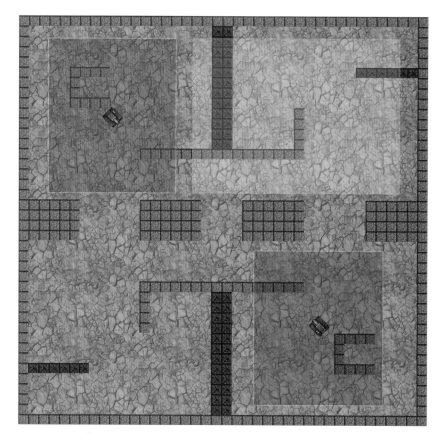

Figure 10-2. *We'll create a large room, much bigger than a normal window (green rectangle), and provide views into it for each of the tanks (red and blue squares).*

You can specify up to eight different views, but you'll probably only need one or two. Let's adapt our game's room to use two views.

Editing the room resource to provide two views:

1. Reopen the main room and switch to the **settings** tab.

2. Set both the **Width** and **Height** of the room to 1280, to create a much larger room.

3. Switch to the **objects** tab and add wall instances to incorporate the extra playing area. Start the tanks close to two opposite corners and add six pickup instances. Also don't forget that the room needs exactly one instance of the controller object.

4. Switch to the **views** tab and select the **Enable the use of Views** option. This activates the use of views in this room.

5. Make sure that **View 0** is selected in the list and enable the **Visible when room starts** option. We will use this view for player one.

6. Under **View in room** set **X** to 0, Y to 0, W to 400, and H to 480. The **X** and **Y** positions of the views don't really matter in this case as we will make them follow the tanks. Nonetheless, notice that lines appear in the room to indicate the size and position of the view.

7. Under **Port on screen** set **X** to 0, **Y** to 0, W to 400, and H to 480. This port will show player one's view on the left side of the screen.

8. Under **Object following** select obj_tank1, then set **Hbor** to 200 and **Vbor** to 240. The form should now look like Figure 10-3.

9. Now select **View 1** in the list and enable the **Visible when room starts** option. We will use this view for player two.

10. Under **View in room** set **X** to 0, **Y** to 0, W to 400, and H to 480.

11. Under **Port on screen** set **X** to 420, **Y** to 0, W to 400, and H to 480. This places the second view to the right of the first view with a little space between them.

12. Under **Object following** select obj_tank2, and set **Hbor** to 200 and **Vbor** to 240.

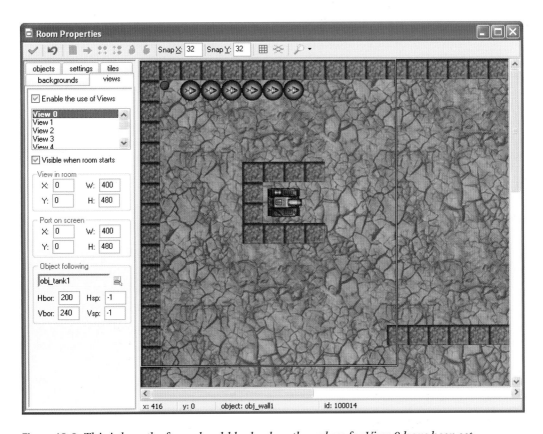

Figure 10-3. *This is how the form should look when the values for View 0 have been set.*

And that's it. Easy, wasn't it? Run the game and you should be able to play in the new split-screen mode.

Tip The empty region between the views defaults to the color black. You can change this in the **Global Game Settings** on the **graphics** tab under **Color outside the room region**.

Have you noticed something strange? The score is displayed at a fixed position in the room so you can only see it if you drive up to it! To fix this we need to draw it at a changing position relative to the player's views. The score for player one needs to appear in the top-right corner of View 0 and the score for player two needs to appear in the top-left corner of View 1. Game Maker provides variables that we can use to obtain the positions of views. `view_xview[0]` and `view_yview[0]` indicate the current x- and y-positions of View 0 while `view_xview[1]` and `view_yview[1]` indicate the x- and y-positions of View 1.

Unfortunately, this does not solve the problem completely. To explain why, you'll need to understand what Game Maker is doing when you use views. For each view, Game Maker draws the whole room, including all the backgrounds, objects, and **Draw** events; clips the visible area to the size of the view; and then copies it to the required position on the window. This means the **Draw** event of the controller object (that draws the score) is called twice, once for drawing each of the views. So, to display the score in the correct place we need to know which view is currently being drawn. Game Maker allows us to check this using the variable `view_current`, which will be 0 for View 0 and 1 for View 1. Therefore, we can test the value of this variable in the **Draw** event of the controller object and draw the score of the appropriate tank relative to the position of the current view.

Editing the controller object to draw the score relative to the view position:

1. Reopen the controller object and select the **Draw** event.

2. Include a **Test Variable** action before the **Draw Variable** action that draws the score for player one. Set **Variable** to `view_current`, **Value** to `0`, and **Operation** to **equal to**.

3. Edit the **Draw Variable** action that draws player one's score. Change **X** to `view_xview[0]+380` and **Y** to `view_yview[0]+10`.

4. Include a **Test Variable** action before the **Draw Variable** action that draws the score for player two. Set **Variable** to `view_current`, **Value** to `1`, and **Operation** to **equal to**.

5. Edit the **Draw Variable** action for player two. Change **X** to `view_xview[1]+20` and **Y** to `view_yview[1]+10`. The action list should now look like Figure 10-4.

Figure 10-4. *These actions draw the scores correctly for each view.*

Run the game to check that the score is displayed correctly.

We'll now add a little mini-map to help the player see where they are. This mini-map shows the entire room, so that both players can see the location of their opponents and the pickups in the room. Creating a mini-map is very simple using views, as we can create an additional view that includes the whole room but scales it down to a small port on the screen.

Adding a view to create a mini-map:

1. Reopen the main room and switch to the **views** tab.

2. Select **View 2** in the list and enable the **Visible when room starts** option.

3. Under **View in room** set **X** to 0, **Y** to 0, **W** to 1280, and **H** to 1280 (the entire room).

4. Under **Port on screen** set **X** to 350, **Y** to 355, **W** to 120, and **H** to 120. No object needs to be followed.

And that finishes the game for this chapter. Run it and check that it all works. There are a few final improvements you might want to make. You should add some **Game Information** and you might want to change some of the **Global Game Settings**. For example, you might not want to display the cursor but might want to start in full-screen mode or add a loading image of your own for the game.

■**Tip** To improve the mini-map and make it more "iconic," you could make the different objects draw something different when the variable `view_current` is equal to 2. For example, the pickup object could simply display a red disk and the walls could draw black squares.

Congratulations

That's another one complete! We hope you enjoyed making this game and playing it with your friends. The final version can be found on the CD in the file Games/Chapter10/tank4.gm6. You encountered some important new features of Game Maker in this chapter, including views, which can be used to create all sorts of different games.

There are many ways in which you could make Tank War more interesting. You could create different arenas for the players to compete in. Some could be wide and open while others could have close passageways. You could also add other types of walls, perhaps stopping shells but not the tanks, or even the other way around. You could create muddy areas that reduce your speed, or slippery areas that make it difficult to steer your tank. Of course, you can also add other types of secondary weapons, such as guns that fire sideways or in many different directions. You could even drop mines or create holes in the ground. You could also add a front-end to the game, displaying the title graphic that is supplied. You're the designer and it's up to you.

We'll be staying with our Tank War example in the next chapter as we explore the game design issues involved in creating multiplayer games. We've got some different versions of the game for you to play and you'll be balancing tanks, so you'd better go and find some king-sized scales!

■ ■ ■

Game Design: Balance in Multiplayer Games

Multiplayer games offer game designers many additional ways to create playing experiences that are fun. Even games that are not very enjoyable on your own can be very addictive when playing with or against other human players. Harnessing this power requires designing games that treat all players fairly but still allow them to make the kind of meaningful choices that make games interesting to play. In this chapter we'll discuss some of the strategies you can use to strike the right balance in your own multiplayer games.

Competition and Cooperation

Competition and cooperation form the basis of all multiplayer games. No matter how convincing a computer-controlled character is, it never produces the same thrill as another human being taking part in the game. In this section we'll discuss some approaches for creating multiplayer game modes and the pros and cons of each.

Independent Competition

The simplest way to create a competitive game mode is to make players take turns playing the single-player game and declare the player who does the best to be the winner. A long time ago, this was a common way of adding a multiplayer mode to a game, but these days players expect more. Another basic method is to split the screen so that both players play the single-player mode at the same time in different sections of the screen. Figure 11-1 shows how the Super Rainbow Reef game from Chapter 6 might look as a split-screen multiplayer game.

The important thing to note about both of these competitive modes is that neither creates interactions between the players—each player is expected to play independently, and their performance is compared at the end of the game. While such approaches offer an easy way to include a competitive mode, the results are generally not nearly as much fun as when there are interactions between the players.

Figure 11-1. *A split-screen multiplayer mode for Super Rainbow Reef might look something like this.*

Dependent Competition

Competitive games that create interactions *between* players provide each player with a game-play experience that is dependent on their opponent. Often this is achieved by setting the gameplay within a shared environment and providing competing goals (as in the Tank War game). However a shared environment is not always necessary: dependent competition could be added to the split-screen Super Rainbow Reef example by including power-up bricks that affect the opposing player's starfish or shell. This would also make each player's experience dependent on the other and add an extra competitive edge to the game.

Dependent competition may harness more of the competitive potential of multiplayer games, but it has its own drawbacks. Independent competition usually gives both players a decent chance to enjoy the game—even if one player is much less skilled than the other. Dependent competitions can often be over very quickly when players' skills aren't equally matched and soon stop being fun for both players. For this reason, many competitive games include features to rebalance the competition, such as handicap settings or weaker characters for more skillful players to use. Many even include hidden catch-up mechanisms, whereby the losing player is given better power-ups to try to even out the competition.

It's also worth remembering that competition is not everyone's idea of fun, and its appeal depends a lot on individual personality. For every player who craves the adrenaline rush of a head-to-head competition, there's another who hates the confrontation that this kind of gameplay creates. Fortunately, multiplayer games don't have to be competitive at all, and many players can get just as much enjoyment from cooperative game modes.

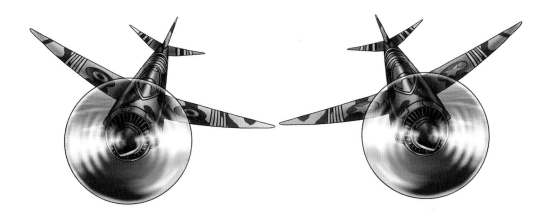

Independent Cooperation

The game *Wingman Sam* provides a multiplayer mode with mostly independent cooperation. It allows players to work toward the same goal, but they are not necessarily required to work together or interact with each other to achieve it. This is usually the most practical way of including a cooperative game mode as it means that each of the players can survive on their own if one player dies. This is fairly essential for coin-operated arcade games, as players would feel cheated if their game ended just because their partner had run out of money! Fortunately, home computer games are free to encourage more collaborative forms of play that require players to interact with each other in order to survive.

Dependent Cooperation

Dependent cooperation encourages players to interact or collaborate in order to achieve the game's goals rather than just both being on the same side. One way of achieving this is to give your players different roles or skills within the game. For example, in Wingman Sam we could make one player control a slow bomber with lots of forward firepower, while the other player has a smaller fighter plane with excellent maneuverability. This then forces players to find collaborative strategies that utilize their own strengths and weaknesses to complete the game's goals.

While multiplayer games that encourage collaboration are often more interesting than those requiring simple cooperation, you can't assume that players will naturally know how to collaborate effectively in your game. Modes in which collaboration is essential may be a culture shock for some players, and may require their own kind of training levels. In general, a game design that rewards players for collaborating rather then punishing them for not collaborating should have a broader appeal.

Mix and Match

In practice, multiplayer games rarely fall neatly into one category. Cooperative games often turn competitive for a while when a health pickup appears on the screen, and competitive games often involve a whole set of unwritten rules that players cooperate to enforce. Even our Wingman Sam example encourages collaboration when one player is about to die, as this ends the game for both players. Multiplayer games rely on human beings interacting with one another, so they are rarely simple or predictable! Nonetheless, they do provide a powerful way to motivate players, allowing designers to create some of the most enjoyable playing experiences around.

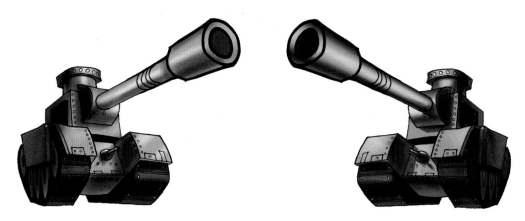

Balanced Beginnings

Although not everyone plays multiplayer games just to win, nobody plays them to lose unfairly. Players need to feel that multiplayer games give them as much chance of winning as other players. Creating different sides with balanced abilities is not an easy task, and is a bit like trying to work out how many apples equal so many pears. In this section, we'll take you through a practical technique for ensuring that your characters are balanced using the Tank War example from the previous chapter.

Equivalent Characters

Providing all players with directly equivalent features is a sure way to guarantee that no player has an unfair advantage. This kind of equivalence is obvious in Tank War, where, aside from their color, the red and blue tanks are identical. Nonetheless, games may often provide a number of characters to choose from that look completely different but play identically in the game. Equivalent characters can be a good option to include for die-hard gamers who want to prove that they're better than their opponents in a straight fight. However, carefully balanced differences between characters can often make a more interesting multiplayer game and increase the longevity of the gameplay.

Balancing Differences

Including gameplay differences between characters provides players with meaningful choices right from the start of the game. However, having such choices soon becomes meaningless if players discover that one character always has an advantage over the others. From this point on, the game degenerates into a competition (or fight) to choose that character first as it usually determines the outcome of the game! The players might as well toss a coin to decide the winner. Making sure that this doesn't happen requires careful planning and thorough play testing. We're going to create heavy and light tanks as balanced alternatives to the basic tank in Tank War. We'll start by making a list of tank characteristics that could be varied to make the game more interesting, as follows:

- Rate of fire—How fast the vehicle can shoot its main weapon

- Shot damage—The amount of damage caused by each shot of its main weapon

- Shot speed—The speed at which shells fly through the air

- Vehicle armor—The proportion of damage that is absorbed by the vehicle's armor

- Vehicle speed—The speed at which the vehicle moves forward

- Rate of turn—The speed at which a vehicle can turn on the spot

- Vehicle size—The size of the vehicle (the larger the size of the target, the easier it is to hit)

We probably won't want to change the vehicle size, but it's worth noting so that we don't accidentally change the gameplay later by making the light tank smaller than the heavy one. Next, let's create a table for each vehicle type and list the strengths and weaknesses we want them to have for each characteristic (see Table 11-1). The idea is to produce a different profile for each vehicle that balances out their abilities. There's not much point in trying to assign relative values to each strength or weakness at this stage. It's not really possible to say, for example, how slow one vehicle's speed should be to compensate for its high shot damage (it's like comparing apples and pears). It may seem safe to assume relationships between some characteristics; if you half the shot speed but double the damage, then it should have the same overall firepower. However, in practice they actually produce two very different weapons that favor different situations and strategies (as should become apparent).

Table 11-1. *Tank Characteristics*

Characteristic	Heavy Tank	Basic Tank	Light Tank
Rate of fire	Weakness	--	Strength
Shot damage	Strength	--	Weakness
Shot speed	Strength	--	Weakness
Vehicle armor	Strength	--	Weakness
Max speed	Weakness	--	Strength
Rate of turn	Weakness	--	Strength

Now we need to create a test bed that allows you to alter all these characteristics for each vehicle while you are playing the game. A test bed is not something that the player gets to use, so it doesn't need to look very pretty or have a fantastic interface, as long as it is practical and doesn't crash. We've already created one for you in Games/Chapter11/new_tank1.gm6 on the CD. This time you'll need to copy it into a directory on your computer along with the file tankdata.txt—that's so the game can read and write to the data file. Now load it up and run the game. Clicking on either tank will cycle between the three different tank types available: light, basic, and heavy. Pressing the Shift key will toggle a test panel at the bottom of the screen, allowing you to tweak the characteristics for each tank (see Figure 11-2). Left-clicking on a value will increase it, and right-clicking will decrease it. The settings are automatically saved and loaded to the data file so that they're not lost next time you play the game. You can look at the contents of this file by double-clicking on it in Windows, and if you're very careful, then you can edit it this way too.

At the moment, the settings for each tank are exactly the same as the original. Your first job is to change them so that they have the strengths and weaknesses given in Table 11-1. It's difficult to know where to start, but just try adding or removing values and seeing what difference they make to the way the tank handles. Changes should take effect immediately, but you may need to close the debug panel for the game to run at full speed again (just press Shift again). Begin by driving and firing each tank on your own until you're fairly happy with the changes that you've made.

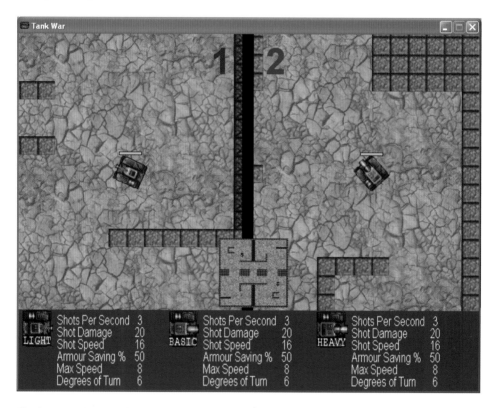

Figure 11-2. *The new version of Tank War features different types of tanks and a panel for changing their characteristics.*

Next, find yourself an opponent (preferably someone who is about the same standard as you) and start playing the game. Systematically play every combination of tanks (see Table 11-2) and battle it out in order to establish whether any of the tanks has an unfair advantage over the others. When you find that one does, make some tweaks to balance things out and try again. Make sure you stick broadly to the original strengths and weaknesses in the table, though—it's no use slowly changing all their settings to be equivalent again! You may have to go through the table several times in order to make sure that your changes haven't unbalanced tanks that you tested earlier. Nonetheless, if you (and your opponent) are prepared to put the effort in, then you should eventually reach a stage where all the tanks are fairly equally matched without being the same.

Table 11-2. *All the Combinations of Tanks*

Your Tank	Your Opponent's Tank
Light	Light
Light	Basic
Light	Heavy
Basic	Light
Basic	Basic
Basic	Heavy
Heavy	Light
Heavy	Basic
Heavy	Heavy

Well done—you will have probably learned more about game balance from this exercise than we could ever teach you from just reading about it, but here are a few things that you may have thought about during this process:

- Which characteristics are the most/least important?

- How does this depend on the player's individual abilities and strategies? (Try always driving backwards, if you haven't done so already).

- How much do the characteristics required for balanced tanks change as players get better at the game? (Try watching some beginners play the game now that it's "balanced.")

- Do you still have a preference for one type of tank? Does this matter?

- Would these same settings be useful for creating progression in a single-player mode against the computer?

- Are your settings realistic, and does it matter if they're not?

Give yourself a pat on the back if you already found yourself asking some of these questions when you were playing the game. Asking yourself questions like this is an important part of expanding your own understanding of game design. Unfortunately, there are often no right answers to questions like these—in fact, there are few answers in game design that apply to every situation you'll come across. Becoming an expert at game design (or anything really) is not about learning a set of "answers" from a book, but using your knowledge and experience to ask the right questions in a given situation. Does it matter if the tank settings are realistic?

Well, it depends on who your target audience is. It probably doesn't for the kind of game we're creating here, but if we were making a combat simulation, then realism might be more important to the player than balance.

Okay, so this is one type of balance—where the characteristics of each player are balanced to provide an equal chance of winning from the start of the game. However, there are other ways to achieve balance in games that involve balancing the range of choices that the players get to make throughout the game.

Balanced Choice

Just because players start off on an equal footing doesn't necessarily mean that the game will remain balanced. In some ways, this is expected—after all, one player has to win the game at some point by gaining an advantage. Nonetheless, it is still important to offer players a fair and balanced opportunity to make choices within the game. In this section, we'll discuss some simple and more advanced techniques for doing this.

Weighting Choices

Imagine Tank War as a strategy game, where—rather than driving a single tank—players have to train squads of tanks and send them off to fight battles and conquer territory. As time progresses, each player accumulates resources that they can spend on creating light, basic, or heavy tanks. However, if all the tanks are equally balanced in combat, then deciding which ones to create is not a very meaningful choice. In this situation, it would be better to have a hierarchy of tanks going from light to heavy and weight the choices accordingly. So a heavy tank may be as good as three basic tanks, but it takes three times as long to accumulate the resources needed to build it. Alternatively, we might make it only take twice as long to build but require the player to invest resources building a heavy armor factory first. In this way, we encourage the players to choose between making an early investment for a delayed reward or making an early decisive strike on the enemy.

Weighting choices in this way helps to make the options that players have in the game both interesting and fair. However, once one player has built an army larger than their opponent, then the outcome of the game becomes fairly predictable. Once a player knows they can easily win outright with their superior might, the remainder of the game becomes less interesting for both players. Including cyclic relationships between the tank types can remove this predictability and ensure that even one-sided battles have to be fought with strategies in order to come out on top.

Cyclic Relationships

If you've ever played rock, paper, scissors, then you've experienced a cyclic relationship (and if you haven't, then you must be from another planet). This ancient game has a balance and simplicity to it that can be applied to more complicated games as well. So far we have discussed a linear hierarchy of tanks where heavy tanks are better than basic tanks, and basic tanks are better than light tanks. This is like rock beating scissors and scissors beating paper. However, paper also beats rock, ensuring that rock doesn't become the dominant choice for players to make. Admittedly, players might get a bit annoyed if their hard-earned heavy tanks could be beaten outright by light tanks, but that doesn't mean that they couldn't be more vulnerable to light tanks than they might otherwise be. After all, heavy tanks are slow and clumsy compared to light tanks that can hit and run more easily. So we could deliberately build in cyclic vulnerabilities into the relationship so that light tanks punch beyond their weight (in many ways) against heavy tanks, heavy tanks do the same to basic tanks, and basic tanks do the same to light tanks (see Figure 11-3).

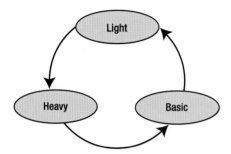

Figure 11-3. *This diagram shows the cyclic relationship in tank types.*

Adding this kind of relationship forces a player to fight more tactically, bringing in different tanks to support each other depending on the type of enemy they are facing. This creates a more interesting game, and one in which a clever tactician can turn the tables on his opponent even when fighting against superior numbers.

This same principle can be even applied to our original single combat version of Tank War. Copy the file Games/Chapter11/new_tank2.gm6 from the CD to the same directory as before. You'll need to make a backup copy of tankdata.txt if you want to keep your old characteristics settings, as this program will write over your old file. If you run the game, you'll see that we've changed things a bit; both tanks now start the game as weaponless tank bodies. The weapons now appear as pickups on the map that give you all the characteristics of the appropriate tank until you collect a different one. This means that you can roam around the map switching tank types more or less as you please. While this is already an interesting variation on the original game, you can improve on it by creating a cyclic relationship between the tanks. Try playing the game with a friend and tweaking the characteristics again until the basic tank has an advantage over the light tank, the heavy tank over the basic tank, and the light tank over the heavy tank. One way to achieve this is to make the light tank so nimble that the heavy tank can't catch it, while making its bullets slow enough that they linger around the map after the light tank has moved on. Combined with moving backward and firing, this makes the light tank a nifty opponent—although you'll need to make sure that the medium tank can beat it!

You'll know when you have the right balance; you should notice it turning into a game of cat and mouse, where the cat and mouse keep switching as players try to gain an advantage. When player one picks up the heavy gun, player two goes for the light gun, then player one goes for the basic gun, and so on. This style of play is a lot of fun and illustrates well how cyclic relationships can improve the playability of your multiplayer games.

Balanced Computer Opponents

Many multiplayer games include the option for computer-controlled opponents to make up the numbers in games. Unsurprisingly, players expect the same level of fairness against computer opponents as human ones. In Chapter 14 you'll make a game with some very simple artificial intelligence (AI), but in this section we'll briefly discuss some of the broader implications of AI for game balance.

Artificial Stupidity

For computer games, the term *artificial intelligence* is deceptive as it suggests that computer opponents should behave as intelligently as possible. In practice, a balanced computer opponent is one that behaves as humanly as possible, which is as much about human failings as human intelligence. A computer-controlled player without any failings is even more frustrating to play against than a human player with an unfair advantage. To a computer, making the perfect shot is child's play—you're in its world and playing by its rules. It has instant access to everything there is to know about the playing world and can process it a million times faster than you can!

Ideally then, computer opponents in multiplayer games should play by the same rules as you. They should refrain from using their god-like knowledge of the world to see past your diversionary attack, they should go to pieces under pressure, and they should occasionally just screw up because they got distracted! However, while these are good aims for a professional AI programmer, there is nothing wrong with using the computer's natural advantages to help you take your first steps in AI. Make use of every advantage the computer has, but remember to add a few random commands to make it look less than perfect. A player only needs to *feel* that the computer doesn't have an unfair advantage, and what they don't know can't hurt them! Given half a chance, players will naturally project human characteristics onto the behavior of computer opponents. An enemy that occasionally doesn't shoot when there's a clear shot can look like they haven't spotted the player. An opponent who randomly spins out on the corner of a racetrack can be seen as caving under pressure. A liberal use of the random command can hide a multitude of programming sins and give your artificial intelligence the apparent human fallibility that it needs.

Summary

In this chapter we've looked at different kinds of balance in multiplayer games, but many of the same principles apply to balancing computer opponents in single-player games as well. Balance is ultimately about ensuring that players have a fair chance of winning the game, and that's what players want in single-player games too. Here's a summary of the main points discussed in this chapter to help you with designing your own multiplayer games:

- Make multiplayer games more fun to play by

    - Including competition and cooperation.

    - Making players' interactions with the game dependent on each other.

    - Balancing the game for players.

- Multiplayer games can be balanced by

    - Providing equivalent characters (less desirable).

    - Providing balanced characters with different strengths and weaknesses.

    - Weighing choices to provide interesting trade-offs.

    - Including cyclic relationships to provide richer gameplay.

- Characteristics can be balanced by

    - Creating a test bed that allows characteristics to be tweaked in real time.

    - Play testing.

    - Play testing.

    - More play testing.

Well, that's it for another part of the book. This is the last chapter on game design, but there's still plenty more to learn about game programming. Prepare yourself for a few frights as you go exploring for ancient treasure in haunted Egyptian tombs. On the way, you'll learn about the deeper workings of Game Maker and discover the power behind the icons—in the form of the programming language GML. Good luck!

PART 5

■ ■ ■

Enemies and Intelligence

You've come a long way, but Game Maker's greatest treasure still lies undisturbed . . . Dare you unleash the arcane powers of GML?

CHAPTER 12

■■■

GML: Become a Programmer

So far we've controlled the behavior of the different objects in our games using events and actions. These actions let the instances of the object perform tasks when certain events occur in the game. In this chapter we are going to define those tasks in an alternative way: by using programs. Programs define tasks through lines of text called *code* that use *functions* instead of actions. This extends the scope of Game Maker considerably as there are only about 150 different actions but close to a thousand *functions*. These *functions* give you much more control than actions, allowing you to define precisely how tasks should be performed in different circumstances.

The text in a program needs to be structured in a very particular way so that Game Maker can understand what you mean. Communicating with Game Maker in this way is like learning a new language with its own special vocabulary and grammar. The programming language Game Maker uses is called GML, which stands for Game Maker Language. If you have written programs before in languages like Java or C++, then you will notice that GML is rather similar. However, every programming language has its own peculiarities, so you will need to watch out for the differences.

Before we go into more detail about GML, you need to know how to tell Game Maker to execute a program using a script resource. Script resources are similar to other resources like sprites and backgrounds in the way they are created and accessed through the resource list. You create a script resource by choosing **Create Script** from the **Resources** menu, and then typing your program into the text editor that appears. Once you've created your script, you can include an **Execute Script** action to call the script in a normal event just as you would for any other action. We'll see how this works in more detail next.

■**Note** You can also use an **Execute Code** action for including GML. Dragging this action into an event will cause the editor to pop up so that you can type the program directly into the event. Although this method is sometimes easier, it is often better to use scripts because they can be reused more easily.

To help you come to grips with GML, in this chapter we're not going to create a whole game but just small examples. Unfortunately, because of its size, we cannot cover all of GML, but we will discuss many key aspects. You can always refer to the Game Maker documentation for a complete overview.

Hello World

We'll start with a traditional program to demonstrate how to write some simple code. We're going to create a script that shows the message "Hello World" on the screen.

Creating a simple script:

1. Start a new game.

2. Choose **Create Script** from the **Resource** menu. The script editor shown in Figure 12-1 will appear.

3. In the **Name** box in the toolbar, give the script the name scr_hello.

4. In the editor, type the following piece of code:

   ```
   {
       show_message('Hello World');
   }
   ```

5. Press the 10/01 button in the toolbar. This will test the program and display an error message if you made a mistake.

6. Close the editor by clicking the green checkmark in the toolbar.

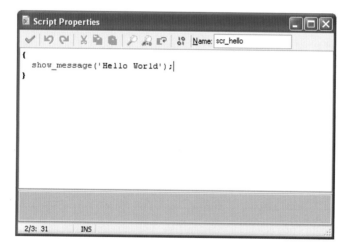

Figure 12-1. *Enter this code in the script editor.*

Note that Game Maker shows parts of the code in different colors. This color-coding helps you know when your code is written correctly. For example, we know that show_message is the correct name for one of Game Maker's built-in functions because it has turned blue. If we had made a spelling mistake, then it wouldn't turn blue and we would know something was wrong. It is also particularly important to give your scripts meaningful names; that way, you can remember what the script does when you use it in an action or some other code.

Before we can see what this code does, we need to execute it. To do so, we must create a new object with a key press event that executes the script.

Executing the script:

1. Create a new object and add a **Key press, <Space>** event to it.

2. Include the **Execute Script** action (**control** tab) and select the scr_hello script from the menu. The arguments can all be left at 0 since we do not use arguments in this script (more about these later). The action should look like Figure 12-2.

3. Create a room and place one instance of the object in it.

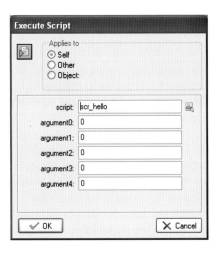

Figure 12-2. *This action executes the scr_hello script.*

Now run the game and press the spacebar. If you did everything correctly, a message box should pop up containing the text "Hello World". If you made a mistake in your script, then Game Maker will report an error when the game loads or when the script is executed. If you do get an error, you should check the script carefully for typing errors. Even using an uppercase letter rather than lowercase can cause an error in GML—so take great care. You'll also find this short program in the file Games/Chapter12/hello_world.gm6 on the CD.

Now let's consider what this script does. The first and last lines contain curly brackets. Different kinds of brackets signify different things in GML, and curly brackets mark the beginning and end of a block of code (a bit like the **Start Block** and **End Block** actions). However, in GML every program must start with an opening curly bracket and must end with a closing bracket. Curly brackets enclose a block of code. Such blocks of code will also be used later at other places.

The program consists of just one command. Such commands are called *statements*. A program consists of one or more statements. A statement ends with a semicolon. In this way, Game Maker understands where one statement ends and the next one begins. Don't forget the semicolons!

The statement in our program is a call to the function `show_message()`. Functions can be recognized because they have a name and then (optionally) some arguments between the parentheses. We have already used such functions before as arguments in actions. For example, we've used the `random()` function in a number of places. Much like actions, functions perform certain tasks. The `show_message()` function has one argument, which is the text to be displayed; `'Hello World'` is that argument. Take note of the single quotes around it as they indicate that this is a string (text). Also note that to make functions easier to recognize and to indicate that you typed their name correctly, they are displayed in a dark blue color.

So when the script is executed, the one statement in it is executed, which shows the alert box containing the text that is provided as an argument. Of course, we could have achieved the same thing using the **Show Message** action. But as we will see later, by using scripts we can do many new things.

Variables

We have used variables in previous chapters. In some cases, we have used the value of a variable (such as an object's position or speed) as a parameter to an action to change its behavior. Sometimes we have used an action to change the value of a variable. Let's now look in more detail at the use of variables, and see how to use them in scripts.

Variables are containers that store values—these values can be changed throughout the course of a game. Such a value can either be a number or a string. A variable is given a name that we can refer to, and we use the name to inspect the current value and to change it. There are a number of built-in variables, like `x` and `y`, which indicate the position of an instance, or like `speed` and `direction`, which indicate the speed and direction in which an instance is moving. Changing a variable in a script is very simple. We use the `=` symbol to assign a new value. For example, to set an instance in the middle of the room, we could use the following piece of code:

```
{
    x = 320;
    y = 240;
}
```

The program starts and ends with curly brackets, as any program must do. There are two statements here, each ending with a semicolon. These both are *assignment statements*, or *assignments* for short. An assignment assigns a value to a variable. The first assignment assigns the value 320 to the variable `x`, which is the horizontal position of the instance. The second assigns the value 240 to the variable `y`, which is the vertical position of the instance. Note that when you type in the piece of code, the variable names will become blue. This color is used for built-in variables.

Rather than assigning a simple value to a variable, we can write a complete expression involving operators (+, -, *, /, and a couple more) and values and other variables. For example, the previous piece of code assumes that the room is 640×480. If we don't know this, we can also write the following:

```
{
    x = room_width/2;
    y = room_height/2;
}
```

Here, `room_width` and `room_height` are two variables that indicate the width and height of the room; by dividing them by 2, we get the middle of the room. We can also use functions in the expressions. For example, as you have seen before, the function `random()` gives a random number smaller than its argument. To move our instance to a random position on the screen, we can use the following code:

```
{
    x = random(room_width);
    y = random(room_height);
}
```

Rather than using the built-in variables, we can also create our own. You do so simply by picking a name and assigning a value to it. Names of variables should only consist of letters and numbers and the underscore (_) symbol. The first character cannot be a number. You should always make sure that your variable names differ from the names of resources or from existing variables or function names. It is vitally important to realize that variable names are case-sensitive—that is, `Name` is not the same as `name`.

Let's make our "Hello World" example a bit more personal. We will ask the player for their name and then greet them in a personal way. You can find the program in the file `Games/Chapter12/hello_you.gm6` on the CD.

```
{
    yourname = get_string('Who are you?','nobody');
    show_message('Hello ' + yourname + '. Welcome to the game.');
}
```

We use a new function here called `get_string()`. This function asks the player to enter some text. The function has two arguments. The first one indicates the question to display, and the second one is the default answer. Note the single quotes around the strings. Also note that the two arguments are separated by a comma. Arguments in functions are always separated by commas. This function returns the text that the player typed in. The assignment assigns this value to a new variable we call `yourname`. Next we use the function `show_message()` again to display a message. The argument, though, might look a bit weird. We include three strings, one of which is stored in the variable `yourname`. When used on strings, the + operator will simply put the strings next to each other—that is, it concatenates the strings. Better try this out in the same way we did for the "Hello World" example.

As you might have realized, the program we just wrote does something that cannot be achieved when only using drag-and-drop actions. It asks the player for some information. Scripts are a lot more powerful than drag-and-drop actions. That is why it is very useful to spend some time learning to write scripts.

You might wonder what happens to the variable `yourname` after the script has finished. Well, it is actually stored with the instance. Later on, in other scripts for this instance, we can still use it. So the user has to enter their name only once. But other instances of the same object or other objects cannot access it directly. It belongs to this particular instance.

There are actually three different types of variables. By default, the variable is stored with the instance and remains available. Each instance can have its own variable using that name. For example, each instance has its own `x` and `y` variables. Sometimes, when you use a variable in a script, you don't want it to remain available when the script is finished. In this case, you need to indicate that it is a variable inside the script, as follows:

```
{
    var yourname;
    yourname = get_string('Who are you?','nobody');
    show_message('Hello ' + yourname + '. Welcome to the game.');
}
```

By adding the line var yourname; we indicate that the variable yourname is defined only in this script. We call it a *local* variable. You can put multiple variables here, with commas separating them. We strongly recommend that you make a variable local whenever possible; it speeds things up and avoids errors when you're reusing the same variables.

Sometimes, though, you want the variable to be available to all instances of all objects. For example, multiple instances might want to use the name of the player once it has been asked using the get_string() function. In this case, we want to make the variable global to all instances. As we have seen in previous chapters, we can achieve this by adding the keyword **global** and inserting a dot in front of the variable name, as follows:

```
{
    global.yourname = get_string('Who are you?','nobody');
    show_message('Hello ' + global.yourname + '. Welcome to the game.');
}
```

Note that the word **global** appears in boldface. It is a special word in the GML language; such keywords are always shown in bold. The word **var** is also a keyword. We will see many more of these in this chapter. In some sense, the curly brackets are also keywords and appear in bold as well.

To summarize, we have three different ways in which we can use variables:

- Belonging to one instance, by simply assigning a value to them

- Local to a script, by declaring them inside the script using the keyword **var**

- Global to the game, by preceding the name with the keyword **global** and a dot

---

Note Global variables remain available when you move to a different room. So, for example, you can ask the player for his name in the first room, store the name in a global variable, and then use that variable in all other rooms in the game.

Functions

Functions are the most important ingredients of a program; they are the things that let Game Maker perform certain tasks. For every action there is a corresponding function, but there are many, many more. In total, close to a thousand functions are available that deal with all aspects of your game, such as motion, instances, graphics, sound, and user input.

We have already used a few functions earlier. Also, you saw two different types of functions. Functions, like the show_message() function, only perform certain tasks. Other functions, like random() and get_string(), return a value that can then be used in expressions or assignments.

When we use a function, we say that we *call* the function. A function call consists of the name of the function, followed by the arguments, separated by commas, in parentheses. Even when a function has no arguments, you must still use the parentheses. Arguments can be values as well as expressions. Most functions have a fixed number of arguments, but some can have an arbitrary number of arguments.

Let's look at some examples. GML provides a large number of functions for drawing objects. These functions should normally only be used in the **Draw** event of objects. There are functions to draw shapes, sprites, backgrounds, text, and so on. If you have registered your version of Game Maker, you also have access to lots of additional drawing functions for creating colorized shapes, rotated text, and even three-dimensional objects. To use some drawing functions, create a script with the following code:

```
{
    draw_set_color(c_red);
    draw_rectangle(x-50,y-50,x+50,y+50,false);
    draw_set_color(c_blue);
    draw_circle(x,y,40,false);
}
```

This piece of code first calls a function to set the drawing color. c_red is a built-in value that indicates the red color. Next, this code draws a rectangle with the indicated corners. The fifth argument, which has the value false, indicates that this must not be an outlined rectangle. Next, the color is set to blue, and finally a filled circle is drawn. To use this script, create an object (it does not need a sprite), and then add a **Draw** event and include an **Execute Script** action to call the script. Add a number of instances of the object to a room and check out the result. You can find the program in the file Games/Chapter12/draw_shapes.gm6 on the CD.

As a second example, let's consider the creation of instances. Often during games you want to create instances of objects. The function instance_create() can be used for doing just this. This function has three arguments. The first two arguments must indicate the position where you want to create the instance and the third argument must indicate the object of which the instance must be created. Assume we want to create a bullet and fire it in the direction of the instance that creates it. This can be achieved with the following piece of code (which assumes that an object obj_bullet exists):

```
{
    var bullet_instance;
    bullet_instance = instance_create(x,y,obj_bullet);
    bullet_instance.speed = 12;
    bullet_instance.direction = direction;
}
```

In this code we first declare a local variable `bullet_instance` that is only available in this piece of code. Next, we call the function to create the instance. This function returns an ID of the new instance, which we store in the variable `bullet_instance`. An ID is simply a number that can be used to refer to the particular instance. To set the speed of this instance, we change the variable speed in the instance to `12`. We do this by using `bullet_instance.speed`, similar to how we addressed variables in objects. In the same way, we set the direction of instance `bullet_instance` to the direction of the current instance.

Conditional Statements

As you know, in Game Maker there are conditional actions that control whether or not a block of actions is executed. When using scripts, you can use *conditional statements* in a similar way. A conditional statement starts with the keyword `if` followed by an expression between parentheses. If this expression evaluates to `true`, the following statement or block of statements is executed. So a conditional statement looks like this:

```
if (<expression>)
{
    <statement>;
    <statement>;
    ...
}
```

The statements between the curly brackets are only executed when the expression is true. In the expression, you can use comparison operators to compare numbers as follows:

- `<` means smaller than.

- `<=` means smaller or equal.

- `==` means equal (note that we need two = symbols, to distinguish the comparison from the assignment).

- `!=` means unequal.

- `>=` means larger or equal.

- `>` means larger than.

You can combine comparisons using `&&` (which means and), `||` (which means or), or `!` (which means not). For example, to indicate that the x value should be larger than `200` but smaller than the y value, you can write something like this: `(x > 200) && (x < y)`.

Note The use of parentheses (like in the previous example) is not always strictly necessary, but it can help make things a lot clearer.

Let's consider an example. We want an instance to wrap around the screen—that is, if its x-position gets smaller than 0 while it is moving to the left, we change the x-position to 640, and when it gets larger than 640 and it is moving to the right, we change it to 0. Here is the corresponding piece of code:

```
{
    if ( (x<0) && (hspeed<0) )
    {
        x = 640;
    }
    if ( (x>640) && (hspeed>0) )
    {
        x = 0;
    }
}
```

Note the use of opening and closing brackets. It is important to carefully check whether they match. Forgetting a bracket is a very common error when writing programs. This code could even be a bit more compact. Note that in a program the layout of the code is up to you. We used a rather standard layout style in this example; we used indents to show which bits of code belong together. Although employing a clear layout style is useful, in this case we've over-done it a bit. Also, when only one statement follows a conditional statement, we do not need the curly brackets. So, we might as well use the following piece of code, which does exactly the same thing:

```
{
    if ( (x<0) && (hspeed<0) ) x = 640;
    if ( (x>640) && (hspeed>0) ) x = 0;
}
```

As with conditional actions, the conditional statement can have an else that is executed when the condition is not true. The structure then looks as follows:

```
if (<expression>)
{
    <statement>;
    ...
}
else
{
    <statement>;
    ...
}
```

For example, assume that we have a monster that should move horizontally in the direction of the player. So, depending on where the player is, the monster should adapt its direction. If the player is an instance of the object obj_player, we can use the following piece of code:

```
{
    if (x < obj_player.x)
    {
        hspeed = 4; vspeed = 0;
    }
    else
    {
        hspeed - -4; vspeed = 0;
    }
}
```

We test whether the x-coordinate of the current instance (the monster) is smaller than the x-coordinate of an instance of object obj_player. If so, we set the motion to the right; else, we set the motion to the left. As we saw earlier, we can address the value of a variable in another instance by preceding it with the ID of that instance and a dot. This time we do it slightly differently, and indicate the object that the instance belongs to. This will work equally well, assuming just one instance of obj_player exists. If there are several player objects, however, only one of them is chosen for comparison and the code may not function as you expect.

Repeating Things

Often in code you want to repeat certain things, and there are a number of ways to achieve this. We call such a piece of code a *loop*. We will start with the easiest way to repeat a piece of code a given number of times: the repeat statement. It looks like this:

```
repeat (<expression>)
{
    <statement>;
    <statement>;
    ...
}
```

The expression must result in an integer value; the block of code following it is executed that number of times. Let's look at an example. In the following program we ask the player for a value and then create the given number of balls at random positions. It assumes that an object obj_ball exists.

```
{
    var numb;
    numb = get_integer('Give the number of balls:',10);
    repeat (numb)
    {
        instance_create(random(640),random(480),obj_ball);
    }
}
```

The program asks the player for an integer number, using the function get_integer(), and stores it in the local variable numb. Next it repeats a piece of code numb times, each time creating a new ball at a random position. The example Games/Chapter12/balls.gm6 on the CD uses this script.

A second way of repeating code is when we want to repeat something as long as some expression is true. For this we use the while statement:

```
while (<expression>)
{
    <statement>;
    <statement>;
    ...
}
```

The while statement is similar to the if statement, but there is an important difference: when the expression is true, the block after the if statement is executed exactly once. However, the block after the while statement is executed for as long as the condition is true. If you are not careful, this code can loop forever, in which case the game will no longer respond.

In this example, we are going to draw 40 concentric circles in different colors:

```
{
    var i;
    i = 0;
    while (i<40)
    {
        var color;
        color = make_color_rgb(random(256),random(128),random(64));
        draw_set_color(color);
        draw_circle(x,y,2*i,true);
        i = i+1;
    }
}
```

■**Note** A color is represented as a number. Such a number consists of three parts, one to indicate the blue component, one to indicate the green component, and one to indicate the red component. Each of these components is a number between 0 and 255. Here we use the function make_rgb_color() to combine these three components (each a random number) into a single color. In order to make the effect prettier, we have biased the numbers toward red and orange by using a larger red component than green and blue. It may seem confusing to use random(256) rather than random(255) to get a number between 0 and 255, but the random() function always returns a number less than the parameter passed in, so if we used 255 we would not get the full color range.

In the program we first initialize the local variable i with a value of 0. Next, we run a loop as long as i is smaller than 40. In the loop we create a random color using the function make_color_rgb(), and set the drawing color. Next we draw a circle with radius 2*i, and finally we increase i. After the loop has been executed 40 times, the condition becomes false and the loop ends. The example Games/Chapter12/draw_circles.gm6 on the CD uses this script to create a rather funny effect.

This type of while loop—in which we first initialize a variable, test the value in the while statement, and increase the variable in every execution of the loop—occurs very often. Hence, there is an easier way to write it: the for loop. It looks like this:

```
for (<initialize>;<condition>;<increment>)
{
    <statement>;
    <statement>;
    ...
}
```

The initialize statement is executed once before the loop starts. The condition is then checked at the beginning of each loop execution to see whether the loop must still be executed. The increment statement is executed at the end of each loop execution. So our circle example can also be written as follows:

```
{
    var i;
    for (i=0; i<40; i=i+1)
    {
        var color;
        color = make_color_rgb(random(256),random(128),random(64));
        draw_set_color(color);
        draw_circle(x,y,2*i,true);
    }
}
```

Note that loops can contain further loops. For example, to create 10 columns comprising eight balls each, we can use the following piece of code:

```
{
    var i,j;
    for (i=0; i<10; i+=1)
    {
        for (j=0; j<8; j+=1)
        {
            instance_create(40*i,40*j,obj_ball);
        }
    }
}
```

Note that we use the expression i+=1. This is a shortcut for i = i+1. It adds 1 to the variable i.

> **Warning** During the execution of a `repeat`, `while`, or `for` loop, no events or actions are processed. So make sure the loop always ends and does not take too long as this might interrupt the game play.

Arrays

Variables are infinitely useful in scripts, but they can only store one value each—in a number of situations you'll want to store a whole collection of values, and *arrays* allow us to do this. An array can store an arbitrary number of values. To get a particular value out of an array you have to specify the index. To this end, you put the index between square brackets. For example, if aaa is an array, you can obtain the fifth element in it by typing aaa[5]. Using arrays in GML is very easy. There is no need to declare them or to specify their length. Only when you want a local array should you declare it using the var keyword. Let's create a simple example in which we compute and store the squares of the numbers 1 through 30, and then draw them on the screen:

```
{
    var i, squares;
    for (i=1; i<=30; i+=1)
    {
        squares[i] = i*i;
    }
    for (i=1; i<=30; i+=1)
    {
        draw_text(10,15*i,string(squares[i]));
    }
}
```

The first loop fills the array with the values, and the second loop draws them on the screen. Note that the function `string()` turns the integer value into a string, which can then be drawn. Clearly this script is a bit useless; there is no need to first store the values in the array. You might as well have drawn them directly.

> **Warning** Make sure that you first store a value into an element of an array before you try to retrieve it.

Let's now consider a slightly more interesting example. Assume we want to make a game containing a number of math questions. The game should ask a random question and then check the answer that the player gives. We can store all questions and answers in an array. We need two scripts: one that fills the array and one that asks the questions. The first script looks like this:

```
{
    question[0] = 'How much is 12+34?';
    question[1] = 'How much is 4*6?';
    question[2] = 'How much is 72/9?';
    question[3] = 'How much is 56-23?';
    question[4] = 'How much is 7*11?';
    question[5] = 'How much is 71+24?';
    question[6] = 'How much is 84/7?';
    question[7] = 'How much is 69-37?';
    question[8] = 'How much is 45+74?';
    question[9] = 'How much is 12*12?';
    answer[0] = 46;
    answer[1] = 24;
    answer[2] = 8;
    answer[3] = 33;
    answer[4] = 77;
    answer[5] = 95;
    answer[6] = 12;
    answer[7] = 32;
    answer[8] = 119;
    answer[9] = 144;
}
```

Note that we do not use local variables. The arrays are now stored in the instance. This script should be called just once when the instance is created. The second script asks a question and checks the answer:

```
{
    var ind,val;
    ind = floor(random(10));
    val = get_integer(question[ind],0);
    if (val == answer[ind])
        show_message('That is the correct answer.')
    else
        show_message('That answer is WRONG!');
}
```

We create a random integer index between 0 and 9. Next we ask the corresponding question and store the result in the variable val. Finally we compare val with the correct answer and display the appropriate message. You can call this script, for instance, in a mouse press event. For an example, see Games/Chapter12/quiz.gm6 on the CD.

▉**Note** The index of an array must be 0 or larger.

The arrays we've seen so far store a row of values. In some situations, we may need a complete matrix of values—for example, to represent the stones in a playing field. This is achieved very simply. Rather than using one index we use two indexes, separated by a comma. So you can write aaa[5,8]. To illustrate, let's create a multiplication table in which mult[i,j] is equal to i*j. The following piece of code achieves this:

```
{
    var i, j, mult;
    for (i=1; i<=10; i+=1)
    {
        for (j=1; j<=10; j+=1)
        {
            mult[i,j] = i*j;
        }
    }
}
```

In the next chapter we will see a number of such 2-dimensional arrays as we represent the playing field for a Tic-Tac-Toe game in this way.

Dealing with Other Instances

As you know, you can apply actions to other instances. Sometimes within a script, you also want to apply some code to other instances or objects. As we saw in the bullet example earlier in the chapter, we can change a variable in another instance or object by preceding it with the index of the instance or object and a dot. To apply more complicated code to other instances, we can use the with statement. In a with statement, you specify the instance or object to which a block of code must be applied. Globally it looks like this:

```
with (<index>)
{
    <statement>;
    <statement>;
    ...
}
```

The index should either be the index of an instance, as obtained when calling the instance_create() function, or the index of an object (normally by giving its name), or the keyword other to apply the block of code to the other object in a collision event. Here is an example that destroys all balls in a game. obj_ball is the ball object.

```
{
    with (obj_ball)
    {
        instance_destroy();
    }
}
```

And here is another example in which we create a bullet with a speed and direction of motion:

```
{
    var bullet_instance;
    bullet_instance = instance_create(x,y,obj_bullet);
    with (bullet_instance)
    {
        speed = 12;
        direction = other.direction;
    }
}
```

Note that we use other.direction within the block of code. Here, other refers to the object for which the code was originally executed.

The with statement is very powerful, and understanding it will help you a lot in creating effective code.

Scripts As Functions

In the **Execute Script** action, you can indicate a number of arguments. The values of these arguments can then be used inside the script. In this way, you can create more generic scripts that can be used at multiple places. Inside the script you can obtain the values of the arguments using the variables argument0, argument1, argument2, and so on. (You can only obtain the values from these variables; you cannot change them.)

Next, we create a script that draws a square and a filled circle at a given position on the screen. We will use four arguments: two that indicate the position and two that indicate the color of the square and the filled circle. Here's the script:

```
{
    draw_set_color(argument2);
    draw_rectangle(argument0-50,argument1-50, argument0+50,argument1+50,false);
    draw_set_color(argument3);
    draw_circle(argument0,argument1,40,false);
}
```

Note that this script is largely the same as the one we showed you earlier, but this time we used arguments to set the color and determine the position for drawing. To use the script we include the **Execute Script** action in the **Draw** event of an object and indicate the value of the arguments, as in Figure 12-3.

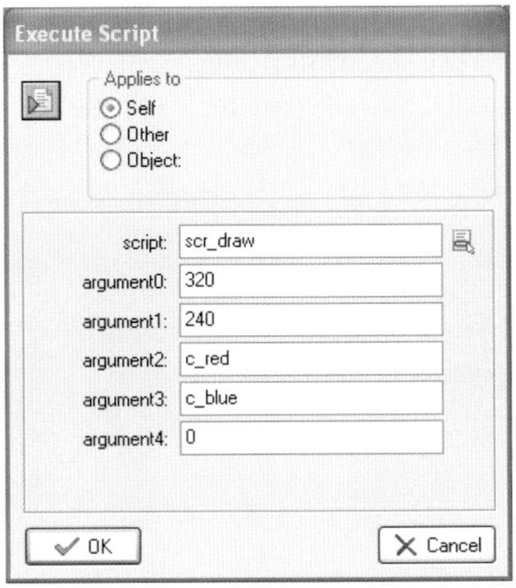

Figure 12-3. *This action executes a script using arguments.*

You can now use this script to draw the shape at other positions and with other colors as well. You could also add the size of the shape as an additional argument to make the script even more generic.

Scripts that you create yourself can be called inside other scripts in exactly the same way as you call functions. You simply use the name of the script and add the arguments between parentheses with commas between them. Remember that even if the script has no arguments, you still need to include the parentheses but just leave them empty.

For example, the following script uses the scr_draw script to draw 100 shapes at random locations with random colors:

```
{
    repeat (100)
    {
        var color1;
        var color2;
        color1 = make_color_rgb(random(256),random(256),random(256));
        color2 = make_color_rgb(random(256),random(256),random(256));
        scr_draw(random(640),random(480),color1,color2);
    }
}
```

You can call this script in the **Draw** event of an object. If you run the program you will notice that the colors and positions change every step. This is of course precisely what we indicated. If you want the positions and colors to stay the same, you could have stored them in arrays. You can find this program in the file Games/Chapter12/draw_wild.gm6 on the CD.

■**Note** Scripts can actually call themselves. This is known as a recursive call. Be very careful with using recursive calls, however, because they can easily lead to errors in which the script continues to call itself forever.

We have seen that functions can return a value that can then be used in expressions. We can also let a script return a value so that we can use it in expressions. For this you use the return statement. Here is an example of a script that returns the squared value of its argument:

```
{
    return argument0*argument0;
}
```

Note that the execution of a script stops after a return statement. The rest of the script will no longer be executed. As an example, here is a script that checks whether all 10 entries of an array are equal to 0:

```
{
    var i;
    for (i=1; i<=10; i+=1)
    {
        if (aaa[i] != 0) return false;
    }
    return true;
}
```

Whenever one of the entries is not equal to 0, the value false is returned and the execution is stopped. Only when all entries are 0 is the final return true; statement executed.

Rather than putting your whole code in one script, it is often a good idea to split it into several scripts and let these scripts call each other. That makes the code more readable and makes it possible to use the same piece of code multiple times.

Debugging Programs

When creating scripts, you can easily make errors. You might misspell a function name or forget a closing bracket. When running the game, this can result in two types of errors.

You might get an error during the loading of the game. This happens when you forget a bracket, for example. The error message indicates in which script and on which line the error occurs, and provides a brief explanation of the error. Carefully reading the error message will help you solve the problem. You can also check for such problems by clicking the 10/01 button in the toolbar of the script editor. A check is performed and when there is an error, this is reported. The editor highlights the line where the error occurs, as shown in Figure 12-4. We strongly recommend that you do this check after each change you make in the script.

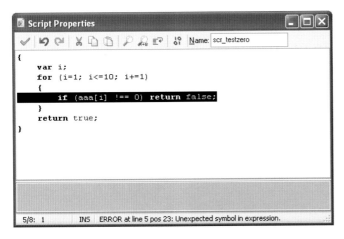

Figure 12-4. *After pressing the 10/01 key, an error is indicated in the script.*

A second type of error can occur while a user is playing of the game—if you use a nonexistent variable, for example. Again an error message is displayed that should help you correct the error. Such errors are more difficult to find. They typically occur when you've misspelled a variable name or when you have used a variable name that was also the name of a resource. So you must be careful when writing code.

Game Maker contains a debugger. When you run the game using the feature **Run in Debug Mode** (located in the **Run** menu), an additional window will pop up, as shown in Figure 12-5.

Figure 12-5. *When running the game in debug mode, this debug window is shown.*

The debug window allows you to pause and continue the game or step through it. Also, you can check the value of different variables and even execute some code. For more details, see the Game Maker documentation.

Congratulations

You have now mastered the basics of programming in the GML language. We hope you have realized that programming is not so difficult after all. Once you get the hang of it, programming in GML is actually a lot easier and faster than using the drag-and-drop actions that you used in previous chapters. Using scripts opens up a whole new set of possibilities in Game Maker. More than half of the documentation of Game Maker deals with functions and built-in variables that you can use to enhance your games in many ways. You will gain a lot more control over instances, rooms, views, sound, and graphics.

We did not describe the GML in full; it provides a number of additional statements and constructions you can take advantage of. But we examined the ones that you will need most. Once you are a bit more experienced with using the language, we recommend that you read the GML section in the documentation, which covers the language in full.

In the next chapter we'll create a game in which we only use scripts. The game will contain just one instance of a single object in which just three scripts are called. This may sound rather simple, but actually it is the first game in which the computer will be intelligent.

■ ■ ■

CHAPTER 13

Clever Computers: Playing Tic-Tac-Toe

In this chapter we are going to create a version of the game tic-tac-toe in which you are pitted against an intelligent computer opponent. This opponent must have a strategy that will regularly beat the player to keep it challenging, but the computer opponent must not be too strong; otherwise the player has no chance of winning, and will quickly become frustrated and give up. We will also show how the computer can adapt its play to the level of the player. The game will be almost completely written using the GML programming language, so make sure you read and understood Chapter 12 on GML before starting this chapter.

Designing the Game: Tic-Tac-Toe

I am sure you'll know how to play *Tic-Tac-Toe*, but even so, it is good to describe it carefully before we start to aid you in making the game.

> *The game of Tic-Tac-Toe is played on a 3×3 grid. The computer player uses red stones while the human player uses blue stones. The players take turns placing a stone of their color on an empty cell. When a player manages to create a horizontal, vertical, or diagonal row of three stones of his color, he wins the game. When all cells are filled and no row is created, the game ends in a draw.*

> *The player uses the mouse to place the stones. The Esc key is used to end the game. The game consists of an arbitrary number of rounds. In each round the player who lost the previous round will start. The number of wins for each player and the number of draws are recorded, and displayed on the game interface for reference. Figure 13-1 shows the game in action.*

The game requires just a few ingredients: the playing field, the stones, and a mechanism to show the number of wins. The most complicated part will be how to determine the moves for the computer player. All the resources can be found in the Resources/Chapter13 folder on the CD.

Figure 13-1. *The Tic-Tac-Toe game looks like this.*

The Playing Field

We will first need two sprites for the stones, a background to contain the playing field, and some sound effects. As this is a game in which the player is supposed to think a lot, background music is not really appropriate, so we won't use it.

Creating sprites, a background, and sound effects:

1. Start a new game.

2. Create a new sprite using the file Stone1.gif from the Resources/Chapter13 folder on the CD.

3. Create another sprite using the file Stone2.gif.

4. Create a background using the file Background.bmp.

5. Finally create sound effects using the files Place.wav, Win.wav, Lose.wav, and Draw.wav.

We will also need a font for our game. We will use this to draw the score, that is, how many games are won by the player and the computer.

Creating a font:

1. Create a new font for the game. We named ours fnt_score. Select a nice font; for example, **Comic Sans MS**, give it a size of 16, and select **Bold**.

The playing field is where all the action happens. We will create just one object in the game, which represents the playing field, and there will be just one instance of this object in the game. This object does not need a sprite, as the field is already drawn on the background.

Creating the field object and the room:

1. Create a new object. Give it the name obj_field. No sprite is required.

2. Create a new room. In the **backgrounds** tab, assign to it the background.

3. In the **settings** tab, give the room an appropriate caption.

4. In the **objects** tab, add one instance of the field object at an arbitrary place.

You might want to run the game just to test that the playing field is indeed there. Obviously, nothing can be done at this stage, as we are yet to specify the behavior for the field object. We will only use scripts for this.

Internally we represent the playing field with a variable field that will be a two-dimensional array. This variable represents the cells in the field, as shown in Figure 13-2. Each entry can have three values: 0 means that the cell is empty, 1 means that the human player placed a stone there, and 2 means that the computer player placed a stone there.

field[0,0]	field[1,0]	field[2,0]
field[0,1]	field[1,1]	field[2,1]
field[0,2]	field[1,2]	field[2,2]

Figure 13-2. *The playing field is represented by a two-dimensional array called field.*

Let's start by creating a script to initialize the field. Call this script scr_field_init. This script must set all the field entries to 0. We will use two local variables for this, and then use a double loop to fill in the entries, as shown in Listing 13-1.

Listing 13-1. *The Script scr_field_init*

```
{
    var i,j;
    // clear the field
    for (i=0; i<=2; i+=1)
        for (j=0; j<=2; j+=1)
            field[i,j] = 0;
}
```

Note Notice the line that starts with //. This line is a comment, so it is not really part of the program. Comments are ignored by Game Maker, and exist purely to help you, or someone else, know what is going on in the code—would you remember what all your variables and loops do when coming back to a piece of code after six months?

The game must store the number of wins by the two players, as well as the number of draws. For this we will use three variables: score_player, score_computer, and score_draw. To initialize the game, we must initialize these variables to 0 and we must initialize the playing field, as shown in Listing 13-2.

Listing 13-2. *The Script scr_game_init*

```
{
    // initialize the score
    score_player = 0;
    score_computer = 0;
    score_draw = 0;
    // initialize the field
    scr_field_init();
}
```

As you can see, we call the first script (scr_field_init) from within this script. Scripts can be used as functions that can be called from other scripts—we will use this technique a lot in our game. The scr_game_init script is executed from the **Create** event of the field object.

Creating and executing the scripts:

1. Create the two scripts, scr_field_init and scr_game_init, as described earlier.

2. Reopen the properties form of the field object by double-clicking on it in the resource list.

3. Add a **Create** event. In it include the **Execute Script** action and indicate the script scr_game_init.

The next step is to make it possible for the player to place stones. When the player clicks the left mouse button on the screen, we must detect which cell the click occurs in. If the click is outside the playing field or on a cell that is already filled, there will be no resulting action.

To determine the cell that has been clicked, we consider the current position of the mouse, which is indicated by the global variables mouse_x and mouse_y. The cells each have a size of 140×140, so to get the correct cell index (0, 1, or 2), we divide the mouse position by 140 and then round it down to the nearest whole number using the floor() function. This would give the correct cell index if our playing field were in the top-left corner of the screen. Because the top-left corner of the field is at position (208,32), we must subtract this offset from the mouse position, as we want the position relative to the top-left corner of the playing field, not the top-left corner of the screen.

So, for example, say the human player clicks at x = 350. The sum we do is (350-208)/140 = 1.01. Rounded down, the result is 1, which tells us that the cursor has been clicked inside one of the middle columns of cells (remember that the array starts at 0, not 1).

If the results of the calculations for x and y are less than 0 or more than 2, we ignore the click. If they *are* in this range, we check whether the corresponding cell is empty. If the cell is empty, we change its value to 1 to place the stone and play the sound effect.

The script looks like the one shown in Listing 13-3.

Listing 13-3. The Script scr_field_click

```
{
    var i,j;
    // find the position that is clicked
    i = floor((mouse_x-208)/140);
    j = floor((mouse_y-32)/140);
    // check whether it exists and is empty
    if (i<0 || i>2 || j<0 || j>2) exit;
    if (field[i,j] != 0) exit;
    // set the stone
    field[i,j] = 1;
    sound_play(snd_place);
}
```

Note that we use a new statement here: exit. The exit statement ends the execution of the script. We need to call this script in the **Global left pressed** event. This event is called when the left mouse button is pressed anywhere on the screen (not necessarily in the field object).

Creating the mouse click script:

1. Create the script scr_field_click, as shown earlier.

2. Reopen the properties form of the field object by double-clicking on it in the resource list.

3. Add a **Mouse**, **Global mouse**, **Global left pressed** event. In it include the **Execute Script** action and indicate the script scr_field_click.

If you run the game now, you will notice that you do hear the sound effect when you click on a cell but that no stones appear. This makes sense, as we have not yet added any code to draw the stones. Rather than using stone objects, we will create a script that draws the stones. Actually, this script will draw everything that is required: the stones and the current score (remember that the field does not need to be drawn as it is on the background image).

The script (shown in Listing 13-4) consists of two parts. First, all cells that are nonempty are drawn. We use a double loop for this. Depending on the value of the field cell at that position, the red or blue stone sprite is drawn. Second, the score is drawn. For this we set the correct font and position, and for each line we set a different color. (Note that the function string() turns a number into a string.)

Listing 13-4. *The Script scr_field_draw*

```
{
    var i,j;
    // draw the correct sprites
    for (i=0; i<=2; i+=1)
        for (j=0; j<=2; j+=1)
        {
            if (field[i,j] == 1)
                draw_sprite(spr_stone1,0,208+140*i,32+140*j);
            if (field[i,j] == 2)
                draw_sprite(spr_stone2,0,208+140*i,32+140*j);
        }
    // draw the score
    draw_set_font(fnt_score);
    draw_set_halign(fa_right);
    draw_set_color(c_blue);
    draw_text(200,340,'Player Wins: ' + string(score_player));
    draw_set_color(c_red);
    draw_text(200,375,'Computer Wins: ' + string(score_computer));
    draw_set_color(c_black);
    draw_text(200,410,'Draws: ' + string(score_draw));
}
```

We must call this script in the **Draw** event of the field object.

Drawing the field:

1. Create the script scr_field_draw as described earlier.

2. Add the **Draw** event to the field object. In it include the **Execute Script** action and indicate the script scr_field_draw.

Now when you test the game, you should be able to place stones. The computer opponent is not yet doing anything, so only your own stones exist. In the next section we will create some simple opponent behavior. The current version of the game can be found in the file Games/Chapter13/tic_tac_toe1.gm6 on the CD.

Let the Computer Play

In this section, we are mainly going to concentrate on completing the first version of the game by adding the logic for a simple computer opponent. But first we need some scripts to test whether the player or the computer won the last game, or if it was a draw. We start with a script to check whether the player did win. There are eight different lines of three stones that can be filled to win: three horizontal ones, three vertical ones, and two diagonal ones. In the script (shown in Listing 13-5), we simply test all of these to see whether the cells contain the correct value. The function will return either the value true indicating that the player did win, or false, indicating that the player did not yet win. The value returned by the script can then be used later as a condition in other scripts. By this point you should know how to create a script, so we will just show the code from here on out. If you are confused at any point, remember that the game is available on the CD in Games/Chapter13/tic_tac_toe2.gm6, so feel free to open it up and have a look.

Listing 13-5. *The Script scr_check_player_win*

```
{
    if (field[0,0]==1 && field[0,1]==1 && field[0,2]==1) return true;
    if (field[1,0]==1 && field[1,1]==1 && field[1,2]==1) return true;
    if (field[2,0]==1 && field[2,1]==1 && field[2,2]==1) return true;
    if (field[0,0]==1 && field[1,0]==1 && field[2,0]==1) return true;
    if (field[0,1]==1 && field[1,1]==1 && field[2,1]==1) return true;
    if (field[0,2]==1 && field[1,2]==1 && field[2,2]==1) return true;
    if (field[0,0]==1 && field[1,1]==1 && field[2,2]==1) return true;
    if (field[0,2]==1 && field[1,1]==1 && field[2,0]==1) return true;
    return false;
}
```

■**Note** To check whether two values are equal, you must use ==, not =, as a single = is the assignment operator. Also remember that once a return statement is reached, the rest of the script is not executed.

Checking whether the computer wins is exactly the same, except that this time, we are testing whether the cells contain values of 2, not 1, as shown in Listing 13-6.

Listing 13-6. *The Script scr_check_computer_win*

```
{
    if (field[0,0]==2 && field[0,1]==2 && field[0,2]==2) return true;
    if (field[1,0]==2 && field[1,1]==2 && field[1,2]==2) return true;
    if (field[2,0]==2 && field[2,1]==2 && field[2,2]==2) return true;
    if (field[0,0]==2 && field[1,0]==2 && field[2,0]==2) return true;
    if (field[0,1]==2 && field[1,1]==2 && field[2,1]==2) return true;
    if (field[0,2]==2 && field[1,2]==2 && field[2,2]==2) return true;
```

```
    if (field[0,0]==2 && field[1,1]==2 && field[2,2]==2) return true;
    if (field[0,2]==2 && field[1,1]==2 && field[2,0]==2) return true;
    return false;
}
```

Checking for a draw is even simpler (see Listing 13-7)—we check all cells; if one is empty we return false as there is still a move possible. Only when all cells are filled do we return true.

Listing 13-7. *The Script scr_check_draw*

```
{
    var i,j;
    for (i=0; i<=2; i+=1)
        for (j=0; j<=2; j+=1)
        {
            if (field[i,j] == 0) return false;
        }
    return true;
}
```

To act on the outcome of these three possibilities, we will use another script, as shown in Listing 13-8. For each possible outcome, the correct score variable is increased; a sound is played; we redraw the screen to actually show the last move and the new score; wait for a second; show a message; and initialize the field again.

Listing 13-8. *The Script scr_check_end*

```
{
    // check whether the player did win
    if (scr_check_player_win())
    {
        score_player += 1;
        sound_play(snd_win);
        screen_redraw();
        sleep(1000);
        show_message('YOU WIN');
        scr_field_init();
    }
    // check whether the computer did win
    if (scr_check_computer_win())
    {
        score_computer += 1;
        sound_play(snd_lose);
        screen_redraw();
        sleep(1000);
        show_message('YOU LOSE');
        scr_field_init();
    }
```

```
    // check whether there is a draw
    if (scr_check_draw())
    {
        score_draw += 1;
        sound_play(snd_draw);
        screen_redraw();
        sleep(1000);
        show_message("IT'S A DRAW");
        scr_field_init();
    }
}
```

We must call this script after each move by either the player or the computer.

But we still need to give the computer the power to make a move. Let's create a very simple mechanism here; in the next section we'll create a much more intelligent opponent. Our simple mechanism makes a random move. We do this as follows. We select a random cell, test whether it is empty, and if so, place the stone there. If the selected cell is not empty, we repeat the search until we find one that is. Finding a random position works like this—we use the function random(3) to obtain a random real number below 3. Using the floor() function, we round this down, obtaining 0, 1, or 2. The script is shown in Listing 13-9.

Listing 13-9. *The Script scr_find_move*

```
{
    var i,j;
    while (true)
    {
        i = floor(random(3));
        j = floor(random(3));
        if (field[i,j] == 0)
        {
            field[i,j] = 2;
            exit;
        }
    }
}
```

This script makes use of a while loop to find a random free cell. while(true) can be dangerous, because as the expression is always true, the loop never exits by itself. In this case, however, we are exiting in our own code as soon as an empty cell is detected, so it is safe as long as an empty cell exists. If there are no empty cells, we already know it is a draw, so we need not worry about that case.

We are going to use this script in an updated version of the script scr_field_click, which we created earlier. When the player has made a valid move, there are three things we must do. First, we check whether the player won or whether there is a draw, in which case the field is initialized again, ready for the next game. Next, we let the computer make a move. Finally, we check whether the computer won or whether there is a draw.

We adapt the scr_field_click script by adding a few lines, as shown in Listing 13-10.

Listing 13-10. *The Adapted Script scr_field_click*

```
{
    var i,j;
    // find the position that is clicked
    i = floor((mouse_x-208)/140);
    j = floor((mouse_y-32)/140);
    // check whether it exists and is empty
    if (i<0 || i>2 || j<0 || j>2) exit;
    if (field[i,j] != 0) exit;
    // set the stone
    field[i,j] = 1;
    sound_play(snd_place);
    scr_check_end();
    // let the computer make a move
    scr_find_move();
    scr_check_end();
}
```

Once you have added the new scripts and made the change to scr_field_click, test the game, and you should find it is now fully operational. You can find it in the file Games/ Chapter13/tic_tac_toe2.gm6 on the CD.

The game as it stands is fine, but it is extremely easy to win as the computer plays random moves. In the next section, we will make the computer a bit more intelligent.

A Clever Computer Opponent

To be able to make a clever computer opponent we must first be clever ourselves. How would you play the game? What would your strategy be? If you have played the game often, here is a strategy you might come up with:

- If there is a move available that will make you win, then play it.

- If there is no winning move available for you, but there is one available for the opponent, you'd better play that move to block them; otherwise you will lose.

- If neither is the case but the center cell is free, then play the center.

- If none of the above is true, play a random move.

This is not the best strategy possible but it is pretty good, and still leaves the player with a chance to win, so let's implement it. To give the game a bit more variation, we will program the computer opponent to only do the third step half times it is presented. We are going to create four scripts, one for each of the four cases. The last one we already have—all we have to do is rename it from scr_find_move to scr_find_random. The other scripts still have to be constructed.

We will start with the script that tests for the existence of a winning move for the computer. If such a move exists, it is made, and true is returned. Otherwise false is returned. The script works as follows—we consider every empty cell. We place a stone there and test whether we won. If so, we return true. If not, we make the cell empty again and proceed with the next empty cell. The script is shown in Listing 13-11.

Listing 13-11. The Script scr_find_win, Which Tries to Find a Winning Move

```
{
    var i,j;
    for (i=0; i<=2; i+=1)
        for (j=0; j<=2; j+=1)
            if (field[i,j] == 0)
            {
                field[i,j] = 2;
                if scr_check_computer_win() return true;
                field[i,j] = 0;
            }
    return false;
}
```

The next script tries to find a potential winning move for the human player. If such a position exists, the computer places a stone there. It largely works the same, except that we are testing for a potential row of three human player stones, not three computer player stones. The cell is then given a value of 2 to place a computer stone there, to block the human player's winning move, as shown in Listing 13-12.

Listing 13-12. The Script scr_find_lose, Which Tries to Block a Winning Move of the Player

```
{
    var i,j;
    for (i=0; i<=2; i+=1)
        for (j=0; j<=2; j+=1)
            if (field[i,j] == 0)
            {
                field[i,j] = 1;
                if scr_check_player_win()
                    { field[i,j] = 2; return true; }
                field[i,j] = 0;
            }
    return false;
}
```

Finally, we need the script that tries the center position (Listing 13-13.) It will only try it once out of every two times.

Listing 13-13. *The Script scr_find_center, Which Tries to Place a Stone in the Center*

```
{
    if (random(2) < 1 && field[1,1] == 0)
        { field[1,1] = 2; return true; }
    return false;
}
```

With all these scripts in place, we have to remake the script scr_find_move that determines the next move of the computer. This script calls the four scripts in order and, whenever one succeeds, it stops further processing because the opponent has made a move. This script appears in Listing 13-14.

Listing 13-14. *The New Script scr_find_move*

```
{
    if scr_find_win() exit;
    if scr_find_lose() exit;
    if scr_find_center() exit;
    scr_find_random();
}
```

That's the whole game. You can find this finished version in the file Games/Chapter13/ tic_tac_toe3.gm6 on the CD. It will be quite a bit harder to beat this opponent, and if you are not very good at the game you will most likely lose a few times! In particular, the game might be too difficult for young children. In the next section, we will see how we can automatically adapt the game to the level of the player.

Adaptive Gameplay

When the player is good, we should confront him with a strong computer opponent. But when the player is a novice, the computer opponent should be weaker. Many games achieve this by letting the user manually select the level of the game (for example, easy, normal, or hard). But it can be more desirable when the game automatically adapts to the level of the player. For our game this can easily be achieved—we maintain the score of the player and the computer, so we know who is winning. When the player is winning a lot, we can make the computer play better, and when the player is losing a lot, we can make the computer play down its abilities.

As an indication of how good the player is, we use (score_player+1) / (score_computer+1). The reason for adding 1 to both values is that we do not want to divide by 0, as this would cause an error. When this value is larger than 1, the player is better than the computer. When it is smaller than 1, the computer is better. In the scr_find_move script where we decide on the computer move, we will also compute this value, and based on the result, we decide which moves we check. When the value is larger than 1.2, we try all moves. When it is smaller than 0.5, we only do a random move. We add in the other two moves as the value increases. The updated version of scr_find_move is shown in Listing 13-15.

Listing 13-15. *Further Adapting the Script scr_find_move*

```
{
    var level;
    level = (score_player+1) / (score_computer+1);
    if (level > 0.5)
        { if scr_find_win() exit; }
    if (level > 0.8)
        { if scr_find_lose() exit; }
    if (level > 1.2)
        { if scr_find_center() exit; }
    scr_find_random();
}
```

You should now let a number of people play the game and see whether the game indeed adapts to their level of play. You might want to vary the numbers in the script to make the game easier or harder for the players.

Congratulations

You have just created your first intelligent computer opponent. Also, you have created some adaptive gameplay, something that is very important for good games. You will find the last version of the game in the file Games/Chapter13/tic_tac_toe4.gm6 on the CD.

You might want to extend the game even further. First, you can think a bit more about the strategy. A very good move in the game is a move where you create two winning positions for yourself in the next move. As the opponent can only play one of the two, you are then assured of winning the game in the next move. You might want to add this to the strategy. Another thing you could do is add a two-player mode in which two people can play against each other. This is relatively easy, as there is no need for an intelligent computer opponent anymore— here you only need to remember and indicate who is to play in each move.

The registered version of Game Maker makes available functions that make it possible to play such a game over a network with two computers, but that is something really advanced.

In this chapter you saw how useful GML code is—we put everything in scripts. In fact, a game like this would have been almost impossible to create without GML. And it wasn't really all that much work. Once you get accustomed to using GML code, you will probably start using actions much less.

Intelligent opponents make games more interesting. In this chapter we had just one intelligent opponent. In the next chapter, we will create a whole collection of intelligent enemies.

CHAPTER 14

■ ■ ■

Intelligent Behavior: Animating the Dead

An interesting and challenging game must involve tricky opponents that require clever thinking or quick reactions to defeat. Up to now, the enemies in our games behaved rather stupidly—they were just following predefined rules or attacking randomly. In this chapter we will make the enemies a bit more intelligent, but care must be taken that we do not make them too clever—we still want the player to be able to win the game.

To facilitate this, we'll introduce some artificial intelligence (AI) techniques in this chapter—this term will probably conjure up images of powerful intelligent robot or cyborg opponents, the likes of which are seen in futuristic movies. This may sound like a complicated topic, but don't worry—the techniques we'll examine are actually rather easy to implement in Game Maker.

Designing the Game: Pyramid Panic

The game we're going to create in this chapter is called *Pyramid Panic*. It is a maze game, like the Koalabr8 game we created in Chapter 7, but the gameplay will be rather different. Here is the story:

> *You play an explorer (see Figure 14-1) who has become trapped while investigating a large pyramid complex. All around lie the treasures of an ancient pharaoh, but pyramids are hazardous places and danger lurks around every corner. Deadly scorpions and beetles will block your progress and mummies will hunt you down. Only by keeping your wits about you can you hope to unravel the secrets of the great pyramid and escape as a rich man.*
>
> *You control the explorer using the arrow keys. Many obstacles will block your path, keeping you from taking the treasures and eventually escaping to freedom. Beetles will only move vertically while scorpions only move horizontally. Mummies move in all directions. These enemies are clever and will react when they see you by trying to catch you and end your explorations. Some wall segments can be pushed, allowing you to reach other areas or hide from enemies. The pyramid also contains scarabs that you can use to make the mummies temporarily vulnerable—allowing you to hunt them for extra points.*

Deep within the center of the pyramid lies its greatest treasure, the fabled sword of the sun god Ra. It is this great treasure that casts the unnatural light which reaches throughout the pyramid and allows you to see your way so clearly. It is precious beyond measure, but in taking it you will upset that delicate system and the pyramid will be plunged into eerie darkness. Only the small glow remaining in the sword will light your way now, and formerly simple puzzles will seem new and challenging. All is not lost, however, for the sword has a second func-tion. When wielding the sword you will be able to press and hold the spacebar to temporarily reactivate its glow. The sword transmutes gold into pure light, lighting your way but reducing your score. When the sword is active, the mummies will flee as they do when a scarab is active, making your journey easier, but draining your wealth.

The basic ingredients of the game are similar to the maze game in Chapter 7, but there is a big difference. We are including enemies that are clever and will react when they see you, which makes the game a lot more interesting to play. All the resources can be found in the Resources/Chapter14 folder on the CD.

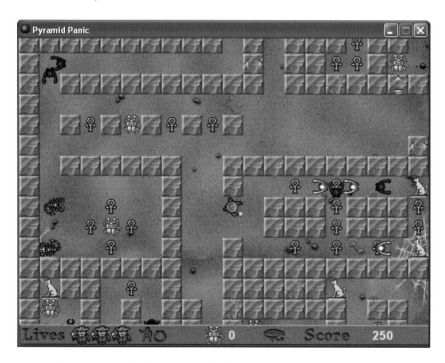

Figure 14-1. *Our intrepid explorer is chasing mummies.*

The Basic Framework

Let's start by creating the basic game framework. This will work in largely the same way as described earlier in Chapters 6 and 7, so we'll only briefly outline it here. If you want to immediately go to the next section, you can load the file Games/Chapter14/pyramid1.gm6 from the CD.

Creating the front-end:

1. Open Game Maker and start a new game using the **File** menu.

2. Create sprites using the following files from the Resources/Chapter14 folder on the CD: Title.gif, Button_start.gif, Button_load.gif, Button_help.gif, Button_scores.gif, and Button_quit.gif.

3. Create two backgrounds using the files Background1.gif and Background2.gif.

4. Create sounds using the files Music.mp3 and Click.wav.

 5. Create a title object using the title sprite. Add an **Other, Game Start** event and include an action to play the music (with **Loop** set to **true**).

 6. Add a **Create** event. Include a **Set Score** action and set the score to 0. Also include a **Set Lives** action and set the number of lives to 3. Finally, include the **Score Caption** action and indicate that the score must not be shown.

 7. Create a start button object using the start sprite. Add a **Left Pressed** mouse event and include an action to play the click sound followed by an action to move to the next room. Add **Key Press** events for the **<Space>** key and the **<Enter>** key, with the same actions.

 8. Create a load button object using the load sprite. Add a **Left Pressed** mouse event and include an action to play the click sound followed by a **Load Game** action.

 9. Create a help button object using the help sprite. Add a **Left Pressed** mouse event and include an action to play the click sound followed by a **Show Info** action.

 10. Create a scores button object using the scores sprite. Add a **Left Pressed** mouse event and include an action to play the click sound followed by a **Show Highscore** action. Use the second background as an image for the high-score list and choose some nice font and colors.

 11. Create a quit button object using the quit sprite. Add a **Left Pressed** mouse event and include an action to play the click sound followed by an **End Game** action. Also add a **Key Press, Others, <Escape>** event, with the same actions in it.

12. Create a front-end room using the first background, and place the title and five button objects in it.

Now follow the next instructions to create the completion screen. Refer to Chapter 6 for a more detailed explanation.

Creating the completion screen:

1. Create a sprite using the file `Congratulation.gif`.

2. Create a new object using this sprite. Add a **Create** event and include a **Set Alarm** action to set **Alarm0** using 60 steps. Also include a **Set Score** action and set the score to `score * 2`. This gives the player an incentive to escape the pyramid alive.

3. Add an **Alarm0** event and include the **Show Highscore** action. Use the same settings as before. Next, include a **Different Room** action to move to the front-end room.

4. Create a completion room using the second background and place an instance of the congratulation object in it.

We also need to create the game information and change some of the Game Maker's default settings for the game.

Changing the game settings:

1. Double-click on **Game Information**, near the bottom of the resource list, and create a short help text based on the game's description earlier.

2. Double-click on **Global Game Settings** at the bottom of the resource list.

3. Select the **other** tab and disable the option **Let <Esc> end the game**, as we'll handle this ourselves.

The next step is to create a controller object for the game. This controller object will have a number of functions. First, it provides the option to return to the front-end screen. Second, it handles the ending of the game when all lives are lost. Finally, later in the chapter, it will display a panel at the bottom of the room with the number of lives left and the score.

Creating the controller object:

1. Create a new object and name it `obj_controller`. It does not need a sprite. Add a **Key Press, Others, <Escape>** event, and include the **Different Room** action to move to the front-end room.

2. Add the **Other, No More Lives** event. Within it, include a **Sleep** action, setting the number of milliseconds to 1000. Next include a **Display Message** action with the message "YOU LOST ALL YOUR LIVES!", or something similar.

3. Still in the **No More Lives** event, include the **Show Highscore** action with the same settings as you used in the completion screen. Finally, include the **Different Room** action to move to the front-end room.

To test what we have so far, we will add a room between the front-end room and the completion room, to act as the game level.

Creating a basic room:

1. Right-click on the completion room in the resource list. From the pop-up menu, select **Insert Room**.

2. Select the **backgrounds** tab and in the middle select the second background.

3. Select the **settings** tab to give the room an appropriate caption and call the room `room_pyramid`.

4. Select the **objects** tab and place one instance of the controller object at the top left of the room.

That completes our basic game framework for Pyramid Panic, which can also be found in the file `Games/Chapter14/pyramid1.gm6` on the CD. Give it a little test to see that it works correctly. Note that the only way to stop the game is to press the Esc key—this returns you to the front-end room.

Creating the Maze and the Explorer

Our next goal is to create the basic maze. Again, this is similar to what we did in Chapter 7, but this time we will use **Execute Code** actions in many places instead of actions. Let's start by creating two wall objects. We'll use two different ones to give some variation, but we'll ensure that they behave the same in the game by making the first wall the parent of the second wall.

Creating the wall objects:

1. Create two sprites using the files `Wall1.gif` and `Wall2.gif`. Make sure that both sprites are not transparent.

2. Create a new object for the first wall and name it `obj_wall1`. Give it the first wall sprite and enable the **Solid** option.

3. Create a new object for the second wall and name it `obj_wall2`. Give it the second wall sprite, enable the **Solid** option, and set **Parent** to the first wall object.

Next we need to create the hero of our game—the explorer. We use four different animated sprites for this. To make sure that the explorer stays correctly aligned with the cells, we'll disable precise collision checking and actually increase the bounding box for the sprites. As a result, Game Maker will act as if the sprites have a size of 32×32.

Creating the explorer sprites:

1. Create a sprite using the file `Explorer_left.gif`. This is an animated sprite. Give it the name `spr_explorer_left`.

2. Disable the option **Precise collision checking**, and select the **Full image** option found under **Bounding Box**. Since the sprite is 32×32, this will make the collision act on a 32×32 box.

3. In the same way, create the three other sprites using the files `Explorer_right.gif`, `Explorer_up.gif`, and `Explorer_down.gif`.

The explorer object must pick the correct sprite depending on its direction of motion. This time, rather than using actions we'll do all the motion using code. When the explorer reaches the area outside the room, he has escaped the pyramid and we can move to the completion screen.

Creating the explorer object:

1. Create a new object for the explorer and name it obj_explorer. Give it the downward moving explorer sprite.

2. Add a **Create** event, and in it, include the **Execute Code** action (**control** tab). Type in the following piece of code:

```
{
    image_speed = 0;
}
```

The image_speed variable we use here stores the speed with which the animation is played. When the explorer is standing still, this is set to 0.

3. Add a **Collision** event with the first wall object and include the **Execute Code** action within it. Here we must stop the motion and set the animation speed to 0. For this, we use the following piece of code:

```
{
    speed = 0;
    image_speed = 0;
}
```

4. Add a **Keyboard, <Left>** event and again include an **Execute Code** action using the following piece of code:

```
{
    if ( !place_snapped(32,32) ) exit;
    speed = 4;
    direction = 180;
    sprite_index = spr_explorer_left;
    image_speed = 0.25;
}
```

In the first line of this code we call the function place_snapped(), which tests whether the instance is aligned with the grid. If this is not the case (remember that the ! sign means not), we exit the piece of code; otherwise we set the speed and direction. The variable sprite_index indicates the sprite that is used, and we set it to the left-facing explorer sprite. Finally, we set the animation speed to 0.25. We use a small value to make sure that the animation looks more realistic and that it doesn't go too fast.

5. Add similar events for the **<Right>**, **<Up>**, and **<Down>** keys. The directions for these events should be 0, 90, and 270, and you should be sure to choose the correct sprite for each.

6. Add a **Keyboard, <no key>** event. If aligned with the grid we must stop the motion here. So include an **Execute Code** action with the following piece of code:

```
{
    if ( !place_snapped(32,32) ) exit;
    speed = 0;
    image_speed = 0;
}
```

7. Add the **Other, Outside Room** event and include the **Next Room** action.

For the time being, this concludes the description of the explorer object. At first, using code may seem harder than using actions, but when you get used to the way code is structured, you will find it faster, because you can more easily change it. It is now time to test the explorer's movement and his interaction with the walls.

Adapting the room:

1. Open room_pyramid by double-clicking on it in the resource list.

2. In the toolbar, set **Snap X** and **Snap Y** to 32, as our maze cells are 32×32.

3. Using the first wall object, create a maze in the room. (Be careful not to remove the controller object.) Make sure there is one exit to the outside. In some places, place an instance of the second wall object instead, to give the walls some variation.

4. Add one instance of the explorer in the room.

Now test the room to make sure the explorer's motion around the maze is working correctly. Once you reach the outside, you should be moved to the completion room. This version of the game can also be found in the file Games/Chapter14/pyramid2.gm6 on the CD.

Expanding Our Horizons

One of the main features of our game is exploration. In most of our previous games we have extended the game by adding extra levels, but for this game we'll do something a little different. Expanding on our use of views in Chapter 10, we'll create the whole pyramid as one huge level. This will provide our intrepid explorer with a worthy challenge, and give you plenty of space in which to devise cunning tricks and traps.

For this game we need a single view that shows the explorer and the pyramid. The view will scroll around the pyramid following the explorer. If any of this doesn't make sense, be sure to go back to Chapter 10 where there is a much more detailed explanation.

Creating the view:

1. Open `room_pyramid` and select the **settings** tab. Change the **Width** to 1920 and the **Height** to 2400. This will be plenty big enough for our pyramid, but you can feel free to make it bigger later on.

2. Select the **views** tab. First enable the option **Enable the use of views**.

3. Select **View 0** in the list. Enable the option **Visible when room starts**.

4. Under **View in room** keep the default values: **X**: 0, **Y**: 0, **W**: 640, **H**: 480. Note that the view is shown in the room.

5. Under **Port on screen** also keep the default values: **X**: 0, **Y**: 0, **W**: 640, **H**: 480.

6. Under **Object Following** click the menu icon and select `obj_explorer`. Set **Hbor** to 300 and **Vbor** to 220. This will keep the explorer nicely centered in the view.

7. Now you can extend your maze to fill the whole room. There's not much to do yet, but don't worry—we'll fix that soon.

It's probably best to try out your game now to check that the view works. As you move around the maze, the view should scroll so that the explorer is always in view. Our next step is to adapt the controller object to draw a status panel with information about the number of lives and the score.

Extending the controller object:

1. Create two sprites using the files `Panel.gif` and `Lives.gif`. Make sure that the panel sprite is not transparent.

2. Create a font that will be used for the score. We used a size 14 bold Arial font.

3. Reopen the properties form for the controller object. Set the **Depth** to -100 to make sure it lies in front of all other objects.

 4. Add a **Draw** event. We need to make sure the panel is drawn in the correct position in the view. To this end, we first move the controller object to the correct position. As explained in Chapter 10, we can use the variables `view_xview[0]` and `view_yview[0]` for this. Include a **Jump to Position** action and set **X** to `view_xview[0]` and **Y** to `view_yview[0]+448`.

 5. Include the **Draw Sprite** action with **Sprite** set to the panel sprite, **X** set to 0, **Y** set to 0, and the **Relative** option enabled. Also include the **Draw Life Images** action, with **Image** set to the lives sprite, **X** set to 80, **Y** set to 2, and the **Relative** option enabled.

 6. Include a **Set Font** action and select the score font. Set **Align** to right. Also include a **Set Color** action and choose a nice yellow for the color. Finally, include the **Draw Score** action with **X** set to 585, **Y** set to 5, the **Caption** set to the empty string, and the **Relative** option enabled.

That's it for the view. Start up the game and check that the panel is drawn correctly. This version of the game can also be found in the file `Games/Chapter14/pyramid3.gm6` on the CD.

Reactive Behavior

It is now time to start dealing with the topic of this chapter: behavior. We want our pyramid to be inhabited with creatures that our explorer needs to avoid. We'll create a number of different enemies; the first ones will be rather stupid, and will be controlled by some simple reactive behavior. Later, enemies will use rules that guide their behavior, and the cleverest enemies will have different states, depending on the current situation.

Reactive behavior is the simplest kind of behavior you can think of. The entity reacts to different events. Actually, this is what we have been doing throughout the book—we have created objects and indicated their reactions to events. You could say that Game Maker is completely based on the idea of reactive behavior. However, this is the first time we have studied the concept in depth, and it does warrant a good deal of discussion when trying to program better games.

Here we will create a beetle enemy that simply moves up and down. It will react to two different events: when it hits a block it will change its direction of motion, and when the explorer is in front of it, it will move toward the player and double its speed of motion. This gives the impression that the beetle notices the explorer and runs to try to catch him, making the game more interesting to play. We'll also create a scorpion that operates in the same fashion, but instead moves left and right.

Before we do this let's create a dummy object called obj_enemy. This object will be the parent of all the enemy objects; this makes it possible to define one collision event for the explorer that deals with all different enemies. We'll also use it to destroy the enemy—our explorer doesn't always go down without a fight! It is a good habit to divide your objects into subgroups and make them share a parent object for common behavior.

Creating the basic enemy object:

1. Create a sound from the file Die.wav and call it snd_die.

2. Create an object and call it obj_enemy. It does not need a sprite.

3. Reopen the properties form for the explorer object, and add a **Collision** event with obj_enemy. Include the **Execute Code** action. Here we'll play the dying sound, reduce the number of lives, redraw the screen, sleep a while, and then set the explorer back to his start position and destroy the enemy:

```
{
    sound_play(snd_die);
    lives -= 1;
    screen_redraw();
    sleep(1000);
    x = xstart;
    y = ystart;
    move_snap(32,32);
    with(other)
    {
        instance_destroy();
    }
}
```

Note the use of the **with** statement. As explained in Chapter 11, with this statement we can execute code as if it were being run on another object. Later in the chapter we will also see how **with** can be used to act on whole groups of objects in the same way.

With the basic enemy defined we'll now create the beetle object.

Creating the beetle object:

1. Create two sprites using the files `Beetle_up.gif` and `Beetle_down.gif`, and give them the names `spr_beetle_up` and `spr_beetle_down`, respectively. In both cases, disable the option **Precise collision checking**, and select the **Full image** option found under **Bounding Box**.

2. Create an object and call it `obj_beetle`. Give it the `spr_beetle_down` sprite, and indicate `obj_enemy` as its **Parent**.

 3. Add a **Create** event and include the **Move Fixed** action. Indicate a downward direction and a **Speed** of 2.

 4. Add a **Collision** event with `obj_wall1` and include a **Reverse Vertical** action.

 5. Add the **Step, End Step** event. Include an **Execute Code** action with the following code, which adapts the sprite to the direction of motion:

```
{
    if ( vspeed > 0 )
        sprite_index = spr_beetle_down
    else
        sprite_index = spr_beetle_up;
}
```

Now if you add some beetles to a room, you will notice that they nicely move up and down, and that the explorer dies when he touches one of them. But this is not very intelligent beetle behavior. We'll now add a piece of code that makes the beetle react to the presence of the explorer. If the explorer is on the same row of the maze as the beetle and in front of it, the beetle will speed up and run toward him.

Making the beetle object more intelligent:

 1. Add the **Step, Step** event, then include an **Execute Code** action containing the following code:

```
{
    speed = 2;
    if ( x == obj_explorer.x )
    {
        if ( (direction == 90) && (y > obj_explorer.y) )
        {
            speed = 4;
```

```
        }
        else if ( (direction == 270) && (y < obj_explorer.y) )
        {
            speed = 4;
        }
    }
}
```

You should now create a scorpion object that acts in exactly the same way as the beetles, only it moves horizontally, not vertically.

Creating the scorpion object:

1. Create two sprites using the files Scorpion_left.gif and Scorpion_right.gif, and give them the names spr_scorpion_left and spr_scorpion_right, respectively. In both cases, disable the option **Precise collision checking**, and select the **Full image** option found under **Bounding Box**.

2. Create an object and call it obj_scorpion. Give it the spr_scorpion_right sprite, and indicate obj_enemy as its **Parent**.

3. Define the behavior of the scorpion object using the same events and similar actions and code as for the beetle object.

You can stop and try your game out now if you like, but I think it's worth waiting until we've put some treasure in before we do that—after all, who wants to dodge all of those deadly monsters without some sort of reward!

Time for Treasure!

Now it's time to add some treasure to the room for the explorer to discover. There will be two different treasure types: the first one will occur many times in the maze, and each piece of this treasure will give the player 10 points. The second treasure type is rarer but much more valuable when collected. You can place it at difficult locations in the room to give the player a real challenge to aim toward.

Creating the treasure objects:

1. Create two sprites using the files Treasure1.gif and Treasure2.gif. For each of them, disable the **Precise collision checking** option and select the **Full image** option found under **Bounding Box**.

2. Create a sound using the Treasure.wav file and call it snd_treasure.

3. Create an object for the first treasure and assign the first sprite to it. Give it a **Depth** of 10 to make sure that enemies appear over it.

4. Add a **Collision** event with the explorer object, and include an **Execute Code** action within it with the following code that increases the score, destroys the treasure, and plays the treasure sound:

```
{
    score += 10;
    instance_destroy();
    sound_play(snd_treasure);
}
```

5. Create an object for the second treasure, assign the second sprite to it, and give it a **Depth** of 10. Add a **Collision** event with the explorer, and include an **Execute Code** action containing the preceding code, except that this time the score increment must be 100 rather than 10.

You should now enhance your level to include some treasure for the explorer to discover and some enemies to guard it. Test your game and see how the beetles and scorpions add to the challenge.

Movable Blocks

To create more interesting challenges, we'll introduce two special blocks that can be pushed by the player. One type of block can only be pushed horizontally, while the other type can only be pushed vertically. Only the explorer will be able to push the blocks. These will be magical blocks, which will return to their original position when the explorer stops pushing them. The original position of each block can easily be determined, as it is always available in the variables xstart and ystart. Then by checking the current position compared to its start position, we can determine which direction the block must move to get back to its original position. We will do this in the **End Step** event to make sure it happens after all other events have been processed.

Creating the block objects:

1. Create a sprite using the file Block_hor.gif, and disable the **Transparent** option.

2. Create a sound from the file Block.wav and call it snd_block.

3. Create an object for the horizontal block and give it the above sprite. Enable the **Solid** option, and indicate the first wall object as the **Parent**, as the block should behave a lot like a wall.

4. Add the **Step, End Step** event. Include an **Execute Code** action and type in the following piece of code, which moves the block instance back toward its start position and plays the sound:

```
{
    if ( (x < xstart) && place_empty(x+2,y) )
    {
        x += 2 ;
        sound_play(snd_block);
```

```
    }
    if ( (x > xstart) && place_empty(x-2,y) )
    {
        x -= 2;
        sound_play(snd_block);
    }
}
```

5. Reopen the properties form for the explorer object and add a **Collision** event with the horizontal block. Include the **Execute Code** action, and indicate the **Other** object at the top under **Applies To**, as we want to move the block. Now type the following code—in it we first check whether the explorer has moved horizontally. If he has, we check whether we can move the block the same amount.

```
{
    if ( obj_explorer.hspeed == 0 ) exit;
    if ( place_empty(x+obj_explorer.hspeed,y) )
    {
        x += obj_explorer.hspeed;
        sound_play(snd_block);
    }
}
```

6. Repeat the previous steps to create the vertical moving block. Create the sprite and the object and include similar pieces of code, this time moving vertically.

░**Note** You might have wondered why we defined the collision event in the explorer object and not in the moving block object. The reason is that we want to replace the default collision behavior with the first wall. Otherwise, the explorer would stop moving.

Now let's test our blocks—add some horizontal and vertical moving blocks to your room. Make sure there is space next to the blocks so that they can be moved. With some careful level design, you can now create one-way doors to add to the maze's challenge, as well as other clever puzzles. The current version of the game can be found in the file Games/Chapter14/pyramid4.gm6 on the CD. Be sure to come back soon, though—we're just about to introduce the big bad guys and you won't want to miss it!

Rule-Based Behavior

To make our ultimate AI opponent, we are going to want some pretty complicated behavior. A convenient way of defining behavior is to use rules. Thinking in terms of rules helps you to clearly describe how entities must behave. A rule indicates that if certain conditions are met, certain actions must be taken. So a rule has the form

conditions ➤ actions

Although you may not have realized it at the time, we have already used a rule in the previous section. We indicated that if the x-coordinates of the beetle and the explorer are equal, the beetle must move fast toward the explorer:

x-coordinates equal and facing explorer ➤ move fast toward explorer

There even was a second, default rule that said that if the x-coordinates of the beetle and the explorer were not equal, or the beetle was facing the other way, then the beetle should move with a slower speed. Also, the collision with a wall can be formulated as a rule. So in total there were three rules:

x-coordinates equal and facing explorer ➤ move fast toward explorer

x-coordinates not equal or facing away ➤ move slowly

collision with wall ➤ reverse vertical direction away from the wall

The first two rules are exclusive, that is, they can never both be true. But the third can be true at the same time as one of the other two. In such a situation, it is important to decide what should happen. Should both actions be executed, or just one, and if so, which one? Does one rule have priority over another, or should a random one be picked? In our previous example the third rule should definitely have priority over the other rules, as the beetle should never be allowed to move into a wall.

Creating rule-based behavior consists of defining a set of rules and indicating what should happen when multiple rules are valid. A rule consists of one or more conditions and the actions that must be followed in the case the conditions are true. Typical conditions that are often used in games are as follows:

- Is a position or direction collision-free?

- Is the enemy near to the player?

- Is the player in a particular direction relative to the enemy?

- Can the enemy see the player?

- Does the enemy or the player carry a particular item?

All these conditions can easily by tested in Game Maker as we'll see in a moment; however, first we need to create the mummy object that can use these conditions to drive its behavior.

Creating the mummy object:

1. Create four sprites using the files `Mummy_left.gif`, `Mummy_right.gif`, `Mummy_up.gif`, and `Mummy_down.gif`. Name them `spr_mummy_left`, `spr_mummy_right`, `spr_mummy_up`, and `spr_mummy_down`.

2. For each of the sprites, disable the **Precise collision checking** option, and select the **Full image** option under **Bounding Box**.

3. Create a new object for the mummy and name it `obj_mummy`. Give it the downward-moving mummy sprite and indicate `obj_enemy` as its **Parent**.

4. Add a **Create** event and in it include the **Move Fixed** action. Give it a downward direction and a **Speed** of 4.

5. Add the **Step, End Step** event. Here we'll set the correct sprite and animation speed. Include an **Execute Code** action and type in the following piece of code:

```
{
    image_speed = 1/3;
    if (hspeed < 0) sprite_index = spr_mummy_left;
    if (hspeed > 0) sprite_index = spr_mummy_right;
    if (vspeed < 0) sprite_index = spr_mummy_up;
    if (vspeed > 0) sprite_index = spr_mummy_down;
}
```

As it stands, the mummy will simply walk through the walls, but don't despair—we'll give it better behavior next.

Walking Around

The first behavior we want to define for the mummy is simply walking around through the level. This is more difficult than it might seem. At each cell there are four possible directions the mummy can choose. Some might be blocked by walls, and are therefore forbidden. Once all of the forbidden choices are removed, we must pick one of the available ones. To ensure natural motion, we'll make sure that we never go back in the direction we came from, unless this is the only possible direction to take (when we go into a dead end). For the other directions, we'll pick a valid one randomly.

How do we turn this into rules? Let ahead, left, and right indicate whether these three positions are free. We have the following rules:

not ahead and **not** left and **not** right ➤ move back

ahead ➤ move straight ahead

left ➤ turn left

right ➤ turn right

The first rule is exclusive from the others, so if the first rule is valid, all others are not valid. The other three rules can all be valid at the same moment, and as we mentioned earlier, we should pick a random valid one.

The next step is to turn this into a GML script (see Listing 14-1). To determine the value of ahead, left, and right, we'll use the function place_free, and to make a random choice we'll use a similar method to Chapter 13. To make the script easier to understand, we have also split the code based on whether the mummy is moving horizontally or vertically.

Listing 14-1. *The Script scr_behavior_walk*

```
{
    var ahead, left, right;
    if ( !place_snapped(32,32) ) exit;
    if (vspeed == 0)
    {
        ahead = place_free(x+hspeed,y);
        left = place_free(x,y+4);
        right = place_free(x,y-4);
        if (!ahead && !left && !right) {direction += 180; exit;}
        while (true)   // forever
        {
            if (ahead && random(3)<1) {exit;}
            if (left && random(3)<1) {direction = 270; exit;}
            if (right && random(3)<1) {direction = 90; exit;}
        }
    }
    else
    {
        ahead = place_free(x,y+vspeed);
        left = place_free(x+4,y);
        right = place_free(x-4,y);
        if (!ahead && !left && !right) {vspeed = -vspeed; exit;}
        while (true)   // forever
        {
            if (ahead && random(3)<1) {exit;}
            if (left && random(3)<1) {direction = 0; exit;}
            if (right && random(3)<1) {direction = 180; exit;}
        }
    }
}
```

Let's analyze this script in detail. We use three local variables to store values that specify whether the three possible positions are collision free. We first test whether the mummy is aligned with the grid. If not, we exit the script, as nothing needs to be done.

Next we distinguish between a horizontal motion (vspeed == 0) and a vertical motion. We'll discuss just the horizontal motion here, as the vertical motion is treated in a similar fashion. We first determine the values of the variables ahead, left, and right. Next, we check whether the first rule is valid. If so, we reverse the direction and exit the code. To pick one of the other rules randomly, we use a loop that continues forever until a rule is picked. To pick a rule with a one-in-three chance we check each time whether random(3)<1. This happens on average one out of three times. So in each execution of the loop we try each rule with a one-in-three chance and, if it is valid, we execute the rule and exit the code. We can even change the chances with which rules are picked. For example, we could give a motion straight ahead a bigger chance by, for example, checking whether random(2)<1. It is essential that we know that at least one rule is valid; otherwise, the loop would run forever—in our earlier example we know this won't be the case.

Note that this time we use a script rather than an **Execute Code** action. This is because we want to use this as a function in later code. For the moment we'll use this script in the **Step** event of the mummy object.

Giving the mummy object behavior:

1. Create the script scr_behavior_walk, as indicated earlier.

2. Reopen the properties form of the mummy object.

3. Add the **Step, Step** event, then include an **Execute Script** action and indicate the script scr_behavior_walk.

Place mummies in some of the rooms and test their behavior; the mummies should traverse the maze successfully.

Moving Toward the Explorer

Our second behavior tries to move the mummy toward the explorer. To this end we must first determine the direction the player is in relation to the mummy. We'll store this in a local variable called dir. This direction between two points can be calculated using the function point_direction(), which gives a value between 0 and 360 degrees. To turn it into one of four choices, we can divide it by 90, round it to the nearest integer number, and make our decision based on the resulting value. This will always be 0, 1, 2, or 3. The value 0 means to the right, 1 to the top, 2 to the left, and 3 to the bottom. We can now give the mummy the following rules to follow:

dir == 0 and can move right ➤ move right

dir == 1 and can move up ➤ move up

dir == 2 and can move left ➤ move left

dir == 3 and can move down ➤ move down

These rules are exclusive. Whether we can actually move in a particular direction depends on whether that direction is collision free in the first place. Also, we want to avoid the mummy reversing its direction. If all rules fail, we call the previous behavior. This can all be achieved using the script in Listing 14-2.

Listing 14-2. *The Script scr_behavior_towards*

```
{
    if ( !place_snapped(32,32) ) exit;
    // find out in which direction the explorer is located
    var dir;
    dir = point_direction(x,y,obj_explorer.x,obj_explorer.y);
    dir = round(dir/90);
    if (dir == 4) dir = 0;
    // the four rules that move the mummy in the explorer's direction
    if (dir == 0 && direction != 180 && place_free(x+4,y))
        { direction = 0; exit; }
```

```
    if (dir == 1 && direction != 270 && place_free(x,y-4))
        { direction = 90; exit; }
    if (dir == 2 && direction !=   0 && place_free(x-4,y))
        { direction = 180; exit; }
    if (dir == 3 && direction !=  90 && place_free(x,y+4))
        { direction = 270; exit; }
    // otherwise do the normal walking behavior
    scr_behavior_walk();
}
```

Try replacing the behavior of the mummy with this new behavior. You will notice that the mummy moves toward you rather rapidly, and it is almost impossible to finish the game—we made the mummy a bit too clever! To make things fairer for the explorer, we should not always use our intelligent behavior. In particular, we should not do it at all if the explorer is far away. This can be achieved using the following behavior. We first compute the distance between the mummy and the player. Then we check whether the mummy can see the player. For this we check whether the line between the centers of the two instances does not collide with a wall. We now use the following rules:

if player can be seen ➤ move toward player

if distance is larger than 200 ➤ walk around

otherwise ➤ with one-in-two chance move toward the player, otherwise walk around

These rules are in order of priority, so we'll execute the first one that is valid. This is achieved using the script in Listing 14-3.

Listing 14-3. *The Script scr_behavior_total*

```
{
    if ( !place_snapped(32,32) ) exit;
    // Calculate distance and visibility
    var dist,vis;
    dist = point_distance(x,y,obj_explorer.x,obj_explorer.y);
    vis = !collision_line(x+16,y+16,obj_explorer.x+16,obj_explorer.y+16,
                          obj_wall1,false,false);
    // Execute the rules in order
    if (vis) { scr_behavior_towards(); exit; }
    if (dist>200) { scr_behavior_walk(); exit; }
    if (random(2)<1) { scr_behavior_towards(); exit; }
    scr_behavior_walk();
}
```

To use the new script, make the following changes.

Improving the mummy object behavior:

1. Create the scripts `scr_behavior_towards` and `scr_behavior_total`, shown earlier.

2. Reopen the properties form of the mummy object.

3. Select the normal **Step** event. Select the **Execute Script** action and change the script to `scr_behavior_total`.

Our mummy now displays some interesting behavior. Try putting some mummies in the pyramid room in interesting configurations, to test out everything we have so far. You can also try to change the behavior—for example, by changing the maximum distance away that the mummy can be before it stops reacting to the explorer, or the chance that the mummy responds when in range. You will find the current version of the game in the file Games/Chapter14/pyramid5.gm6 on the CD. You might find the game with the mummies is a bit hard at this point, but don't worry too much as we'll modify them next to provide a more realistic challenge.

Dealing with States

We have so far created some interesting behavior for our pyramid denizens using rules. However, think about real life; people don't just behave according to one set of rules—they adapt their behavior based on the current situation. We could add this type of thing in Game Maker using rules, but that would make the collection of rules huge and hard to keep consistent.

Instead, it is easier to introduce states. For each situation, a character will choose an appropriate state. By creating a state for each situation, we can keep the number of rules for each state small but still create complicated and realistic behavior. When something happens, a character can change state, which can result in different behavior. To start, we'll give our mummy three states: wandering around, searching for the explorer, and chasing the explorer.

State changes can occur when particular events happen, or they can occur according to rules. For example, the wandering mummy changes into a searching mummy when it gets close to the explorer. This one in turn becomes a chasing mummy when it can see the explorer. Such a system, with a finite number of states and events that cause state changes, is called a *finite-state machine*. It is common to draw such a finite-state machine as a diagram in which nodes correspond to the states and arrows correspond to state changes. For our mummy, such a diagram would look like Figure 14-2.

For each of these states, we can then define behavior. In the wandering state, the mummy just walks around. In the searching state, the mummy moves toward the explorer from time to time. Finally, in the chasing state the mummy always moves toward the explorer. We have all of the basic behaviors for this already. We'll use the states to control how they are used.

Using states is very simple in Game Maker. We'll just use a different object for each state. We'll keep our mummy object, but we'll remove the behavior from it, and use it as a parent for the other mummy objects. Remember that the mummy object still has the enemy object as its parent, so our new objects will inherit behavior from both. Three objects are then created for the three different states. In the step event of these objects, we call the correct behavior script.

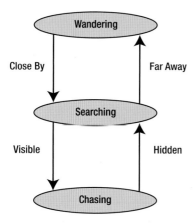

Figure 14-2. *The finite-state machine consists of three states.*

The only remaining thing to do is to indicate the state changes. We use the **Begin Step** event for this. This event is executed at the beginning of each step, which is a good time to test whether the state should change. If we do need to change state, we'll use the instance_change() function to transform the object into the appropriate type. As well as changing the behavior of the mummies in each state, we'll change the speed. This will make the mummies a little easier to avoid, and after all, mummies just wandering about the pyramid are hardly going to move at the same speed as the ones who are chasing our explorer!

Creating a different mummy object:

1. Reopen the properties form of the mummy object.

2. Select the normal **Step** event and click the **Delete** button to remove it.

3. Create a new object and call it obj_mummy_wander, give it the downward-looking mummy sprite, and indicate obj_mummy as its **Parent**.

4. Add the **Step, Step** event. Include an **Execute Script** action and indicate the script scr_behavior_walk.

5. Add the **Step, Begin Step** event. Here we want to tell the mummy to change into a searching mummy when we get close to the explorer (the searching mummy must still be created). Because the searching mummy goes at a slightly faster speed, we also need to check that our position is snapped to a grid at that new speed (in this case 2). Without this check, the mummies can get out of alignment with the grid and move through walls. Include an **Execute Code** action and type the following code:

```
{
    speed = 1; // wandering mummies go slowly
    if ( point_distance(x,y,obj_explorer.x,obj_explorer.y) < 200 )
    {
        if (!place_snapped(2,2) ) exit;
        instance_change(obj_mummy_search,false);
    }
}
```

6. Create a new object and call it obj_mummy_search, give it the mummy sprite, and indicate obj_mummy as its **Parent**.

7. Add the **Step, Step** event. Include a **Test Chance** action and indicate 2 for the number of sides. Include an **Execute Script** action and indicate the script scr_behavior_walk.

8. Next Include an **Else** action and another **Execute Script** action, and indicate the script scr_behavior_towards. This gives us our search behavior as described earlier.

9. Add the **Step, Begin Step** event. Here we want to change back into a wandering mummy when we get too far away from the explorer or into a chasing mummy when we see the explorer. Again we need to check that we are snapped to the grid at the new speed (although we can ignore this for the wandering mummy as all positions are snapped to 1 pixel). Include an **Execute Code** action and type the following code:

```
{
    speed = 2;
    if ( !collision_line(x+16,y+16,obj_explorer.x+16,obj_explorer.y+16,
                         obj_wall1,false,false) )
    {
        if ( !place_snapped(4,4) ) exit;
        instance_change(obj_mummy_chase,false);
    }
    if ( point_distance(x,y,obj_explorer.x,obj_explorer.y) > 200 )
    {
        instance_change(obj_mummy_wander,false);
    }
}
```

10. Create a new object and call it obj_mummy_chase, give it the mummy sprite, and indicate obj_mummy as its **Parent**.

11. Add the **Step, Step** event. Include an **Execute Script** action and indicate the script scr_behavior_towards.

12. Add the **Step, Begin Step** event. Here we want to change back into a searching mummy when we no longer see the explorer. Note that we don't need to check whether the place is snapped here because any place that is snapped to 4 is also snapped to 2. Include an **Execute Code** action and type the following code:

```
{
    speed = 4;    // chasing mummies really shift
    if ( collision_line(x+16,y+16,obj_explorer.x+16,obj_explorer.y+16,
                        obj_wall1,false,false) )
        instance_change(obj_mummy_search,false);
}
```

13. Delete the script `scr_behavior_total`, as we no longer need it.

14. In the pyramid room, replace all the mummy instances with wandering mummy instances.

Now test the game again. The new mummies should be more realistic, and carefully sneaking past them should be a fun challenge. You can find this version of the game in the file `Games/Chapter14/pyramid6.gm6` on the CD.

Scarabs

If you add a lot of mummies to your game, it is still pretty difficult to escape the pyramid alive. To give the explorer a better chance against the mummies, we're going to introduce a scarab object. When the explorer uses a scarab, the mummies become temporarily vulnerable and the explorer can destroy them. To this end we need an additional state for the mummy—the afraid state. When the mummy is afraid, it will no longer move toward the explorer but will instead simply wander around. If the player catches a mummy, the mummy will be destroyed and the player's score will increase. Our new finite-state machine will now look like Figure 14-3.

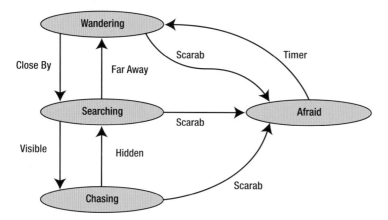

Figure 14-3. *The extended finite-state diagram contains four states.*

To implement this, we add a new mummy object for the afraid state. The afraid mummy will have the same behavior as the wandering mummy, but its state changes are handled differently.

Creating the afraid mummy object:

1. Create a new object and call it `obj_mummy_afraid`, give it the mummy sprite, and indicate `obj_mummy` as its **Parent**.

2. Add the **Step, Step** event. Include an **Execute Script** action and indicate the script `scr_behavior_walk`.

Next we must create the scarab object.

Creating the scarab object:

1. Create a sprite using the file `Scarab.gif`.

2. Create a new object, call it `obj_scarab`, give it the scarab sprite, and give it a **Depth** of `10`. It does not need any behavior.

Next we'll extend the explorer object to deal with scarabs. As well as collecting scarabs, the explorer needs to be able to use them. For this we'll create a **Key Press, <Shift>** event where we turn all mummies into afraid mummies, and we'll set up some alarms to turn the mummies back when the scarab is used up.

Extending the explorer object:

1. We need some sounds for when we activate the scarab power, so create `snd_power_start` with the file `PowerStart.wav` and `snd_power_end` with the file `PowerEnd.wav`.

2. Reopen the properties form for the explorer object. Select the **Create** event and change the code by setting the variable `scarab_count` to `0`. We'll use `scarab_count` to check how many scarabs the explorer is carrying and whether he can use one to chase the mummies away. The new code should look like this:

```
{
    image_speed = 0;
    scarab_count = 0;
}
```

 3. Add a **Collision** event with `obj_scarab`. Include an **Execute Code** action and add the following code, which plays a sound, increases the score, and destroys the scarab object. It also adds 1 to the explorer's scarab count.

```
{
    sound_play(snd_treasure);
    score += 50;
    scarab_count += 1;
    with (other) instance_destroy();
}
```

 4. Add a **Key Pressed, <Shift>** event. Include an **Execute Code** event with the following code, which sets **Alarm0** to `300` (10 seconds) and turns all mummies into afraid mummies. We also set **Alarm1** so that we can play the end sound slightly before the timer ends so the explorer has some warning. But before this is done, the code checks to see that the explorer has collected a scarab, and if he has, it reduces `scarab_count` by 1 to indicate that the scarab has been used.

```
{
    if ( scarab_count > 0 )
    {
        with (obj_mummy) instance_change(obj_mummy_afraid,false);
        alarm[0] = 300;    // scarab timer
        alarm[1] = 240;    // end of scarab sound timer
```

```
            scarab_count -= 1;
            sound_play(snd_power_start)
        }
    }
}
```

 5. Add the **Alarm0** event. Include an **Execute Code** action with the following code, which turns all surviving mummies back into wandering mummies:

```
{
    with (obj_mummy) instance_change(obj_mummy_wander,false);
}
```

 6. Add the **Alarm1** event. Include a **Play Sound** action with snd_power_end to play the end of power sound.

Next we define a collision event between the explorer and the scared mummy. Here we play a sound, increase the score, and destroy the mummy instance. As this event overrides the collision event with the basic enemy object, the explorer is not killed in this case.

Handling the collision between the explorer and the scared mummy:

1. Create a sound with the name snd_scared using the file Scared.wav.

2. Reopen the properties form for the explorer object.

 3. Add a **Collision** event with obj_mummy_afraid. Insert an **Execute Code** action and add the following code, which plays a sound, increases the score, and destroys the mummy:

```
{
    sound_play(snd_scared);
    score += 100;
    with (other) instance_destroy();
}
```

The explorer can now collect and use scarabs, but there is no indication of how many he has collected. In order to make this clearer to the player, let's extend our display at the bottom of the screen to include the explorer's scarab count.

Extending the score display:

1. Reopen the properties form for obj_controller.

 2. At the end of the **Draw** event add a **Draw Sprite** action with **Sprite** set to spr_scarab, **X** set to 290, **Y** set to 1, and the **Relative** option enabled.

 3. Add a **Draw Variable** action and choose obj_explorer.scarab_count as the variable. Set **X** to 340 and **Y** to 5, and enable the **Relative** option.

In order to help the player we'll visually indicate whether or not the mummy is afraid. We can achieve this by changing the color of the sprite. We'll actually take this a step further and also use different colors for the searching and chasing mummy. This will make it clear to the player when he must be careful.

Note Changing the sprite color is only possible in the registered version of Game Maker. If you do not have a registered copy, you must solve this differently—for example, by using a different sprite or by indicating the status on the panel at the bottom.

Changing the color of the different mummy objects:

1. Reopen the properties form for obj_mummy_afraid, and select the **Step** event. Include the **Color Sprite** action from the **main1** panel. Indicate a blue color.

2. Reopen the properties form for obj_mummy_wander, and select the **Step** event. Include the **Color Sprite** action and indicate a white color.

3. Reopen the properties form for obj_mummy_search, and select the **Step** event. Include the **Color Sprite** action and indicate an orange color.

4. Reopen the properties form for obj_mummy_chase, and select the **Step** event. Include the **Color Sprite** action and indicate a red color.

Before we finish this section, we've got one more trick up our sleeves. With plenty of mummies in the game, it's still pretty hard, so to help the player out let's add some health potions to give the player extra lives.

Creating the potion object:

1. Create a sprite spr_potion with the Potion.gif file.

2. Now create an obj_potion object and assign the spr_potion sprite. Give it a **Depth** of 10 so that enemies move on top of it.

3. Reopen the properties form for the explorer object.

4. Add a **Collision** event with the obj_potion object and insert the **Execute Code** action. In the code window type the following code:

```
{
    lives += 1;
    with (other) instance_destroy();
}
```

Add some scarabs, potions, and some more mummies and test the game thoroughly. If it seems too hard, you can add extra scarabs or potions. If it is too easy, adding some more mummies will fix that. Now that the explorer has a way to fight back, you should begin to find that the game is much more fun to play and that balancing it is much easier. You will find the current version of the game in the file Games/Chapter14/pyramid7.gm6 on the CD.

Let There Be Light

As the final touch for our game, we'll be adding a second objective. As well as escaping alive, our explorer will be searching for the pyramid's biggest treasure, the Sword of Ra. The Sword of Ra will be worth a staggering 5,000 points, but it won't be all positive. Drawing the sword will switch off all of the lights in the pyramid. The explorer will be able to use the dim light that the sword still produces to light his way, and it will also scare away the mummies, but every second it is activated will drain his score and reduce his eventual wealth.

▓**Note** This section requires a registered version of Game Maker because it uses some features that are not available in the free version.

To implement this, we need a couple of ingredients. First, we need a way to show only part of the world. We'll use a global variable called `global.swordon` to indicate whether or not the sword is activated. This will tell us whether our light should light only close to the explorer or further out. We'll also extend the controller object to control the light. In its **Create** event, we'll set `global.swordon` to false to indicate that the sword is not activated. When the player presses or releases the spacebar, we switch the value from false to true and back. Finally, in the draw event of the controller we must hide the part of the world that cannot be seen. To make sure that the panel at the bottom of the screen is unaffected, we'll do this draw step before drawing the panel.

To hide part of the room, we use a special form of blending. We add the image in Figure 14-4 as a background, and then subtract this image from the room image. Normally images we draw replace the background image. But we can change the blend mode to get different effects. Don't forget to set the blend mode back to normal afterward.

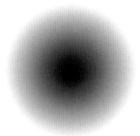

Figure 14-4. *We subtract this image from the room image.*

As this image is black (0) in the center, nothing is subtracted there, but more is subtracted as you go toward the outside of the image, until the image is completely white on the outside. At that point everything is subtracted, leaving the area outside the image completely black (we simply fill this area with black rectangles as nothing can be seen there). You can see the result in Figure 14-5, which is pretty impressive and results in a creepier feeling.

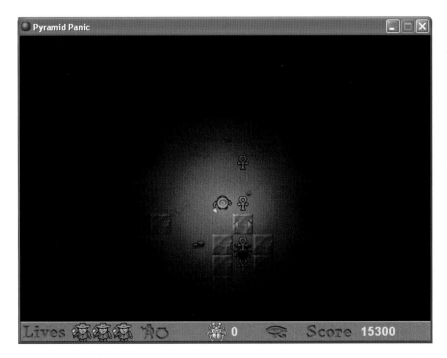

Figure 14-5. *Subtracting the image from the room gives a creepy feeling.*

The script in Listing 14-4 achieves this. As arguments, the script gets the location of the light. Depending on the value of the variable global.swordon, it determines the size of the lit area. Next, it draws black rectangles about this area. Finally, it sets the blend mode, draws the light image in the correct size, and sets the blend mode back to normal.

Listing 14-4. *The Script scr_light*

```
{
    // Only draw if the explorer has found the sword
    if ( !obj_explorer.has_sword ) exit;
    // First determine the size of the lit area
    var x1,y1,x2,y2,ww;
    if ( global.swordon ) ww = 800 else ww = 300;
    x1 = argument0-ww/2;
    x2 = argument0+ww/2;
    y1 = argument1-ww/2;
    y2 = argument1+ww/2;
    // Hide things that are far away by drawing black rectangles
    draw_set_color(c_black);
    draw_rectangle(0,0,x1,room_height,false);
    draw_rectangle(x2,0,room_width,room_height,false);
    draw_rectangle(0,0,room_width,y1,false);
    draw_rectangle(0,y2,room_width,room_height,false);
    // Now hide nearby stuff by subtracting the light image
```

```
        draw_set_blend_mode(bm_subtract);
        draw_background_stretched(back_light,x1,y1,ww,ww);
        draw_set_blend_mode(bm_normal);
    }
```

The script must be called at the beginning of the **Draw** event of the controller object.

Extending the controller object:

1. Create a background resource from the file `Light.bmp` and name it `back_light`.

2. Create the script `scr_light` as described earlier.

3. Reopen the properties form for the controller object.

4. Add the **Create** event and include the **Set Variable** action, with **Variable** set to `global.swordon` and **Value** to false.

5. Select the **Draw** event. At the start of the list of actions include the **Execute Script** action. As **Script** select `scr_light`. As **Argument0** indicate `obj_explorer.x+16`, and as **Argument1** indicate `obj_explorer.y+16`. This will center the light on the explorer.

Next we need to create the sword object.

Creating the sword object:

1. Create a sprite from the file `Sword.gif`.

2. Create an object using this sprite and call it `obj_sword`. Set the **Depth** to `10`. No events or actions are required.

Now we need to edit the explorer object to handle collision with the sword, and to allow the player to use the sword's power when it is needed.

Extending the explorer object:

1. Reopen the properties form for the explorer object. In the **Create** event, open the **Execute Code** action and add the line `has_sword = false;`. This makes sure that the explorer starts out without the sword.

2. Now add a **Collision** event with `obj_sword`. Include the **Execute Code** action and type the following code:

```
    {
        score += 5000;
        sound_play(snd_treasure);
        show_message("As you draw the mighty Sword of Ra the lights go out!" +
                    "##Frighten the mummies, but don't lose your treasures. ");
        has_sword = true;
        with (other)  instance_destroy();
    }
```

This is very similar to the **Collision** events with the other types of treasure, but we also set the variable has_sword to true and show a message. Showing a message like this helps to indicate to the player that something really special has happened and makes the player feel a real sense of achievement.

3. Add the **Keyboard, <Space>** event, and include the **Execute Code** action. Add the following code:

```
{
    if ( has_sword && (score > 0) )
    {
        global.swordon = true;
        with (obj_mummy) instance_change(obj_mummy_afraid,false);
        score -= 10;
    }
}
```

This checks that the explorer has found the sword, and also that he still has score to feed it. If both of those things are true, it changes all of the mummies into scared mummies and subtracts 10 from the score. Because this event happens every step that the spacebar is held, this subtracts 300 points per second. You'll soon spend all 5000 points the sword gave you if you're not careful!

4. Add the **Key Release, <Space>** event. Include the **Execute Code** action and type the following code:

```
{
    if ( has_sword )
    {
        global.swordon = false;
        if ( alarm[0] <= 0 )
        {
            with (obj_mummy_afraid) instance_change(obj_mummy_wander,false);
        }
    }
}
```

This sets global.swordon back to false and turns all of the mummies back to wandering mummies. Before it does this, though, it double-checks that **Alarm0** is not running. This ensures that it does not turn the mummies back if a scarab is currently in use.

And there you go. Put one instance of the sword object at a special place in the pyramid room and test that it works. But before we finally wrap this game up, there's one more change to make to the mummies. Now that the lights are out, it would be a bit unfair if the mummies still detected the explorer from the same distance. To change that, let's check the obj_explorer.has_sword variable; if it is true we'll make the distance smaller to reflect the small amount of light.

Adapting the behavior of the mummy object:

1. Reopen the properties form for the wandering mummy, select the **Begin Step** event, and double-click on the **Execute Code** action. Now change the code as follows:

```
{
    var maxdist;
    if ( !obj_explorer.has_sword )
        maxdist = 200
    else
        maxdist = 75;
    speed = 1; // wandering mummies go slowly
    if ( point_distance(x,y,obj_explorer.x,obj_explorer.y) < maxdist )
    {
        if ( !place_snapped(2,2) ) exit;
        instance_change(obj_mummy_search,false);
    }
}
```

2. Reopen the properties form for the searching mummy, select the **Begin Step** event, and double-click on the **Execute Code** action. Change this code as follows:

```
{
    var maxdist;
    if ( !obj_explorer.has_sword )
        maxdist = 200
    else
        maxdist = 75;
    speed = 2;
    if ( !collision_line(x+16,y+16,obj_explorer.x+16,obj_explorer.y+16,
                          obj_wall1,false,false) )
    {
        if ( !place_snapped(4,4) ) exit;
        instance_change(obj_mummy_chase,false);
    }
    if ( point_distance(x,y,obj_explorer.x,obj_explorer.y) > maxdist )
    {
        instance_change(obj_mummy_wander,false);
    }
}
```

That finishes the changes we must make. You will find the final version of the game in the file Games/Chapter14/pyramid8.gm6 on the CD. Now you should take some time to complete your masterpiece. Be sure to get some friends to test out the game for you to ensure that it isn't too hard, and have fun—there are a lot of great objects to play with here, so be sure to go wild!

Looking to the Future

This is the last game project in the book, but it's just the beginning of your game design career. Taking this game as a springboard, you could explore lots of directions. Maybe you want to add a whole set of different pyramids, each with different treasures and devious new traps. Or perhaps it's time for our explorer to break free of claustrophobic corridors and step out in a new direction—plunging deep in the rainforests of the Amazon or perhaps fighting winds across the icy wastes of Antarctica. You might even feel like adding some totally new game mechanics to the game—perhaps the explorer has to take to the skies in his trusty biplane, navigating through deadly desert sandstorms and avoiding terrible swarms of man-eating locusts on the way to his next target.

The fun doesn't stop with this game. Using the game design skills you have picked up so far in this book along with the advice in Chapter 15, you are in the perfect situation to start designing your own games. Imagine yourself an unlikely dustball hero, create yourself an unstoppable army of weasels, travel into deep space to play ping-pong with stars—the only limit is your imagination. Go forth and design—you have nothing to lose but your boredom!

■ ■ ■

Final Words

So that's it—you've made it to the end. You've completed all the challenges this book has to offer and, we hope, learned a lot about creating games in the process. You've battled demons, flown spacecrafts, dodged crates, juggled starfish, rescued koalas, commanded tanks, survived dogfights, hidden from mummies, and still had time for a game of tic-tac-toe along the way! We hope you've enjoyed this journey. Just because this book has come to an end, it doesn't mean that your gaming projects have to. So before we say a final farewell, we'll quickly mention some other directions you could explore if you want to continue enhancing your game development skills.

Creating Resources

As we said at the start, you're free to use the graphics, music, and sound effects provided with this book for your own Game Maker projects. However, those of you with artistic or musical talents will eventually want to try making your own resources for your games. In this section, we'll briefly mention some of the tools available for doing this. In each case we've chosen to focus on free tools, as you'll lose nothing from giving them a try before looking elsewhere.

Artwork: The GIMP

The GNU Image Manipulation Program—GIMP for short—is a professional-quality 2D art package, which is free to download and use on your PC (see Figure 15-1). It has many more features than the Image Editor in Game Maker and is comparable to Adobe Photoshop—the main 2D art package used in the games industry (and in this book). It's not the easiest package to learn how to use, but if you're serious about creating game artwork, then the GIMP will allow you to stretch your artistic talents while learning some professional techniques. Visit the GIMP website for more information and to download the program to your machine: http://gimp-win.sourceforge.net.

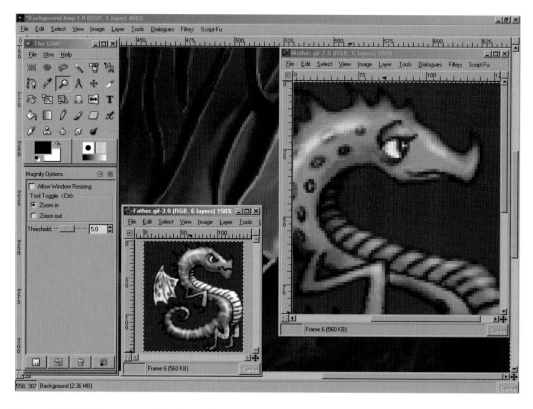

Figure 15-1. *This is a screenshot from the GIMP.*

While Photoshop and the GIMP are great packages, they can be a bit too much for beginners to handle, particularly when trying to use them to create sprites. HUMANBALANCE Co.'s GraphicsGale and Cosmigo's Pro Motion are cheap alternatives that are easier to use and designed specifically for creating sprites. You can download trial versions of these packages from the following websites:

- www.humanbalance.net/gale/us (GraphicsGale)

- www.cosmigo.com/promotion/index.php (Pro Motion)

Music: Anvil Studio

Music can add a lot of atmosphere to games as well as being a great deal of fun to create. Willow Software's Anvil Studio (see Figure 15-2) is a free beginner's package, which includes loads of features as well as helpful tips and tutorials to get you on your way. Packages like Anvil are MIDI based, and allow you to compose MIDI music files that are small in size and easy to include in your Game Maker games. MIDI music is the computer equivalent of writing down music on paper and getting the computer to perform the piece of music each time it needs to be played. This means that the way it sounds depends on the computer's sound card, so the music will often sound different on different computers. You can get around this by recording a performance of a MIDI song on your computer as a WAV file and including this in your game. The music will then sound exactly the same on every computer, but the WAV file will be much larger in size than the original MIDI. You can download Anvil Studio from the following website: www.anvilstudio.com.

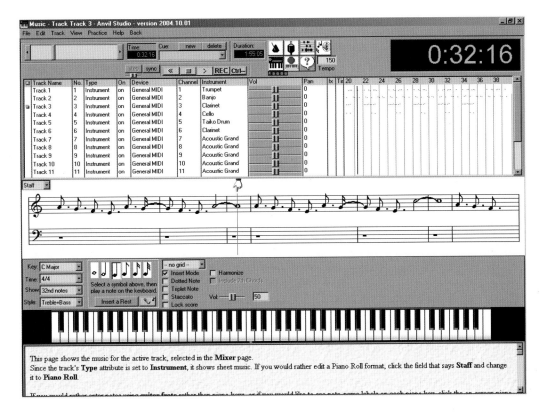

Figure 15-2. *This is a screenshot from Anvil Studio.*

Although Anvil is a fine place to start with making music, MIDI Tracker (from RF1 Systems) is a little simpler to use and not expensive to buy online. In fact, most of the MIDI files from the games in this book were originally composed on MIDI Tracker. Steinberg's Cubase SE is an entry-level music production package in the same range as those used in professional game development. This was the package used to create the MP3 music files included in this book. However, packages like this require special kinds of sound cards in order to work properly, so don't rush out and buy one without reading up on them first.

- www.rf1.net/software/mt (MIDI Tracker)

- www.steinberg.de (Cubase SE)

Sound Effects: Audacity

Audacity (see Figure 15-3) is an excellent open source program for recording and editing sound effects. With a reasonable sound card and a microphone, it should provide all you need for creating sound effects for your games. It's easier to create sound effects if your sound card is full-duplex—that is, it can both record and play sounds at the same time. Most modern PC sound cards can do this, although some laptop sound cards don't. You can download Audacity from http://audacity.sourceforge.net.

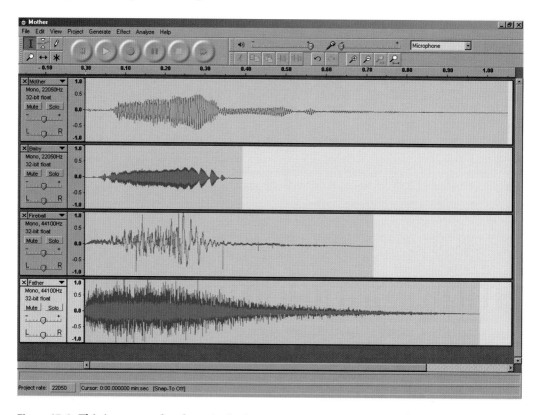

Figure 15-3. *This is a screenshot from Audacity.*

If you feel the need to use something more professional, then Sound Forge Audio Studio is the package used to create the sound effects in this book. This is an entry-level version of the Sound Forge packages that are used to create sound effects in professional games. You can find more information at www.sonymediasoftware.com (the website of Sony Media Software, the publishers of Sound Forge).

The Game Maker Community

Whatever you go on to do with Game Maker, we hope that you will join the online Game Maker community (see Figure 15-4) and share your ideas, knowledge, and expertise with other users. The Game Maker forum has over 20,000 worldwide members and is a great place to get help or advice at any time of the day or night. You'll even find advice on the tools described in the previous section, as well as a whole host of others.

Figure 15-4. *You'll want to join the Game Maker community.*

Point your web browser to http://forums.gamemaker.nl and you'll be in contact with Game Maker users from all around the world in no time at all. From time to time you may even see us contributing to the discussions.

▌Caution   Remember that it's not a good idea to give out personal information (like your full name, school/college, or home address) on any kind of Internet forum.

Note to Teachers

Game Maker is already used in a growing number of clubs and schools worldwide as an engaging activity for students from ages 7 to 70. It is certainly ideal for students from 14 up, and you can find out more about some of the projects happening worldwide through the teacher's forum at www.gamelearning.net.

Good Luck

Twenty years ago every self-respecting computer enthusiast owned a collection of books about programming games for the simple computers of the day. These books usually made the reader type in pages of code, which generally contained a generous helping of typing errors and bugs to work around. If you were lucky, then hours of painstaking labor might eventually be rewarded with the chance to control the letter O as it was chased around the screen by a couple of nasty-looking As. Nonetheless, it was books just like these that inspired us to write this one, because they were responsible for starting us down a path that lead to the game-related careers that we have today.

These days it's tools like Game Maker that will provide the first step on the ladder for games industry professionals of the future. It's exciting to think that some of you may go on to work in the games industry and help to define the shape of game development over the decades to come. It's difficult to predict how far games will have evolved by then, but you can be sure that they will look quite different from the 2D games that you've worked on in this book. Nevertheless, despite the technological advancements that the future will bring, it's unlikely that their game mechanics will be such a far cry from the ones you've explored here. We wish you the best of luck and hope that you'll remember your first game development projects as fondly as we remember our own.

Jacob and Mark, 2006

Goodbye!

Bibliography

The design chapters in this book are founded on over two decades of amateur and professional experience developing computer games. Nonetheless, the following texts have helped to add structure and conviction to many of the ideas and concepts discussed therein:

Crawford, Chris. *The Art of Computer Game Design*. Out of print: available online at www.vancouver.wsu.edu/fac/peabody/game-book/Coverpage.html, 1982.

Crawford, Chris. *On Game Design*. Indianapolis: New Riders Publishing, 2003.

Loftus, Geoffrey and Loftus, Elizabeth. *Mind at Play: The Psychology of Video Games*. New York: Basic Books, 1983.

Malone, Thomas and Lepper, Mark. "Making Learning Fun: A Taxonomy of Intrinsic Motivations for Learning." In *Aptitude, Learning and Instruction: III. Conative and affective process analyses*. Hilsdale, NJ: Erlbaum, 1987, p. 223–253.

Rollings, Andrew and Morris, Dave. *Game Architecture and Design*. Scottsdale, AZ: Coriolis Group, 2000.

Rollings, Andrew and Adams, Ernest. *On Game Design*. Indianapolis: New Riders Publishing, 2003.

Salen, Katie and Zimmerman, Eric. *Rules of Play, Game Design Fundamentals*. Cambridge, MA: MIT Press, 2004.

Wilson, Phil. *Hogs of War: Supplementary Game Design (original concept by Ade Carless)*. Unpublished design document, 1999.

Index

Find it faster at http://superindex.apress.com/

Find it faster at http://superindex.apress.com/

Find it faster at http://superindex.apress.com/

You Need the Companion eBook

Your purchase of this book entitles you to its companion eBook for only $10.

We believe this Apress title will prove so indispensable that you'll want to carry it with you everywhere, which is why we are offering the companion eBook for $10 to customers who purchase this book now. Convenient and fully searchable, the eBook version of any content-rich, page-heavy Apress book makes a valuable addition to your programming library. You can easily find, copy, and apply code—and then perform examples by quickly toggling between instructions and the application. Even simultaneously tackling a donut, diet soda, and complex code becomes simplified with hands-free eBooks!

Once you purchase this book, getting the $10 companion eBook is simple:

❶ Visit **www.apress.com/promo/tendollars/**.

❷ Complete a basic registration form to receive a randomly generated question about this title.

❸ Answer the question correctly in 60 seconds and you will receive a promotional code to redeem for the $10 eBook.

2560 Ninth Street • Suite 219 • Berkeley, CA 94710

eBookshop

THE EXPERT'S VOICE™

Offer valid through 12/06.

License Agreement